FEMINISM AND ECOLOGICAL COMMUNITIES

Feminism and Ecological Communities: An Ethic of Flourishing is one of the first books radically to take stock of the ecofeminist movement. Acknowledging and addressing as important the arguments against ecofeminism that have been made by postmodern and other anti-essentialist wings, Chris J. Cuomo nevertheless argues that much of the recent work on ecofeminism has been strong on criticism but weak on activism, leaving ecofeminist thought at a crossroads. Taking up this challenge, *Feminism and Ecological Communities* formulates a fascinating new blueprint for ecofeminist thought.

Opening by tracing the emergence of ecofeminism from the ecological and feminist movements, Chris J. Cuomo clearly shows how environmental ethics can benefit by incorporating feminist insights on the limitations of traditional philosophical conceptions of ethics. To develop this picture, she asks challenging questions of many ecofeminist assumptions. Must ecofeminists be committed to the view that women are closer to nature than men? What are the common goals of feminism and environmentalism? How is the oppression of women related to the degradation of nature?

Feminism and Ecological Communities addresses these key questions by drawing on recent work in feminist ethics as well as the work of diverse figures such as Aristotle, John Dewey, Aldo Leopold and Donna Haraway. Although presenting searching new arguments against ecofeminist approaches that rely on simplistic analyses of gender, caring and moral agency, Chris J. Cuomo passionately defends ecofeminism throughout against simplistic anti-essentialist criticism. Paving a new way forward for ecofeminist theory and practice, *Feminism and Ecological Communities* will be essential reading for all those interested in gender studies, environmental studies and philosophy.

Chris J. Cuomo is Assistant Professor of Philosophy at the University of Cincinnati.

FEMINISM AND ECOLOGICAL COMMUNITIES

An ethic of flourishing

Chris J. Cuomo

London and New York

First published 1998
by Routledge
11 New Fetter Lane, London EC4P 4EE

Simultaneously published in the USA and Canada
by Routledge
29 West 35th Street, New York, NY 10001

© 1998 Chris J. Cuomo

Typeset in Sabon by
J&L Composition Ltd, Filey, North Yorkshire
Printed in Great Britain by
Clays Ltd, St Ives plc

British Library Cataloging in Publication Data
A catalogue record for this book is available from the
British Library

Library of Congress Cataloguing in Publication Data
Cuomo, Chris J.
Feminism and Ecological Communities: An Ethic of Flourishing/Chris
J. Cuomo
p. cm.
Includes bibliographical references and index.
1. Ecofeminism 2. Human ecology 3. Feminist theory I. Title
HQ1233.C86 1998
305.42′01—dc21 97–11037

ISBN 0–415–15805–2 (hb)
0–415–15806–0 (pb)

This book is dedicated to the memory of
Emily C. Svetlik,
who taught me how.

CONTENTS

ACKNOWLEDGEMENTS

I've written this book while living and thinking in three different communities, and it is with warmth and incredible gratitude that I recall what it felt like to work in these places, in the company of such wonderful friends and colleagues. In Madison, Wisconsin, I was advised and inspired by Claudia Card, who inspires me still. This project was also shaped from its earliest stages in conversations with Gwen Bialic, Lori Saxe, Tara Ayres, Barb Sparrow, and Jim Anderson. Sandy Seuser provided nurturance and friendship, while the Others in Education, including Laurie Fuller and Fong Hermes, helped pull me out of dogmatic slumbers. The comments of Paula Gottleib, Steve Nadler, and Elizabeth Ellsworth also provided helpful guidance.

In Ithaca, where I was fortunate to spend a year in the Department of Science and Technology Studies at Cornell University, I benefitted immeasurably from the intellectual and emotional support of Ruth Vanita, Archana Prasad, Karen Jones and Jenny Davoren. Conversations with Sheila Jasanoff, Henry Shue, Kathy Abrams, Steven Yearley, Paula Moya, Linda Alcoff, Peter Taylor, Herbert Gottleib, and Anna Marie Smith helped in the seemingly impossible task of clarifying and articulating my thoughts.

Here in Cincinnati, in the last stages of preparing this manuscript, Madeleine Pabis, Ursula Roma, Linda Weiner Morris, Ted Morris, Catherine Raissiguier, Lycette Nelson, Karla Goldman, and Kristin Naca helped keep me sane and silly. I am thankful also for the support of the members of the Department of Philosophy, especially Don Gustafson, and Bob Richardson, and the Program in Women's Studies, especially Robin Sheets, Lisa Hogeland and Maura O'Connor. Special thanks to Julie Fitzgerald, Cate Sherron-Ferrell and Kim Lockwood, for providing some green life and puppy energy just when I thought I had forgotten why I was writing this book.

This book was also written in the company of communities not easily locatable in space. More than anything else, the ideas in this book have been shaped and influenced by a brilliant and nurturing group of feminist philosophers: The Midwest Society for Women in Philosophy. I would especially like to thank Amber Katherine, Vicky Davion, Kim Hall, María Lugones, Alison Bailey, Lori Gruen and Claudia Card for the gifts of their friendship and wisdom. Over the years, I've also been influenced by the words and work of Jacquelyn Zita, Jeffner Allen, Sarah Hoagland, Ann Leighton, Jackie Anderson, Marilyn Frye, Joyce Trebilcot, Nancy Tuana, Lisa Heldke, Alison Jaggar and Sandra Bartky. So as to avoid a litany of names (too late, I know), I'll just say that this book — and this philosopher — would not have been possible without the friendship, support and work of the members of Midwest SWIP. If you don't like what I have to say, you could blame them.

I appreciate the kindness of other writers who have allowed me to reprint their work here. Excerpts from 'Fire' by Joy Harjo (from *What Moon Drove Me to This?* Berkeley: I. Reed Books, 1978), 'Our Stunning Harvest' by Ellen Bass (copyright 1985, Ellen Bass), and 'Kopis'taya,' ('A Gathering of Spirits') by Paula Gunn Allen, all appear with permission of the poets.

This manuscript benefitted greatly from the careful attention of Lori Gruen, Vicky Davion, Ruth Vanita, and Val Plumwood. Thanks also to Tony Bruce and Adrian Driscoll, from Routledge, for their patient assistance, and thank you to Lindsey Brake for careful copyediting. Generous support in the form of money was provided by the Rockefeller Foundation (which funded my postdoc in Science and Technology Studies at Cornell University in 1994–95), as well as the Taft Faculty Board and University Research Council of the University of Cincinnati. Generous support in the form of love was provided by my wonderful family: Bonnie, Peter, Judy, Gina and Lou Cuomo, and Nicolle Ahles. Generous assistance in the form of walking on my computer keyboard was provided by Sappho and Sojourner.

Although I thought I wanted to deviate from the practice of thanking the girlfriend last, it does seem right to end by thanking the person who had to endure the most annoying effects of writing, and the most unsavory parts of me, while I wrote this book. For friendship, for food, for sweet email messages and revivifying distractions, I thank Karen Schlanger, who reminds me that if there is a reason to care about the earth, or to care about ourselves, it is because of real, bodily love.

INTRODUCTION
Thinking at the crossroads

> The story never really begins nor ends, even though there is a beginning and an end to every story, just as there is a beginning and an end to every teller. One can date it back to the immemorial days when a group of mighty men attributed to itself a central, dominating position vis-à-vis other groups; overvalued its particularities and achievements; adopted a projective attitude toward those it classified among the out-groups; and wrapped itself up in its own thinking, interpreting the out-groups through the in-group mode of reasoning while claiming to speak the minds of both the in-group and the out-group.
>
> Trinh T. Minh-ha

This book is an attempt to articulate an ecological feminism, and to exhibit its potential as a source of environmental and social ethics. Feminist environmentalism begins with noticing similarities and connections between forms and instances of human oppression, including the oppression of women, and the degradation of nature. A central position grounding ecofeminism is the belief that values, notions of reality, and social practices are related, and that forms of oppression and domination, however historically and culturally distinct, are interlocked and enmeshed. It follows that our strategies – both theoretical and practical – for resisting oppressions must attend to these connections.

Before proceeding further, let me give an example of the kinds of connections that concern ecofeminists. One month last year, I felt bombarded by bad news: six women in my circle of friends and family were found to have cancer – all of the cervix, uterus, or breast. In the midst of my fear, I pondered histories of inadequate health care for women and the poor, the ways in which women's and nonwhite bodies are devalued, the fact that the meaning of women's lives is so often reduced to their reproductive functions, and the character of a profit-driven, increasingly toxic world. At about the same time, in the city where I live, the Ku Klux Klan was erecting a cross on the downtown square. Enraged, I thought of the misogyny,

1

ethnocentrism, and homophobia, the unapologetic violence, and the general lack of interest in widespread human and ecological flourishing expressed by 'radical' right-wing movements in the United States. And I considered how legacies of hatred were being played out on the bodies of people I love.

Yet no story is ever simple. Cancer, of course, seems to have many different causes. And alongside the fact that women's bodies are devalued, our bodies are also glorified, and men's bodies are devalued, too. And, as for that processed world – at the moment, I can't say that I long for a world without my computer, and frequent-flier miles, and a large selection of food that can be put into my mouth only minutes after deciding I want it. Is it possible to tease the usefulness of products away from their questionable relationships to militarism, class oppression, and alienation? Is it possible, in the face of complexity, to construct theories, practices, and selves, that are mindful of connections? At the very least, the complexity of reality, of the stories that compose our lives, our desires, our histories and communities, call for complexity in our practices, our responses, our analyses and recommendations for the future.

When we pause to consider the implications of our choices, it becomes clear that if we want to be thorough and consistent, and to make choices that seem good, then careful attention must be paid to the contexts in which seemingly isolated elements of reality occur. What is the racial composition of your neighborhood, and how many toxic dumps are nearby? Why is that tough, safe, gas-guzzling four-wheel-drive vehicle so attractive to me? To which relationships in our lives do we devote the most time and energy? What assumptions and contradictions concerning human society lie behind the single-issue environmental movements and organizations we support? How might we most effectively interrupt conservative political rhetoric that promotes regressive notions of woman, family, nation, and racial privilege, even when it pretends to be (merely) about taxes and property rights?

We certainly don't want to drive ourselves crazy with analysis. Theory should not make us so obsessed with causes, connections, underlying factors and implications that we cannot act or move, or leave us so overwhelmed or distracted that we stop caring about whatever brought us to theory in the first place. Even when crazy-making, theoretical work should help its audience negotiate or know whatever the writing aims to clarify – be it a piece of art, a bit of information, or a political identity. Ethical theory, in particular, ought to help us negotiate our personal, social, and institutional relationships.

Where organic well-being beyond oneself is concerned, and in so far as choice is possible, a matter is ethical. The concept of ethics is used to locate a particular category of human problems: one involving the interests of other people, or other 'morally valuable' beings, as factors, and one which calls upon agents to make choices according to socially sanctioned, or 'appropriate,' criteria. Aristotle noted that one of the distinguishing features of virtue, his concept for ethical responses to relationships and situations, is the fact that it involves choice. According to the norms recorded by him and other influential thinkers in the history of ethics, ethical issues involve the exploration of 'the good,' and 'right and wrong,' and their attempted realization in human interactions.

The norms concerning ethical concepts and matters, or the meanings of good and appropriate actions and attitudes, have been debated from the beginning of philosophy. But these discussions of norms are undergoing dramatic, unparalleled upheavals on the wave of social movements for liberation and political change. Two influential, multifaceted, and intertwined sites of controversy in ethics have been at the intersections of academic philosophy and feminism, and philosophy and environmentalism. From these unfixed locations have come some very basic claims with almost incomprehensibly complex implications: nonmale, nonwhite, nonowning, and otherwise nonprivileged people, and nonhuman beings, and the interests of all of these entities that are constructed variously as Other to the paradigmatic Knower, Thinker, Politician and Party to the Contract have been inadequately represented, and dangerously misrepresented, in the history of philosophy. This erasure and distortion is of particular interest when it occurs in ethical thought, since ethics is ostensibly supposed to promote justice and good behavior. Yet, as history shows, ethical arguments can be molded to justify all kinds of actions and identities.

In efforts to unearth unfriendly references to women and other Others in the history of philosophy, and to include them *qua* women, people of color, workers, ecosystems and cows (rather than wives and mothers, slaves, exotics, foreigners and lower classes, Nature and meat) in philosophical explorations, several parallel agendas have emerged as central in feminist and environmental philosophies. One such agenda is to locate and debunk false characterizations, and to map out their often hidden influences and implications. For example, Aristotle's belief that women are essentially, naturally passive helps shape his claims that only certain men count as citizens, and that the political realm entails men's interactions with each other. Women and slaves are backgrounded in his conception of the *polis*, though their work enables its existence. Similarly, Descartes' insistence that nonhuman animals more closely resemble clocks than rational persons, and that their responses to unpleasant stimuli are not true expressions of pain, betrays his predisposition to discount responses that are not uniquely human in his discussion of what knowledge is and how it functions.

Beyond this critical move, feminist and environmental philosophers also look at the implications of including subordinated groups and individuals among those who count as theoretically significant and morally considerable in traditional philosophical systems. Controversies inevitably arise about how to represent 'them,' how to avoid universalization or reduction (what are 'women,' and what is 'nature,' anyway?), and whether traditional frameworks are capable of accommodating as full subjects those castigated as Others by those very frameworks. An inevitable project is a detailed exploration of how counting historically discounted Others as relevant seriously undermines or revises the assumptions and prescriptions of traditional ethical frameworks.

This book sits at the crossroads of feminism and environmentalism in two ways. First, it begins from a concern with the *problems* that have given rise to both environmentalism and feminism: the mistreatment of the natural world, and the subordination of women and other Others, and the ways these are interrelated and influenced by each other. Second, it turns to the separate world of feminist and environmental *analyses* to illuminate solutions to, or means of addressing these problems. I am after ethics that explore connections among related but distinct phenomena, and in my search I bring together varied philosophical and ethical perspectives.

> It is only the dissatisfied who have the urge to live differently,
> and hence the need to find out what ways of living differently
> would be improvements.
>
> Julia Annas

For many good reasons, people drawn to read a book on feminism and environmentalism are likely to be wary of ethics, because its language is so strongly associated with rules, norms and evaluative criteria put forward by the powerful in order to control others and maintain privilege. An example is current conservative talk of 'family values' in the US, which is actually used to justify the silencing and unfair treatment of lesbians and gay men, and to impart blame for urban crime and the federal deficit upon unmarried women who have children and receive welfare payments. Ruling social codes of morality have rarely promoted women's interests or the interests of members of other subordinated groups, and as Nietzsche noted, have helped create cultures founded on guilt, abnegation, denial and lies. In addition, so-called moralities that aim to justify incredible cruelty toward and exploitation of nonprivileged groups of humans, and nonhuman beings and communities, motivate serious, legitimate mistrust of talk of morality. One need only look at what has been carried out against people and against land in the name of 'just war' to acquire a healthy suspicion of moral claims.

Some ethicists have attempted to distance their writing from repressive social or religious rules of correct behavior by referring to their own work as 'ethics,' and to customary and religious codes as 'morality.' In this scheme, ethics is a matter of agents deciding upon good behavior or dispositions through rational consideration of arguments and information, while morality includes unquestioned, unquestioning, rule-following, or unreflective goose-stepping in sync with authorities. Although I do not utilize it

4

here, this distinction makes some practical sense, and also has a basis in the history of the meanings of the terms. 'Moral' is derived from the Latin *moralis*, which refers to manners and customs, while the Greek ancestors of 'ethics,' *ethos* and *ethikos*, refer respectively to character and custom, and the technical art of perfecting them. 'Ethics,' if a technical practice, carries connotations of thoughtful agency and of the potential for change and controversy regarding how one ought to act in social contexts, while 'morality' is merely appropriate rule-following.

Whether or not Cicero was motivated by a desire to conflate them in the literate mind when he translated *ethikos* as *moralis*, the terms have extensive overlap in current meaning, and both refer to the same categories of human actions and dispositions: those in which it makes sense to talk of right and wrong, good and bad, responsibility, duty, and virtue. I therefore use the concepts of ethics and morality interchangeably, keeping in mind the extent to which rational consideration of arguments is always socially embedded, and that rote rule-following does not exempt one from questions of responsibility.

In putting forward arguments toward ethics that are both feminist and environmentalist, I am not advocating universal rules or restrictive guidelines. I am seeking ways of thinking, and of evaluating actions, policies, and values, that challenge destructive and oppressive modes of interaction, and that encourage deep thought and carefulness in the face of lies and illusions, commingled with facts and observations, that are terribly influential and powerful, and that enable oppression and exploitation. Needless to say, I am also motivated by a desire to participate in discussions about 'what to do' about the oppression and exploitation of women, people of color, of workers and the poor, of lesbians and gay men, about the presence and legacies of ethnocentrism and colonialism, about the torture of nonhuman animals in laboratories, and about toxic dumping and dwindling wilderness, and about how to engage in transgressive practices.

Like all philosophy, ethics is always about ideals – as much about what we aspire to do or be as it is about who we actually are. But ideals can function in real relations. Rather than cling to pure abstract truth while meeting inevitability, we sometimes have opportunities to make choices that redirect the path of what seems entirely likely or predisposed. Sometimes these moments feel grand and revolutionary. Sometimes they are local and personal. Perhaps they are more available than they seem at the end of the twentieth century, from 'the belly of the beast,' (as Donna Haraway refers to American society). Hope, possibility, alternative, tradition, history, and creativity can be remarkably powerful in the face of danger and absurdity.

CONFESSIONS OF A RELUCTANT ECO/FEMINIST

Although I've been attracted to thinking at the intersections of feminism and environmentalism for years, I hesitate to call myself an ecofeminist.

Indeed, I prefer to think of my work as *ecological feminism*, in an effort to keep the emphasis on feminism, and also to distance my approach some-what from other work done by self-titled ecofeminists. Though I share moti-vations with the authors of such work, I am sufficiently critical to be uncomfortable with the label. Accordingly, in these pages, 'ecofeminism' is an umbrella term referring to forthright attempts to link some versions of feminism and environmentalism, and 'ecological feminism' refers to the particular subset of ecofeminist approaches I wish to articulate and endorse here. On the whole, I find that a large amount of ecofeminist work has focused too exclusively on the objects of oppression (such as women and nature), and has not adequately explored the connections among the vari-ous forms and functions of oppressive systems.

Throughout this book I distinguish between two different approaches to thinking about connections between feminism and environmental ethics. Some ecofeminists, including many spiritual writers and activists, look pri-marily at the connections and similarities among the objects of oppressive and exploitative thought and action. This approach might be thought of as object-attentive, because of the way it zooms in on women. Unfortunately, this tight focus too often results in false universalizations about women, based on the experiences and interests of women with privilege and power.

Of course, it is possible for a more critical object-attentive approach to take the category 'woman' as referring to a diverse, multifarious group of differing and complex individuals. The clear and present commonalities, patterns and connections among women's gendered positions and experi-ences necessitate a feminism that focuses on those of us who fall under the category 'woman.' None the less, it conceives of the category as multiplici-tous, complex, and even contradictory, and realizes that improving the lives of women therefore necessarily entails working against all oppressions experienced by anyone in the category 'woman.' As Elizabeth Spelman points out, gender oppression cannot be sliced out from women's experi-ences or identities. There is no pure gender, or instance of sexism, not coex-istent with race, class, and sexuality, and accompanying oppressions and privileges. Feminists stand contrary to women's oppression, and 'woman' is always formed within social relations other than gender. Any feminism that aims to deconstruct 'women's oppression,' conceptually or materially, must recognize that even where aspects of oppression can be identified as being 'about gender,' they are commonly, intimately, linked with other oppres-sions. Feminism cannot therefore merely involve promoting anything that can be characterized as simply 'in women's interests.' Because other social categories, such as race, class, and sexuality, fundamentally shape gendered relations and identities (and vice versa), it is incoherent to promote a femi-nism that does not address oppressions based on these categories as well. On this view, connections between 'woman' and 'nature' exist because women are part of 'nature,' as are all humans, and the suppression and hatred of nature is played out in specific ways on women's bodies, activities, and conceptual frameworks. These connections are relevant because both women and nature are categorically devalued, with their distinct and similar qualities.

Another way of noting the interconnections among oppressions is based on an analysis of the ways oppressions function. Accordingly, ecological feminism focuses on the links and patterns among the treatment of oppressed, exploited, or undervalued beings and entities – that is, among forms and instances of oppression and degradation, and common ethical and ontological bases for maltreatment. This approach is not inconsistent with the insights of the first approach, which complicates understandings of moral objects, subjects, and agents. But a focus on oppression employs the notion that different forms and systems of oppression are interwoven, and they therefore strengthen and fuel each other. These approaches emphasize the logical similarity and interdependence of various forms of oppression, the recurrent themes and tools used to harm people and limit their lives, and the ways that members of oppressed groups are actively discouraged from noticing these connections and acting in solidarity to fight common enemies. This approach to interconnection is evident in the work of Karen Warren and Val Plumwood, who emphasize conceptual and practical connections in defining ecological feminism.

Though the work of many earlier ecofeminist thinkers, as well as a good deal of ecofeminist activist rhetoric, could be described as strictly object-attentive, more recent ecofeminist theoretical work departs from attempts to articulate similarities between those mythical entities 'women and nature.' I count my perspective among those voices critical of ecofeminist appeals to femininity or women's corporeality as naturally and essentially more closely linked to the nonhuman world, of characterizations of nature as feminine, or radically separate from culture, and of claims that women are particularly responsible for saving the earth. Rather, the perspective I present here begins with a recognition of the connections among various types and aspects of oppression and exploitation. But instead of rejecting all ecofeminism out of hand, I argue that it is important to recognize that because entities like 'women' and 'nature' are socially, discursively, historically constructed, attention to the particularities and mechanisms of those constructions (seen partially in their 'treatment') will inevitably result in conclusions about what they *are*. Conversely, discussion of what some ecofeminists refer to as bonds or connections between women and nature are not necessarily rooted in essentialist understandings of what they 'are,' but can be based on observations of the meanings, functions, and dispositions of women and natural entities within a given discursive universe.

There is a tension in this book between my aim to describe an existent worldview, and my desire to present it persuasively as a useful ethical alternative. While I aim to create a coherent picture of ecological feminist thought, I move between a descriptive presentation of ecofeminism as it is and normative arguments for ecological feminism as it ought to be. Put differently, part of my project entails sifting through various ecofeminist approaches in order to illuminate their strengths and weaknesses, though I want also to build upon the strengths and suggest fruitful directions for further development.

My discussions of ecofeminism ought not to be interpreted as implying that the only feminists interested in nature – its destruction, its protection, its promise, its historical links with women and femininity – are those who think of themselves as 'ecofeminists,' or who focus explicitly on the practical and conceptual issues in which connections between gender, race, class, and constructions of nature are apparent. Emphasis on nature, pets or companion-animals, vegetarianism, and ecologically-sound practices have often permeated feminist politics and cultures, and feminists have long noticed connections between women and nature. Though in these pages I am primarily attentive to explicitly feminist/environmentalist expressions, I hope also to remain mindful of the extent to which certain versions of feminism have always been environmentalist.

Any piece of philosophy is merely part of a conversation. This book is meant to be a voice in conversations that include, but are not limited to, American academic/activist radical politics. My contribution to these conversations focuses on ecofeminist and other theoretical and literary work from the US, and its relation to Western philosophical traditions. In addition, my discussion of feminism and environmentalism is very much informed by the ways in which these movements exist, in the US, and at the intersections of theory and practice. Feminisms, ecofeminism, and environmentalisms take many different shapes around the world – and within our own communities – and some understandings of these will be at odds with my not-disinterested presentation. Because ecofeminism is a near-global phenomenon, it would be absurd to take one version to exhaust the valuable possibilities for thinking at the crossroads of feminism and environmentalism. For example, it is undeniably true that rural women and poor women, including women in the Third World, have been the leaders in efforts to create practices and institutions that aim jointly to empower women and to restore devastated ecosystems.[1] But while there is certainly significant overlap, there are different requirements for effective political resistance and social change in different contexts. While there is a tendency in Western ecofeminist theory to describe the work of rural Third World women as paradigmatic ecofeminist activism, one sees little effort (in the literature) to

1 For examples, see Leonard 1989; Braidotti *et al.* 1994; Shiva 1994; Nussbaum and Glover 1995.

develop specific models that examine the politics of 'first world' mega-consumption on ecofeminist grounds.

The ecological feminism I describe is a philosophical feminism that attempts to map carefully its constituent concepts, logics, knowledge, and justifications, and which stands on the shoulders of the wealth of feminist philosophical work of the last few decades. In stating this, I mean to point out my own intellectual foundations as well as a body of work that has influenced other thinkers concerned with issues at the crossroads of various systems and modes of oppression. From my focus on the philosophical issues central to ecological feminism, it will be evident that I am preoccupied with the conceptual realm. Though I don't believe that concepts or ideas determine reality, are entirely separate from material, or that they are always easily identifiable, I do believe that conceptual gridlock can be deadly, and that conceptual shifts are a necessary aspect of significant social change.

THE CHAPTERS

Though I admittedly had some linear progression in mind when I put the sections of this book together, not every reader will be best served by following their numerical order, or by reading every piece presented here. Certainly, feminists, environmentalists, philosophers, and other readers who are curious about, yet unfamiliar with, ecological feminism come to these pages with different priorities. With this in mind, I've tried to provide enough background to welcome interested readers, while avoiding overly didactic tangents or unmarked detours into rarefied realms of inquiry.

The opening prelude is meant to provide some context for feminist readers who are not well-acquainted with ecological thought or environmental ethics. Here I locate ecological feminism in the context of other work in ecology and social justice, and discuss the distinction – central to environmental ethics – between instrumental and noninstrumental value. In Chapter 1, I set out the terms of the ecofeminist project – the broad effort to highlight connections between women's oppression and environmental degradation. Here I discuss the difference between ecofeminism and ecological feminism, and argue for an ecological feminism that begins where feminism begins: with a rejection of oppression, and with regard for those who have been labelled 'Other' by oppressive conceptual and political regimes.

Chapter 2 provides a background discussion of feminist ethics, and establishes the 'starting points' of ecological feminist ethics. From this 'foundation,' in the following chapter I present an ethic of flourishing that draws on Aristotelian insights and a sensibility that values the *dynamic charm* of living beings and systems. After developing a general picture of what flourishing in an ethical sense requires, I am left at the end of Chapter 3 with the longing for a useful, nonromantic, ecological and feminist conception of human flourishing. For a brief Interlude, I consider models offered by both

Donna Haraway and María Lugones of multiplicitous, border-dwelling, and resistant selves.

In Chapter 4, I compare ecological feminism to other influential environmental philosophies in terms of its ethical starting points. Consistent with the wealth of literature in feminist ethics, ecofeminist ethics are rarely focused on developing systems of rules and principles to guide behavior. I argue that ecological feminism differs significantly from ethical theories that assume a liberal conception of moral agents, and need not assume that ecological communities are harmonious systems. In contrast, ecological feminists see selves as social and ecological, and see nature as valuable, though chaotic.

In Chapter 5 my aim is to defend ecofeminism, and hence ecological feminism, against simplistic anti-essentialist critiques. Here I argue that ecofeminism is neither as static nor as essentialist as its critics believe, and that feminist 'glorifications' of nature and female embodiment entail more than an unquestioning acceptance of problematic givens. Although most of the positions against which I argue have been put forward by writers who identify their work as 'postmodern,' my agenda does not include a complete dismissal of poststructuralist approaches to feminism or environmentalism, or of the substance of every debate within feminism that has been prompted by the emergence of feminist poststructuralism.

Without losing sight of the potential of the ecofeminist project, in Chapter 6 I examine the problematic philosophical foundations of several popular ecofeminist theories. Concurring with commentators who have traced the problems with early ecofeminist conceptions of 'woman,' and outlining problems in ecofeminist uses of care ethics, dualisms, and diversity and unity, I go on to show how and why this work has none the less been useful in generating alternative paradigms. Chapter 6 is an updated version of the article, 'Unravelling the Problems in Ecofeminism,' that appeared in the journal *Environmental Ethics*.

Chapter 7 is a slightly revised version of 'Toward Thoughtful Ecofeminist Activism,' which was previously published in *Ecological Feminist Philosophies*, edited by Karen J. Warren. The discussion of activism in this chapter is motivated by my belief that moral and political philosophy are most fruitful when they are made relevant to what is affectionately known as 'real life.' Here I engage a question with relevance far beyond the field of environmental ethics: what is the relationship between abstract ethical and political theory and the applications of those theories? I show that the line between theoretical and applied ethics is far more permeable than philosophers generally acknowledge, and only through constant dialogue with applications and real ethical problems can ethical and political theory be made relevant. I argue for ethics at the crossroads of ethical and political theory and practice, and for the practical importance of radical philosophizing.

Prelude

SITUATING ECOLOGICAL FEMINISM

About the book. I'll see if I can make any sense about it briefly. The theme remains what I have felt for several years it would be: Life and the relations of Life to the physical environment . . . Of course everyone knows by this time that the whole world of science has been revolutionized by events of the past decade or so. I suppose my thinking began to be affected soon after atomic science was firmly established . . . So it seems time someone wrote of Life in the light of the truth as it now appears to us . . .

I still feel there is a case to be made for my old belief that as man approaches the 'new heaven and the new earth' – or the space-age universe, if you will, he must do so with humility rather than arrogance . . . And along with humility I think there is still a place for wonder.

Rachel Carson, to Martha Freeman (1958)

In the United States, distinctly ecologically-minded feminisms arose concurrently with the ecology movement. The larger pro-nature movement, loosely based on popular interpretations of ecological science and symbolized in mainstream culture by the creation of Earth Day in 1970, was accompanied by new developments in intellectual and activist environmentalism. This new environmentalism emerged from a history sprinkled with influential white thinkers, including Henry David Thoreau, Aldo Leopold, John Muir and Rachel Carson, who all wrote lovingly of nature, and argued that human practices that alter natural processes should be engaged in cautiously.[1] Most early 'nature writing' exhibits two kinds of valuing discussed in environmental ethics – instrumental and noninstrumental value – and recommendations based on both kinds of valuing echo throughout contemporary ethical debates concerning our interactions with nature.

---

1 And of course these writers in turn had their sources of literary inspiration, including European Romanticism and nonWestern thought. Thoreau, for example, was influenced by Wordsworth, Coleridge, and the *Bhagavadgita*.

11

Instrumental value refers to use value. Something with (only) instrumental value is valuable in so far as it is useful to moral agents, or persons. In contrast, beings with noninstrumental value have additional, ethically significant value above and beyond their use value. Most beings (humans are the most obvious examples) that have noninstrumental value also have instrumental value. An important difference between beings with noninstrumental value, and those that are only valuable in so far as they can be used, is that things with noninstrumental value can themselves be harmed – we can do wrong directly unto those beings. If Dooley, a dog, is only valuable for instrumental reasons, I cannot wrong her. If I disable or neglect her, the only wrong I've done is to her *owner*. If Dooley has moral, noninstrumental value, when I cause her pain or suffering, normative concepts apply to my interactions *with her*. She is not just 'property,' or a 'resource,' she is an entity capable of being harmed or exploited, and against whom I can do wrong. She is morally considerable – she is herself an object of ethical deliberation and action.

Many environmentalists and environmental ethicists see their work as fundamentally rejecting a purely instrumental conception of nonhuman entities, and broadening the category of morally considerable entities. When I discuss 'environmental ethics' in these pages, I refer to positions which assert that at least some nonhuman organic entities ought to be valued for reasons not reducible to their use value.

Many well-known thinkers in the history of American environmentalism, including Carson and Muir, advocated and embodied complex moral and aesthetic attitudes toward nature, including both instrumental and noninstrumental values. None the less, their views are often contrasted with the views of *conservationists* – those who invoke reminders of the instrumental value of nature to argue that preserving the natural world in its 'untouched' states is beneficial for long-term human interests. Conservationists believe that instrumental value is the only reason to consider the interests of nonhuman natural entities. In the words of Gifford Pinchot, chief of the early Federal Forestry Division, written in 1910,

> The first great fact about conservation is that it stands for development. There has been a fundamental misconception that conservation means nothing but the husbanding of resources for future generations. There could be no more serious mistake. The first principle of conservation is development, the use of the natural resources now existing on this continent for the benefit of the people who live here now.
>
> (1990: 76–77)

Tracing the roots of American environmentalism, historian Roderick Nash argues that a unique pro-nature sensibility grew from a sense of national identity and nationalism grounded in a high, ambiguous regard for unspoiled wilderness and 'living off the land.' He attributes this characteristically American position to the belief that land was wild and plentiful and natural resources were inexhaustible, coexistent with a drive toward Progress, conceived as necessarily involving the domination of nature. Given its constituent ambiguities, this same American nationalism helped set the stage for the rapid environmental exploitation that accompanied popular, sentimental calls for conservation of the land.

> In purely American terms, progress demanded the conquest of the wilderness, an imperative fortified by God's command to 'Be fruitful and multiply, and fill the earth and subdue it.' It was not truly a wilderness, of course, for it supported thriving civilizations and networks of constantly traveled roads and trails, all markedly at variance with the meaning of 'wilderness.' But Indians and their works did not qualify as human in the same sense as Spaniards or Englishmen, even though the latter secured a foothold in this wilderness only with the crucial aid, freely given or forcibly compelled, of its human inhabitants . . . A progressively westward struggle with this wilderness had in fact been a dominant theme of American history since the advent of Columbus.
>
> (Utley 1983: 33)

In this context, 'conservation' connoted the preservation of a context, or environment, which was necessary to maximize the liberty of the already-free (men, whites, landowners), and thus helped enable their nearly unfettered pursuit of progress. Material conditions, including an abundance of relatively unspoiled land made possible a widely-held 'national park ideal,' typified by groups such as the Sierra Club, founded by John Muir and others in 1892 (Nash 1990: 35–36).

Ironically, Nash asserts that a significant public preoccupation with human rights provided rhetorical and affective references upon which environmentalism could draw. It is certainly possible that, although human rights were not extended universally, Enlightenment ideals, including rights, justice, and liberty, provided a language for conservationists and other early environmentalists. Still, we should not lose sight of the ways in which this complicated ideology was also shaped by the optimistic colonialist, capitalist character of American identities, immigrant histories, the slavery of Africans and slaughter of Native Americans, and corresponding racial hierarchies. For example, US environmentalism grew in complex relation to indigenous tribal peoples in ways similar to other colonial and postcolonial environmental policies and practices around the world. Native Americans' lives, cultures, communities, and technologies have served as both targets for racist, colonialist, and genocidal Euro-American practices, and romantic models for environmentalists, whose attention has often been less than respectful. Robert M. Utley discusses eighteenth- and nineteenth-century examples of how 'the Indian' roamed 'deeply, darkly, and mirrorlike through the American psyche.'

The idea of progress focused on the Indian in two ways. First, he was a central feature of the wilderness, and by definition, conquest of the wilderness entailed conquest of the Indian. Second, he was living confirmation of the very idea of progress itself. Progress came to be seen as rise from savagery to civilization. In the Indian whites saw the lower order from which they themselves had progressed, and thus in themselves they saw the higher order to which the Indian might one day progress ... Critics of the established order portrayed the Noble Savage as a simple child of nature dwelling idyllically in a forested paradise, a living reproach of the artificiality and decadence of industrial society ... Another [example] was the rise in American literature of the 'Boone figure' – the white frontiersman who acquires the outdoor skills of the Indian, indeed becomes part Indian, as an essential weapon in the white conquest of the wilderness.

(Utley 1983: 34)

When Native Americans are visible in contemporary environmental movements, it is still not unusual for their presence to be as moral or mythic models rather than as individuals and communities with political and economic interests. As literary critic Paula Gunn Allen says of the tales of American aboriginal life spun by early Anglo and European raconteurs,

These stories were all untrue to a greater or lesser extent because they were partial, they reflected the values and perceptions of the travelers and their world-view, and they were bereft of context. However, the conventions developed through these accounts continue to inform present political, social, creative, religious, and educational writing about American Indian life, past and present ... In the main, the writing of these and other non-Indians raises the noble savage convention to a mystical and spiritual height from which the Indian falls at his or her great peril.

(1986: 128–129)

CONNECTING NATURE AND JUSTICE

Despite its history, its current political and intellectual location may lead many readers to think of environmentalism as a good example of a 'left'-leaning political position. But in fact, movements, ideologies and philosophies that might be considered environmentalist by some minimal standard (say, because they value nature, for instrumental or noninstrumental reasons, and therefore advocate significantly limiting its manipulation) do not necessarily include or imply positions regarding human social issues. Such basic ecological thinking can coexist with a wide spectrum of political and ethical positions regarding human relationships with each other. Pro-nature themes linking human ideals, such as civility and civilization, with ethical

14

and aesthetic appreciation of animals, trees, and 'pure,' 'untouched' land, have been common in a wide variety of scientific and political discourses, including German National Socialism (Ferry 1995; Thomas 1995). In the history of ideas, it is not at all uncommon to see concern for the natural world coupled with misanthropic or otherwise harmful ideologies (Haraway 1989). More commonly, influential American environmentalist theorists did not explicitly address human social issues. When Muir, Leopold and Carson emphasized the need for human epistemic humility regarding the role of each being and species in the organic whole, their opinions on the importance of human interests and rights remained mostly undisclosed.

Clearly, care and consideration of nonhuman entities does not *require* sensitivity to social justice, and vice versa. Hence, when the relationships between 'nature and society,' or between human treatment of the natural world and interpersonal and social ethics are addressed, the approaches and conclusions vary immensely. While some idealize the purity of nature and uphold it as a model for social control, others notice the commonalities among the assumptions behind various types of cruelty and mistreatment. Historically, European thinkers of the latter stripe tended to advocate basic ethical ideals of freedom, compassion, and universal rights for nonhuman animals, or all sentient beings. A number of key figures in the early history of European movements against human chauvinism saw their goals and values intricately tied to issues of human social justice, often claiming that nonhuman animals possessed rights or moral worth via an extension of given systems of ethics. Many began by renouncing all forms of cruelty, including cruelty to animals.

Writing in 1789, Jeremy Bentham, founding parent of Utilitarianism, made an analogy between prejudice based on skin color and prejudice based on species identity (Bentham 1844). Several founders of the British Royal Society for the Prevention of Cruelty to Animals, founded in 1824, were former leaders in the antislavery movement (Nash 1990: 25). In 'Cruelties to Civilization,' written in 1897, feminist and humanitarian Henry Salt wrote that the emancipation of men and the emancipation of animals 'are inseparably connected, and neither can be fully realized alone.' He believed that humans and animals are kin, and that 'capitalism victimized both nature and people' (Nash 1990: 29). Making specific material connections between different forms of oppression, Frederick Douglass wrote,

> Not only the slave, but the horse, the ox and the mule shared the general feeling of indifference to the rights naturally engendered by a state of slavery. The master blamed the overseer, the overseer the slave, and the slave the horses, oxen and mules, and violence fell upon the animals as a consequence.
>
> (Quoted in Spiegel 1988: 94)

Given this tradition, perhaps we should not be surprised that Peter Singer, one of the first contemporary philosophers to consider the limits of human-centered ethics, argued that if we are truly committed to social justice and equality, there is no good reason not to extend rights to nonhuman animals.

Roderick Nash describes US environmentalism as a linear, historical extension of traditional ethical norms, from concern with the rights of individual humans to inclusion of biotic communities in the realm of rights-holders. Those who agree with Nash believe the trajectory of the development of environmental ethics in the US and Britain is a story of *ethical extension* – that current environmental ethics entail an expansion of the range of beings considered, in their own right, by traditional liberal ethics and values. Hence the changes necessary for environmental well-being do not pose a radical threat to given notions of society, personhood, morality and individual rights. This characterization melds harmoniously with the explicit statements of humanitarian, conservationist, and environmental thinkers who justify calls for the rights of animals, and exhortations to observe the value of plants and communities, with analogies to similar, traditionally liberal ethics based on the rights and values of human persons. Such moves call for extending the logic of human ethics to include nonhuman entities that possess requisite qualities, such as the ability to cognate, or to suffer. The history offered by Nash describes environmental history in terms of ethical extensionism; Nash and others also *recommend* ethical extensionism as a *good* ethical position. But this analysis, which reduces a variety of diverse opinions and approaches to a core liberal agenda, cannot accommodate the efforts of self-described radical environmentalists, including ecofeminists, to question liberal conceptions of the self, human nature, and rationality, and to create analyses and politics that address the intersections of different forms of oppression.

Sketching a more textured history of various competing political agendas, Paul Gottlieb also describes the efforts of those concerned with preserving the environment as a resource, but the major players in his environmentalist history include campaigners for social justice who valued natural entities and communities in their own right (Gottlieb 1993). For example, contemporary movements highlighting ecological well-being, its direct effects on human health, and its correlation with social justice and the distribution of wealth and resources, had interesting precursors in the Settlement House movement begun by Jane Addams and her associates in Chicago in the late nineteenth century. Though 'by no means the only force for social and environmental reform in the Progressive Era,' this movement 'became both the meeting ground and a key symbol of the movement for change contesting the urban and industrial order of the period' (Gottlieb 1993: 60). Addams, Alice Hamilton, the creator of the field of public health, and Florence Kelley, an influential industrial reformer, were astutely aware of the extent to which environmental factors fundamentally determine social and personal well-being.

In her 'feminist-vegetarian critical theory,' Carol J. Adams outlines how 'many notable feminists who have written since early modern times have either responded to animals' concerns or become interested in vegetarianism' (Adams 1990: 167). Committed nineteenth-century feminist vegetarians included Frances Willard (feminist, vegetarian, and temperance leader), Clara Barton (founder of the American Red Cross), Matilda Joslyn Gage (author of *Woman, Church and State: The Original Exposé of Male Collaboration Against the Female Sex*), and Edith Emma Cooper and Katharine Bradley, the lesbian poet couple who published their work jointly as 'Michael Field.' Emerging from this history is a fascinating and growing tradition of work that conceives of women's oppression and the oppression of people of color as directly linked with the mistreatment of animals, a perspective exemplified by a contemporary organization that names itself Feminists for Animal Rights.

The rudimentary socially-minded environmentalism evident in early movements against the exploitation of animals and for environmental health, though obviously motivated by a desire to promote the well-being of humans and other sentient beings, illuminates some of the limitations of a strictly 'conservationist' approach to environmental problems. Despite various shortcomings, early women's movements for environmental and occupational health provide examples of social thought and activism that investigated the *social* reasons behind the degradation of our environments. Conservationists, on the other hand, fight for the preservation of species and beautiful landscapes, often for the enjoyment of hunters and other 'sportsmen,' without noticing the relationships between the fact that when wilderness vanishes someone is profiting, and the fact that the most economically and politically powerless members of society are nearly always the most severely harmed by industrial waste, poor air and water quality, and the rampant environmental ugliness that tends to accompany urban poverty.

While Rachel Carson's *Silent Spring*, *The Closing Circle: Nature, Man, and Technology*, by Barry Commoner, *The Limits to Growth*, by Donell Meadows *et al.* and E. F. Schumacher's *Small is Beautiful*, all advocating cautious, long-term consideration regarding the effects of human manipulation of nature, were some of the more influential books in the ecology movements of the 1970s, the wave of social activism that came to be known as the 'ecology movement' was also influenced by movements against pesticides and for farm workers' rights, including the work of Cesar Chavez and the National Farm Workers' Union, and by New Left ecological thought, including the work of Herbert Marcuse, Paul Goodman, and Murray Bookchin. These theorists developed neo-Marxist and anarchist critiques of 'the consumer society and its related way of life, the prominence of science and technology in establishing such a system, and the system's new forms of domination of both human society and Nature' (Gottlieb 1993: 92). Critics of science and technology, from the Luddites to the Frankfurt School to the New Science movement, were another source of attention to and criticism of relationships between the exploitation of nature and the oppression of individuals and social groups.

Radical environmentalisms calling for the replacement, not just the extension, of given ethical norms are better understood through Gottleib's lens, as they do not take for granted the sufficiency of given moral and political institutions as bases for ecologically sound practices and values. Radical movements take aim at traditional liberal assumptions that moral agents are discrete, utility-maximizing atoms, and that reform is sufficient for addressing oppressive histories. Though not all such ecologies focus on social justice, or successfully subvert liberal humanism, their existence and influence render linear, evolutionary political histories of environmental thought inadequate.

ENVIRONMENTALISM AND PHILOSOPHY

Controversies concerning the foundations and implications of environmentalism, or of valuing the nonhuman world, permeate various sectors of the environmental movement, including conferences and meetings, activist newsletters, books, discussions, and academic journals. Within the academy, along with the growing popularity of ecological science, environmental literature, and the creation of environmental studies programs, the field of environmental philosophy, and environmental ethics in particular, grew around professional philosophers' attempts to engage and clarify some of the burning ethical, political, and metaphysical debates at the heart of environmental struggles. First published in 1979, the journal *Environmental Ethics* provides a forum for those philosophical discussions, and for meta-level debates about the nature and domain of the field of environmental ethics. The topics explored in this journal include the philosophical ground of the value of nonhuman entities and analyses of the conceptual contributors to ecological destruction. A primary concern expressed there, and one which was slower to emerge from non-feminist communities and thinkers, involved the connections between relationships of human beings with nature and relationships of human beings with each other. Though some thinkers persisted in framing environmental problems and issues as a matter of humans versus nature (how 'we' treat 'it'), others confronted deeper issues about the agents of environmental destruction, the ethics and ontologies behind this destruction, and the connections between these and the 'mindsets' which motivate and allow for human oppression and exploitation. Among the latter thinkers are social ecologists and ecofeminists. The Institute for Social Ecology, created by anarchist environmentalist Murray Bookchin, helped give birth to some of the earliest ecofeminist work (by Ynestra King), as well as other perspectives and projects aimed to promote radical social transformation and ecological well-being.

18

Of course, socially-minded environmentalists and environmentally-concerned social critics continue to disagree, across and within discourses, on numbers of points, some more fundamental than others. The contours of the debates among environmental philosophers are riddled with controversies over essentialism, the basis of ethical value, ideal societies, human nature, rules and values, rights of nonhuman entities, activist strategies, and anthropocentrism, or human-centered thinking.

FEMINISM AND ENVIRONMENTAL ETHICS

Ecofeminism offers necessary criticism not only of systems of masculinist domination and exploitation, but also of nonfeminist environmentalisms, because it exhibits the inadequacy of environmentalisms that take no account of the implications and cross-pollinations of the social and the environmental. Ecofeminist philosophies and social movements aim to take these connections seriously by offering critiques of the ways in which the social and ecological worlds are gendered, and by articulating alternative perspectives on the world. Like other environmental movements concerned with social justice, ecofeminist positions consider the ethical significance of broader ecological issues such as environmental health, the preservation of wilderness, and economic development. Echoing both earlier feminist vegetarian traditions and Peter Singer's more recent critiques of factory farming, ecological feminist philosopher Lori Gruen discusses how the oppression of animals (especially female animals) mirrors and reinforces women's oppression:

> In order to keep dairy cows in a constant state of lactation, they must be impregnated annually. After her first infant is taken from her at birth, she is milked by machines twice, sometimes three times, a day for ten months. After the third month she will be impregnated again. She will give birth only six to eight weeks after drying out. This intense cycle of pregnancy and hyperlactation can last only about five years, and then the 'spent' cow is sent to slaughter . . .
>
> One-third of all dairy cows suffer from mastitis, a disease that infects the udders. The most common mastitis is caused by environmental pathogens that result from squalid housing conditions, particularly from fecal contamination . . . The result for the cow is bleeding and acute pain, particularly during milking (which is always done by machine).
>
> Dairy cows are always artificially inseminated. According to farmers, this method is faster, more efficient, and cheaper than maintaining bulls. With the use of hormone injections, cows will produce dozens of eggs at one time. After artificial insemination, the embryos will be flushed out of the womb and transplanted into surrogates through

incisions in their flanks . . . The Bovine Growth Hormone (BGH) is being touted as a revolutionary way to increase milk yields without raising feed costs. Cows are already producing more milk than their bodies should and more than the market demands. With the advent of BGH, the already shortened and painful life of the dairy cow may become even shorter and more painful.

(1993: 73–74)

But ecofeminists see farms as sites of human oppressions as well. In the United States,

eighty to ninety percent of the approximately two million hired farmworkers are Latino, followed by African-Americans, Caribbeans, Puerto Ricans, Filipinos, Vietnamese, Koreans, and Jamaicans. It is estimated that as many as 313,000 farmworkers experience pesticide-related illnesses each year. Not suprisingly, Hispanic women generally show higher levels of pesticides in their milk than white women do

(Wright 1995: 60)

and the miscarriage rate for female farmworkers in general is seven times the national average (O'Loughlin 1993: 151). In general, low-income communities and communities of color have to deal with more occupational hazards and more environmental pollutants than those who are middle-class and/or white. In addition, people of color and people with low income and poor education tend to be less protected by health insurance, to suffer more from toxic-induced or -aggravated diseases, and to spend a higher proportion of their income on medical health care (Bryant 1995).

RESPONSES TO ECOFEMINISM

When mainstream and even more radical male environmentalists refer to the work of ecofeminists, they tend to characterize it as outside central eco-political debates, completely on the fringe of worthwhile political discourse, and in terms that make it appear trivial, spiritualist, or utopian. For example, in the recent collection *The Politics of Nature: Explorations in Green Political Theory*, there appears one thinly-argued anti-ecofeminist chapter in a section entitled 'Green Political Theory: The Boundaries' (Dobson and Lucardie 1993). And although several of the authors in the volume mention the influence of feminism on 'green thinking,' there is no significant exploration of feminist and ecological criticism of science, technology, the state, liberal politics, and exploitative economic relations. Typically, Alan Carter characterizes 'feminist contributions' primarily in terms of influence on political processes, such as anti-hierarchical organizing, within political and activist groups (Carter 1993). In fact, the potentially powerful impact of feminist thought on environmentalism through its analysis of environmental problems as always social and nearly always dependent on false dualisms, and its articulations of innovative solutions, derives in part from real women's expertise in ghettoized, so-called 'natural,' caretaking practices. But it comes as no surprise to feminists when anything that focuses on women is treated as though it were concerned with 'special,' or fringe interests, or were reducible to a more touchy-feely approach to life, and when more substantive arguments are completely ignored by our detractors. Lori Gruen illustrates how J. Baird Callicott, who has been in dialogue with Karen J. Warren and other feminist philosophers for years, characterizes the ecofeminist project as a cacophonous collection of stories based on what he supposes to be a rejection of 'essentially masculinist' practices like theory-building (Gruen 1994). Rather than attempt to uncover the theoretical assumptions within the ecofeminist project, as most philosophers would do when confronted with the work of other philosophers, Callicott dismisses ecofeminism as 'anti-theoretical.' Gruen responds by outlining the ways in which ecofeminism, 'a theory which always examines the social context in which epistemic and moral claims are generated,' produces moral knowledge 'from the recognition of the interdependent nature of science and society, reason and emotion, facts and values, and the complex ecological crises that the planet now faces' (Gruen 1994: 134).

Misrepresentations of feminist work, and a lack of serious attention to feminist concerns within the majority of ecologically-minded political debates, are noteworthy not because the attention of radical male ecologists is vital or definitive, but because their inconsistencies and contradictory positions help point the way to a more coherent politics. In addition, as I hope to illustrate, rampant mischaracterizations sometimes evince a need for clearer, or perhaps more intentional, articulations of our politics, and our responses can therefore include more careful thinking about political and discursive strategies. My intention here is to focus on the issues and controversies central to ecological feminism – a form of socially-minded environmentalism, a specific site of critique, and a position from which alternative anti-oppressive and nonexploitative ethical and philosophical insights might be derived.

1

THE ECOFEMINIST PROJECT

Man seeks in woman the Other as Nature and as his fellow
being. But we know what ambivalent feelings Nature inspires
in man. He exploits her, but she crushes him, he is born of her
and dies in her; she is the source of his being and the realm
that he subjugates to his will; Nature is a vein of gross
material in which the soul is imprisoned, and she is the
supreme reality; she is contingence and Idea, the finite and the
whole, she is what opposes the Spirit, and the Spirit itself . . .
Woman sums up Nature as Mother, Wife and Idea; these
forms now mingle and now conflict, and each of them wears
a double visage.

Simone de Beauvoir

In this chapter I introduce, with broad strokes, the ecofeminist project – a
project which includes all consciously feminist attempts to articulate and
address links between feminist and environmental concerns. Upon setting
out, I ought to make clear that there is no one, unified, paradigmatic
ecofeminist perspective, movement, or work. However, there clearly is a collection of efforts and positions, related as much by family resemblance as by
commonalities, that are suitably characterized as part of an ecofeminist
project. These positions share, at least, intentions that are explicitly both
feminist and environmentalist, although their implicit understandings of
feminism and environmentalism, women and nature, oppression and liberation, can vary widely.

In following chapters, I will be most interested in *ecological feminism*, a
cluster of perspectives that constitutes a subcategory of the ecofeminist project, and which is noteworthy in its emphasis on the similarities and relationships between and among various forms of oppression, exploitation,
and domination. Where some ecofeminist projects focus on similarities
between the objects of oppression, say 'women' and 'nature,' ecological
feminists maintain that these similarities are philosophically and practically
significant in so far as they evidence patterns of domination. For example,
some object-attentive ecofeminists see both women and nature as inherently
feminine and therefore oppressed by masculine or phallocratic regimes of
meaning and power. These ecofeminists tend to respond to cults of masculinity by upholding femininity as the superior mode of being.

In contrast, ecological feminists argue that both women and nature are considered and constructed as feminine, that the inextricability of masculinity and femininity as concepts and as cultural products make it impossible to reclaim one without assuming the other, and that 'femininity' is a potent tool for domination and control in general. Ecological feminists point out that there is a logical inconsistency in some versions of ecofeminism, because ecofeminists who cling to femininity fail to question the dualisms which, I will illustrate below, the ecofeminist project so vehemently rejects. So 'femininity,' and other features (embodiment, mystery, resistance to reason) supposedly shared by subjugated beings and classes, are problems to be scrutinized, not qualities to be uncritically celebrated. While ecological feminists may end up valuing some of those features, they do so because the features are valuable or useful, not merely because of their associations with the oppressed. In addition, ecological feminists believe that emphasizing the similarities between women and natural states or entities maintains a lack of attention to the ways in which men are natural beings, and women are also dominators and oppressors.

This chapter is about the ecofeminist project in its broadest terms – including ecological feminist and other ecofeminist approaches. Although it is not a history of ecofeminism, the following pages are meant to provide a sense of the relationships between ecofeminist projects and other strains of feminist and environmental thought, and of how ecological feminism in particular has developed as questions about the nature of gender and the solidity of nature have become more perplexing.

CONSTRUCTING CONNECTIONS

Feminist writers and activists began explicitly articulating abstract analyses and practical politics that paid close attention to the similarities and connections between patriarchal mistreatment of women and the mistreatment of nature in the 1970s.[1] The work of these feminist thinkers, and activists similarly concerned with connections between 'women and nature,' has come to be known as *ecofeminist*, marking a distinction between specifically environmentalist feminisms and those concerned solely with women's interests, and human oppression. A foundational aspect of ecofeminism is the belief that for feminism adequately to address the realities and specificities of women's oppression, we must pay explicit attention to how that oppression relies on and fuels the devaluation and exploitation of nonhuman,

1 For a sense of the variety of early works exploring the connections between feminism and environmentalism and/or women and nature, see Atwood 1972; Ruether 1975; Griffin 1978; Dodson Gray 1981; King 1981; McAllister 1982; d'Eaubonne 1981; Gearhardt 1984. For a more complete list see Karen Warren's bibliography in *The American Philosophical Association Newsletter on Feminism and Philosophy* 1991.

'natural' beings and entities. While many ecofeminists describe their work as an expansive *feminism*, they also challenge ecological and environmental approaches that do not look at gender, race, class, or the connections among destructive ideologies and practices. Thus ecofeminists place themselves at the crossroads of feminist, anti-racist, and environmentalist movements, as well as critiques of capitalism, heterosexism, homophobia, and other forms of oppression based on the dualistic construction and maintenance of inferior, devalued, or pathologized/naturalized Others.

Ecofeminist writing emerged from feminist movements in the 1970s, but the versions of feminism grounding ecofeminist positions are as varied as feminist thought itself. Although in *The Dialectic of Enlightenment* (1993) Theodor Adorno and Max Horkheimer introduced a critical theory concerning the role of reason and technology in creating intermingled systems of domination, European and American feminists (including Francois d'Eubonne, Ynestra King, Mary Daly, Susan Griffin, Barbara Deming, and others involved in the Women's Peace Movement) were among the first to discuss in print the deep conceptual connections between men's mistreatment of women and what some called 'the rape of the Earth.' Citing connections between the mistreatment of women and the mistreatment of nonhuman nature, and rejecting women's traditional roles as housekeepers, Mary Daly wrote,

> Rachel Carson, whose credibility was weakened by her sex, was greeted with superficial attention and deep inattentiveness. Ecologists today still deny her recognition, maintaining dishonest silence. Meanwhile the springs are becoming more silent, as the necrophilic leaders of phallotechnic society are carrying out their programs of planned poisoning for all life on the planet.
>
> I am not suggesting that women have a 'mission' to save the world from ecological disaster. I am certainly not calling for female Self-sacrifice in the male-led cause of 'ecology.'
>
> (Daly 1978: 21)

While these white women were certainly not the first to notice connections between environmental degradation and women's mistreatment, they were committed to constructing a feminism that addressed these connections specifically. Feminists who first drew attention to connections among the mistreatment of women, animals, and nature, took these entities at face value, and to a large degree relied on common discursive understandings instead of questioning the accuracy and universality of categories like 'woman' and 'nature.' To many contemporary feminists, their reliance on these categories seems naive and romantic, and denotes a lack of critical attention to the fluidity of concepts, identities, and meaning. At the same time, it is clear that despite their use of Enlightenment rhetoric and spiritualistic imagery, early ecofeminists questioned given norms, descriptions, and boundaries around 'woman,' 'nature,' and 'human.' This occurred in the context of a tradition of feminist reclamation and an emerging feminist literary aesthetic that drew powerful connections between women, or females, and the natural world. From a variety of cultural identities, poets, novelists, and activists stressed the 'naturalness' of women's bodies and perspectives, women's tendency toward involvement in relational, 'private sphere' activities, and the revolutionary potential of these tendencies.[2]

> look at me
> i am not a separate woman
> i am a continuance
> of blue sky
> i am the throat
> of the sandia mountains
> a night wind woman
> who burns
> with every breath
> she takes
>
> Joy Harjo

Every time a sister learns that she is not born to live in a world of fear, to be dominated, every time a sister sits down with a glass of water in front of her and understands that she is intimately tied to water and that all life is tied to water she is gradually building an inner strength that gives her armour to go out and fight the world.

> Luisah Teish

> What good will one woman never again using plastic bags do
> in the face of tons of plutonium, recombinant DNA
> a hundred thousand rapists?
> What good does it do that I feed my daughter organic rice
> purple beets, never sugar?
> What good that I march with other women
> and we yell WOMEN UNITED
> WILL NEVER BE DEFEATED
> banshees into the night?
> These things will not save my daughter . . . .
> And I want to save her.
> Oh Mother of us all, I am a mother too
> I want to save her.
>
> Ellen Bass

2 See, for example, Atwood 1972; Rich 1976, 1978; Daly 1978; Griffin 1978; Jordan 1983; Teish 1983; Lorde 1984, 1992.

Elizabeth Dodson Gray's anti-hierarchical *Green Paradise Lost*, Susan Griffin's *Woman and Nature* and Carolyn Merchant's *The Death of Nature* were published between 1978 and 1981, Leonie Caldecott and Stephanie Leland's *Reclaim the Earth* appeared in 1983, and ecofeminist issues and theories were subsequently visible in various feminist and lesbian-feminist journals and periodicals. Merchant's *The Death of Nature*, published in 1980, presented a systematic account of the effects of the scientific revolution on conceptions of women and nature. Her work provided historical and scientific arguments to justify the leanings of many feminists toward a sense of solidarity with the nonhuman world, and toward theory that analyzed women's oppression as part of a larger scheme of domination, mistreatment, and exploitation. This scheme was described variously as a rape mentality, a patriarchal mindset, a drive to conquer, and power-over thinking. None the less, it wasn't until the late 1980s and early 1990s that books specifically devoted to ecofeminist theory began to appear. *Healing the Wounds: The Promise of Ecofeminism* and *Reweaving the World: The Emergence of Ecofeminism* were early collections of ecofeminist theory. Numerous books and scholarly discussions followed.[3]

Though the Marxist and New Left backgrounds of many feminists resulted in attention to matters of class exploitation, and there was varying attention to race, the most developed positions in early ecofeminist work looked simply at gender, as though 'woman' could be sliced away from race, sexuality, and other identities and social locations. One reason for this mistaken conception of 'woman' is the fact that the working assumption for many white feminists has been that looking at 'race' means looking at racism, or looking at women of color, as though race is not always relevant in gender, as though white women are not products of racialist constructions, and as though the maintenance of the category 'white' is not significantly related to dualistic norms regarding nature and culture. In feminism in general, issues of race did not begin to be adequately fleshed out until women of color began to bring them to the table. The words of doris davenport, written in 1981, often still apply.

> We experience white feminists and their organizations as elitist, crudely insensitive, and condescending. Most of the feminist groups in this country are examples of this elitism . . . It is also apparent that white feminists still perceive us as the 'Other,' based on a menial or sexual image: as more sensual, but less cerebral; more interesting, perhaps, but less intellectual; and more oppressed, but less political than they are.
>
> (1983: 86)

---

3 Influential books include Shiva 1988, 1994; Diamond 1994; Diamond and Orenstein 1990; Spretnak 1991; Gaard 1993; Mies and Shiva 1993; Plumwood 1993.

DIFFICULT INTERSECTIONS

In *The Death of Nature*, Carolyn Merchant illustrates how, historically, conceptualizations of nature in science and religion have dramatically shaped the form and force of human impact on natural entities and communities. Merchant and others identify Baconian thought as the culmination of a gradual, multifaceted shift from thinking of nature as imbued with spiritual force to thinking of it as inert matter. This shift interwove with and enabled the development of forms of science unhindered by a previous tendency to respect, however fancifully, many aspects of nonhuman organic life. The 'turn' away from seeing nature as enchanted, mysterious, and fecund, enabled the development of scientific systems that regarded natural entities and phenomena as under the jurisdiction of man. As a result, technology, science, and other material practices and institutions *instrumentalized* nonhuman entities. That is, they defined and interacted with the natural world primarily as an instrument for human manipulation, consumption, and speculation, as a sphere of being in which nothing possesses the special qualities that would make it worthy of moral respect. They thereby strengthened stalwart conceptual divisions between human and nonhuman reality, and the devaluation of nature.

But, of course, Baconian science did not occur in a social vacuum. Placing the work of this 'father of modern science' in its political and economic context, Merchant also traces the ways in which his descriptions and metaphors were influenced by violence against women, specifically the inquisition of women accused of witchcraft throughout Europe during the early seventeenth century.

> *For you have but to follow and as it were hound nature in her wanderings, and you will be able when you like to lead and drive her afterward to the same place again.* Neither am I of opinion in this history of marvels that superstitious narratives of *sorceries, witchcrafts, charms,* dreams, divinations, and the like, where there is an assurance and clear evidence of the fact, should be altogether excluded . . . howsoever the use and practice of such arts is to be condemned, yet from the speculation and consideration of them . . . A useful light may be gained, not only for a true judgment of the offenses of persons charged with such practices, *but likewise for the further disclosing of the secrets of nature. Neither ought a man to make scruple of entering and penetrating into these holes and corners, when the inquisition of truth is his whole object – as your majesty has shown in your example.*
>
> (1980: 168)

By investigating the ways in which negative constructions of femininity and hence women's subordinate roles, identities, and material circumstances were interwoven with the devaluation of nature, historical work sets the stage for ecofeminist philosophical inquiry. It also lends support to feminists' long-standing tendencies to draw attention to connections among male-dominated science, technology, the destruction of the natural world, and the oppression of women and members of other feminized, naturalized, and subjugated groups whose instrumental use is emphasized and abused by men with power. At the same time, any explanatory theory that mines history for hidden causal connections and conceptual linkages runs the risk of oversimplifying an impossibly complex story.

In any given era, there is rarely a lack of dissent among philosophers, scientists, or theologians regarding the nature of existence, the significance of matter, and the norms of moral behavior. But even given dissent, and the likelihood that no narrative fully represents the whole truth, it is possible to trace the ways in which some ideas or ontologies have reached prominence, and it is worthwhile to consider how the ideas of the powerful tend to maintain their power. Which ideas fell by the wayside? When and how? Why were certain ideas more widely disseminated? Even if there is no essential 'Western worldview,' it is clear that a group of ideas, values, and methodologies has been more influential than others in shaping the history of culture and science in the West. Although the precise causal relationships between hierarchical philosophical and theoretical views that encourage and justify domination, on the one hand, and practices, moral systems, and institutions, on the other, are opaque and controversial, correlation is less difficult to ascertain. As critical work in science studies emphasizes, theoretical understanding comes at least as much from positing or creating explanatory mechanisms as discovering them (Jasanoff *et al.* 1995). Much of social and natural science entails describing perceived phenomena in ways that render them comprehensible and consumable – at least for other scientists. These descriptions emerge from and into social, discursive, and political spaces, and are credible, persuasive, and influential only in so far as they fit other aspects of those spaces. Merchant's is an important story about the ways metaphors and understandings of nature that emerged with the scientific revolution fit into an ideological nexus that posited 'woman' as means to the ends of men. Environmental ethics cannot ignore critical assessments of discursive and material correlations and coincidences which point to hot spots in the history of human interactions, even if the causal story of how associations developed is murky. The similarities among the current treatment of instrumentalized, feminized, and naturalized entities are simply overwhelming.

Though organic life, its material constituents, and all that supports them are physically real, firm distinctions between 'nature' and 'culture' are not accurate ontological markers. Rather, they are discursive creations that shift in response to political, economic, aesthetic, and epistemic forces and agents and that in turn *create* changes in human practices and institutions. As the subtitle of Donna Haraway's *Simians, Cyborgs, and Women* intimates, attempts to reconsider human relationships with nature paradoxically entail a 'reinvention of nature.' In fact, Haraway's thoughts about nature *begin* with the acknowledgement that 'nature' is an invention. The meanings of 'nature' – the concept referring to that stuff which is usually neither human nor human-generated (sometimes humans do count) – vary with their uses and contexts, as do meanings of 'culture.' Yet, even when they are suspect, the universal or near-global patterns of the significance and significations of concepts need not always be completely abandoned. Even the most fluid concepts can be useful and meaningful, and therefore can be theorized. Although relationships between concepts and practices are not linear causal chains, it is possible to trace to some extent their influences on each other and on human reality. For example, conceiving of and responding to natural beings and communities as active, rather than inert, calls to attention qualities and potentialities that will otherwise remain unseen. Philosophical work in environmental ethics requires such interrogations, especially because as we determine how to reconsider our actions and relations with nature, we inevitably reinvent nature and ourselves.

Ecofeminists notice that the language, practices, and values behind women's oppression are often similar and sometimes identical to those through which 'nature' is radically altered and sometimes irreparably destroyed.

> Women are described in animal terms as pets, cows, sows, foxes, chicks, serpents, bitches, beavers, old bats, old hens, mother hens, pussycats, cats, cheetahs, bird-brains, and hare-brains . . . 'Mother Nature' is raped, mastered, conquered, mined; her secrets are 'penetrated,' her 'womb' is to be put into the service of the 'man of science.' Virgin timber is felled, cut down; fertile soil is tilled, and land that lies 'fallow' is 'barren,' useless. The exploitation of nature and animals is justified by feminizing them; the exploitation of women is justified by naturalizing them.
>
> (Warren 1994: 37)

Carol Adams' work on the symbioses between misogynist and meat-eating cultures in *The Sexual Politics of Meat* illustrates the extent to which sexism and the consumption of meat are interwoven in contemporary Western societies. Her analysis is similar to Alice Walker's discussion in her essay 'Am I Blue?' of how racism gets justified, enacted, and hidden in ways similar to the mistreatment of animals. Similar concepts and hierarchies, of masculinity and femininity, reason and emotion, or 'civilized' and 'primitive,' enable various systems of oppression, and these conceptual tools of oppression and domination are transferred across different systems of dominance and subordination. Some of the connections among different oppressions are evident in stark material terms, while others are less obvious. Karen J. Warren argues that several pressing environmental issues, including deforestation, water pollution, and food scarcity, are deeply shaped by gendered divisions of labor and the invisibility and devaluation of women's work (Warren 1994). In any case, giving attention to the relationships among different systems of oppression is imperative not only for theoretical integrity, but because these connections are enacted on and through the lives and bodies of those who exist at the intersections of the institutions and enactments of dominating power. Yet the testimony from those located 'on the intersections' also tells us that this attention should not amount to the reduction of different systems and institutions to each other, or to one 'basic oppression.' As Audre Lorde wrote to Mary Daly,

> To imply . . . that all women suffer the same oppression simply because we are women is to lose sight of the many varied tools of patriarchy. It is to ignore how those tools are used by women without awareness against each other . . . The oppression of women knows no ethnic nor racial boundaries, true, but that does not mean it is identical within those differences.
>
> (1984: 69–70)

A crucial challenge for those engaged in ecofeminist projects is taking seriously connections, patterns, similarities, and interwoven features of different forms of domination and exploitation without either obscuring difference and particularity through reduction, or resting in preoccupation with various forms of domination *only* in so far as they are related to each other.

THE FEMINISM IN ECOFEMINISM

Wondering about the feminist basis of ecological feminism, Karen Warren neatly describes the commonalities and disagreements among feminists:

> All feminists agree that the oppression of women (i.e., the unequal and unjust status of women) exists, is wrong, and ought to be changed. But feminists disagree markedly about how to understand that oppression and how to bring about the necessary changes.
>
> (1987: 8)

Warren then assesses the adequacy of 'four leading versions of feminism,' – liberal feminism, traditional Marxist feminism, radical feminism, and socialist feminism – as defined by Alison Jaggar in her book *Feminist Politics and Human Nature* – as potential foundations for ecofeminism. She concludes that none of these versions is adequate, and that a new, 'integrative and transformative' feminism is necessary, one which moves us beyond the current debate over the four leading versions of feminism and makes a responsible ecological perspective central to feminist theory and practice (1987: 18). Though I concur with some of Warren's criticisms of sectors of feminist thought, I find her overall approach to a discussion of 'feminisms' problematic, and I disagree with the conclusion that inevitably follows from her taxonomic approach.

Many feminist and nonfeminist philosophers utilize Jaggar's discussion of four leading feminist theories and their links to four correlative conceptions of human nature. But taking Jaggar's early 1980s characterization of feminist politics at face value is problematic. Jaggar herself stresses the dynamic aspects of political theory and the ensuing difficulty of categorizing aspects of a relatively young social movement:

> The most obvious difficulty is that theory changes constantly, partly in response to changing social realities, partly in response to new theoretical perspectives. Women's situation is changing rapidly at the present time and feminist theory, in consequence, is constantly developing. Partly because feminist theory is a new intellectual discipline, moreover, feminist theorists are not working within an established paradigm and consequently often challenge their own fundamental assumptions.
>
> (1983: 10)

In reference to her own categorization of 'four conceptions of women's liberation,' she writes, 'the present analysis can be useful as a description only for a relatively short time, although I hope that its critical or prescriptive value may be longer lasting' (1983: 10). Still, Jaggar's characterization of 1970s radical feminism, which both Warren and Jaggar identify as the origin of a great deal of ecofeminist thought, is not uncontroversial. In a review of *Feminist Politics and Human Nature*, Marilyn Frye argued that there is actually little significant difference between radical and socialist feminisms, even regarding their conceptions of human nature, and that Jaggar misrepresents a significant number of radical feminist thinkers who were publishing theory in the 1970s (Frye 1992).

Even if the picture Jaggar presents of 1970s Euro-American radical feminism is accurate, the influences of postmodernism, ecology, media studies, postcolonialism, the literary, theoretical and political work of women of color, and, above all, concrete social and political changes, have affected feminists on all points of the political and theoretical spectrum. The increased academization of feminist theory through Women's Studies programs, and the integration of feminism into most academic disciplines, has created a large number of professional feminist theorists representing a multitude of methodologies and political perspectives. The popularity of interdisciplinary studies has contributed to the cross-pollinated influences and disciplines that have long been characteristic of feminist inquiry. To use Jaggar's categories without acknowledging the dynamic nature of feminist theory and the ongoing conflicts within supposedly similar schools of thought, is to neglect the potential and actual historical intermingling of types of feminist thought with other influences and with each other. Certainly we need to think about how ecofeminism emerged from non-environmentalist feminisms, and what aspects of feminism are necessary for the further development of ecological feminist ethics. But rather than reify or amend the infamous 'categories of feminism' and the positions they are thought to represent, I would like to consider more thoroughly the values and theoretical presuppositions that have grounded and are currently grounding the whole range of ecofeminist theory and practice. What has been effective and accurate? What is destructive or disempowering?

The widespread feminist focus on oppression – on disclosing its existence and planning its demise – and the notion that women's and other forms of oppression are central to the construction of gender and to women's positions and experiences in the world, partially explains the early interest of radical feminists in preventing cruelty to animals and the destruction of the planet. Although there is much disagreement on the roots, causes, and locations of oppression, most feminists agree that to be feminist is to be against oppression in all of its forms. It is therefore no mere coincidence that feminist gatherings have always tended to be places where vegetarianism, recycling, and non-intrusive technologies have been encouraged. This is by no means meant to imply that feminists agree about the nature of oppression, or what counts as oppressive, or about whether the focus of feminism ought to be on oppressions other than women's oppression, or that feminism ought to focus on oppression at all. None the less, though feminists might themselves exploit and oppress, an argument that justifies oppression *qua* oppression is not a feminist argument.

Oppression is more than harm, and though oppression is often painful, it is morally problematic for reasons not accommodated by a utilitarian perspective that is concerned only with pleasure and suffering, or perceived utility. In other words, oppression is unethical even when it does not cause pain and even when it could be said to cause some pleasure. A system that creates happy slaves is unacceptable from an anti-oppressive perspective. So what is oppression if it is not merely a form of pain, or obvious harm? One dictionary defines the verb *to oppress* as *to keep down by the cruel or unjust use of power or authority; to crush; to trample down; to overpower* (Webster's New World 1994). The concept of 'keeping something down,' is more subtle, more deep and comprehensive than pain and suffering. Iris Young defines oppression as consisting in:

> Systematic institutional processes which prevent some people from learning and using satisfying and expansive skills in socially recognized settings, or institutionalized social processes which inhibit people's ability to play and communicate with others or to express their feelings and perspectives on social life in contexts where others can

listen. While the social conditions of oppression often include material deprivation and maldistribution, they also involve issues beyond distribution.

(1990: 38)

Her list of 'five faces of oppression' – exploitation, marginalization, powerlessness, cultural imperialism, and violence – describe some of the correlates of oppression, or tools of subjugation that coexist with and enforce oppression. Another correlate is domination, which Mark Blasius defines in *Gay and Lesbian Politics: Sexuality and the Emergence of a New Ethic* as an expression of power that 'allows the actions of one to elicit and guide or command the actions of another with a high degree of certainty' (1994: 21). In an early essay that set out to define and describe women's oppression in ways not effectively captured by Marxism, Marilyn Frye suggests that oppression entails molding or immobilizing the oppressed by reducing their options in the world (Frye 1983). Using a metaphor of particular interest to ecofeminists, she characterized the position of oppressed women as being like entrapment in a birdcage. A system of many individual wires limits the freedom of a bird in a cage, although each wire in and of itself hardly appears to be an impediment to movement. When options are greatly reduced by diffuse causes that are historically, economically, and psychologically entrenched, pain might not be the best indicator of when we have been immobilized or compromised. A stunningly pernicious aspect of oppression is how it can effectively create desires in the oppressed that are not in their own interest, including, for example, women who want to be with men who seriously, physically threaten their lives.

These definitions are made more complex by the fact that multiple systems of oppression coexist, intertwine, and overlap in societies and persons. The result is that an individual or group may experience itself as fully occupying dominant and subordinate identities (as in a woman who is also white, or groups of middle-class men who are gay). Therefore, because of who women are, and because they are present in nearly every sector of any society, any feminism that aims to address the complexities of 'women's oppression' must be much more than a simplistic attempt to uplift females. Much of the most groundbreaking feminist work of the last fifteen years has been done by lesbians, radical women of color, and working-class feminists who are attempting to create feminisms focused on the intersections among various forms of social mistreatment and oppression. Contrary to some popular characterizations, such feminisms have radical, often positive implications for men who are also victims of the oppressive systems feminists aim to unravel, such as class. Feminism is also admittedly not always experienced as liberatory by women for whom the significance of gender oppression is greatly shaped and overshadowed by their possession of race, class, geographic, or heterosexual privilege.

Instead of pointing toward a new, transformative feminism to ground ecofeminism, we should recognize that, at the risk of sounding grandiose, the world is full of new feminisms. In fact, 'new' feminisms and women-centered movements arise according to women's needs, concerns, and interests. So ecofeminism and ecological feminism are themselves 'new' feminisms – born out of the histories of feminism and environmentalism but, as they evolve, influenced by various other pertinent academic and political movements, including literary and cultural criticism, Third World women's and other postcolonial movements, peace movements, and science and technology studies. Though a key aspect of ecological feminism, and one of its primary contributions to ethical theory and practice, is its thorough analysis of forms of oppression and moral agency in oppressive contexts, an analysis of oppression is not sufficient ground for ethics. In fact, a rejection of oppression is logically dependent on an affirmation of some alternative. Hence, I ultimately find it most important to focus on the ways in which ecological feminism aims to promote the flourishing of both human and nonhuman life. The backward-looking ecofeminist focus on oppression should not be taken as the beginning and end of its analysis.

Perceptions of a practical need for anti-racist feminist environmental ethics depend on an interpretation of history that shows the extent to which both nature, women and other Others have been damaged, ignored, reduced, romanticized, and essentialized, however ambiguously, and how destructive practices both rely on and shape the philosophical underpinnings that justify, propagate, and alter them. Because 'nature' is as much a relative, socially-constructed concept as a category of beings, entities, and relationships, environmental ethics ought to begin with a tenuous relationship to conceptions of 'nature' as fixed, or secured on every side by impermeable walls. My goal in this book is to explore some aspects of feminist, contextualist, environmental ethics that do not *fix* nature, yet which still offer normative suggestions and practical guidance for human action concerning, and within, nature. Such a project also entails a constructive response to fallacious, fixed notions of culture, gender, and race.

Although nature and human nature cannot provide universal, static norms, it is still meaningful to characterize the social/natural world as comprised of ethical agents and objects with interests and levels of well-being. It is therefore possible to articulate and develop feminist, ecological ethics that aim toward human and ecological flourishing without representing humans, women or nature in ways that are static and bounded. Given our criticisms of gender and sexuality, and our desire to construct more fluid concepts and practices, it is particularly important for feminists to explore the possibilities of ethics that are mindful of the shifting terrain of nature and culture. Such a move, which might be characterized as anti-essentialist, is atypical among nonfeminist environmental ethicists, who tend to rely on fixed or given conceptions of nature to ground or illustrate their claims.

FROM ECOFEMINISM TO ECOLOGICAL FEMINISM

Reweaving the Web of Life: Feminism and Nonviolence, published in 1982, traced the history of feminist pacifism and antinuclear politics, and contains many early ecofeminist sentiments. Here one of the organizers of the Women's Pentagon Action, Donna Warnock, writes,

> Thus man has come to deify 'rational' thought, also known as mechanistic thinking, in which each component of a problem to be solved is analyzed independently, mechanistically, isolated from its environment. Ecological and human consequences are overlooked. Emotion is absent.
>
> (Warnock 1982: 24)

In 'Only Justice Can Stop A Curse,' Alice Walker unflinchingly claims,

> If we have any true love for the stars, planets, the rest of Creation, we must do everything we can to keep white men away from them . . . They who have never met any new creature without exploiting, abusing, or destroying it. They who say we poor and colored and female and elderly blight neighborhoods, while they blight worlds.
>
> (Walker 1982: 265)

Though there are certainly common features among various examples of ecofeminist and ecological feminist thought, the differences among them are equally relevant to our discussion. As feminist theorists reject some versions of feminism as inadequate, shallow, or inconsistent, so must we critically consider the underlying principles and values to which ecofeminists implicitly or explicitly subscribe.

In the following pages I will sometimes be deeply critical of the theoretical underpinnings accepted by a number of ecofeminist writers. None the less, I am favorably disposed toward the ecofeminist project – the attempt to bring together both feminist concerns, analyses, and ethical insights and ethical concerns for the well-being of nonhuman species and environments. Ecofeminists are preoccupied with connections and intersections among different forms and instances of oppression, and this focus can provide important insight and direction for environmental ethics and feminist politics. The positions of feminist and other critical theorists who articulate connections among various forms of human oppression without also analyzing and addressing the mistreatment of nature are different from ecofeminist positions, because ecofeminism relies also on rejecting the belief that membership in the human species should be the sole, ultimate designator of moral value. In fact, ecofeminist arguments are meant not only to uncover the connections between misogyny, sexism, or institutions of gender and the exploitation of the so-called natural world, but also to make explicit connections among these and other forms of oppression. Ecofeminists are particularly interested in the ways oppression depends on hierarchical, dualistic

35

thinking, and values that propagate the glorification of qualities supposedly 'naturally' held by those with economic, sexual, racial, hegemonic power.

Still, ecofeminist methodologies are multifarious, and some are more useful and accurate. A number of ecofeminists take discursive and practical connections between women and nature at face value, believing them to be a result of similarities among oppressed entities. Others – ecological feminists – theorize such connections as indicators of similarities in subjugating ideologies and constructions of the meanings of 'woman' and 'nature.' Among the latter in even her early writings, Ynestra King asserts:

> We live in a culture which is founded on repudiation and domination of nature. This has a special significance for women because, in patriarchal thought, women are *believed to be* closer to nature than men. That gives women a particular stake in ending the domination of nature – in healing the alienation between human and nonhuman nature [my emphasis].
>
> (Rothschild 1983: 18)

Ecological feminist emphasis, not on connections between women and nature, but on complex causal explanations and implications of various, interlocking oppressions has been similar to, and often relies on, work that makes explicit links among misogyny, racism, class oppression, and heterosexism and homophobia. Ecological feminist attention to connections, or to perceivable/constructable points of intersection among understandings of woman, nature, race, and labor that help justify devaluation, should not be presented, by ecofeminists or their critics, as a totalizing or grand schema that attempts to explain and address the root cause of all oppression. Rather, it is best seen as a perspective that can be uniquely illuminative of some aspects of oppression, exploitation, mistreatment, and degradation.

For example, 'environmental racism' is the term that has been used to refer to the ways in which racism is perpetrated *through* environmental harm:

> On still days, when the air is heavy, Piedmont has the rotten-egg smell of a chemistry class. The acrid, sulfurous odor of the bleaches used in the paper mill drifts along the valley, penetrating walls and clothing, furnishings and skin. No perfume can fully mask it. It is as much a part of the valley as is the river, and the people who live there are not overly disturbed by it. 'Smells like money to me,' we were taught to say in its defense, even as children.
>
> (Gates 1994: 6)

The mostly African-American residents in the 85-mile area between Baton Rouge and New Orleans, better known as Cancer Alley, live in a region which contains 136 chemical companies and refineries. A 1987 study conducted by the United Church of Christ's Commission for Racial Justice found that two-thirds of all Blacks and Latinos in the

United States reside in areas with one or more unregulated toxic-waste sites. The CRJ report also cited race as the most significant variable in differentiating communities with such sites from those without them. Partly as a result of living with toxic waste in disproportionate numbers, African-Americans have higher rates of cancer, birth defects, and lead poisoning than the United States population as a whole.

(Riley 1993: 192)

Ecological feminist analyses of environmental racism are crucial, as they help provide a theoretical framework for detecting and analyzing the depth of correlation among various oppressions. This is due mostly to its preoccupation with intersections – a focus that any theory or movement hoping to do something as simple as 'improve the lives of women' must have. Though we cannot underestimate the importance of getting more people to notice (or care) that when the earth gets dumped on so do people of color, ecological feminist analysis also pushes the following kinds of questions. How does ethical, economic and aesthetic rhetoric help justify racist, toxic policies? How do alienation and disempowerment make it particularly difficult for communities to fight against a system that is poisoning them and their immediate environment? How do current racist conceptions of people and urban spaces as unclean and hopeless help justify mistreatment? How, in male-dominated contexts, are women disproportionately affected by the minute and mundane effects of toxins?

Regarding environmental racism and injustice, ecological feminism can offer helpful questions, and perhaps point to promising alternatives. For example, activists might draw on feminist empowerment and consciousness-raising models to create community discussion of issues. Feminist politics also require that the knowledge, insights, and questions of women of color are central in shaping understandings of the problems and solutions at hand. A feminist lens might also be necessary to create activist strategies that do not replicate oppressive gender roles and identities. Without special attention to the needs and interests of girls and women of particular races and classes, it is likely that their particular, gendered experiences of, complicity in, and resistance to environmental harm will not be noticed. Ecological feminist values and analyses also insure that 'environmental racism' is not thought of as just a problem for people, and that the interests of the nonhuman life through which human communities are built are considered as well. *But the fact of its usefulness by no means implies that ecological feminism is the only analysis needed.* Any consideration of 'community problems' that does not include the lives of women and nonhuman beings is grossly inadequate, as is any analysis that is not highly attentive to the racial formations within environmental issues. Various lenses, concerning the history and meanings of racism and economic oppression in the US, epidemiological patterns, workers' issues with regard to toxic chemicals, and urban and industrial planning and policy, and the relationships between domestic dumping of US waste and global economic practices, must all inform theoretical and practical responses to environmental racism and injustice.

The 'power and promise' of ecological feminism lies in its challenges to the assumptions of various other political ecological perspectives, its feminist philosophical foundations, and its positive recommendations for options that take seriously intersections among different systems of domination. This thinking at the crossroads can be an important contributor to the kind of political and ethical discourse and conversation that we need right now, not as the answer to all of our problems, or a primary bottom-line analysis, but because its attention to patterns and connections forecloses dead end single-issue politics and the acceptance of practices and policies that actually contradict our goals.

THE SUBSTANCE OF ECOLOGICAL FEMINISM

By way of summary, I offer the following synopsis of ecological feminist positions which ground the discussion of ethics throughout the rest of this book.

(1) Ethical systems and values born out of conceptual universes that relegate what is considered feminine or natural to an inferior status help justify and implement both that relegation and the mistreatment of those groups and entities. The most obvious examples are ethical systems that allow for no moral consideration of those entities, that specifically claim that women, nature, tribal people, foreigners, or slaves are not included in a given moral universe. But it is also true that moral systems based on deeply rooted and exclusionary conceptions of moral agents and objects can import problematic beliefs in more clandestine ways. Ecological feminist ethics therefore follow in the footsteps of feminist ethics in exploring values and practices that derive from a foundation that takes women, nature, and other commonly excluded beings or groups seriously as morally relevant. This might include focusing on their particularities as (for humans) moral agents, or as objects of ethical decision-making.

(2) When nature gets harmed, women and other Others (the poor, people of color, indigenous communities, laborers, and members of other categorically disempowered social groups) are inevitably harmed, or harmed more than the socially and economically privileged. The devaluation of women and other oppressed groups justifies

(a) devaluing, and consequently harming, other 'feminine' things;
(b) disregarding their interests by plundering or neglecting land that they own, control, or rely upon;
(c) ignoring or minimizing their assertions that land, water, or animals be

treated more carefully (even when women or agricultural workers, for example, may have more intimate knowledge of the objects in question);

(d) preventing them from ownership and decision-making that might result in less destructive practices.

(3) 'Woman' and 'nature' are socially created concepts, each referring to highly varied categories of beings and objects. The concepts do not belie essential or necessary truths about beings and objects, but their definitive power helps constitute and regulate material realities. In Western and other hierarchical dualistic cultures, women and nature are likened to each other and identified with femininity and corporeality – opposite and inferior to masculinity, reason, and their associates. These definitions render the realm of the feminine suitable for domination, although the strange mechanisms of oppression sometimes place the feminine in glorified positions imbued with purity, mystery, and fertility. These and similar false generalizations are also made concerning other groups who come to be metaphysically or practically associated with femininity and/or nature, including 'primitives' and sexual 'deviants.'

(4) In the process of exploring and creating ethical options and alternatives, reclamations of traditional ideas and practices might be helpful, but they must be critically evaluated in terms of present contexts as well as their historical embeddedness. When the substance of a moral claim cannot be logically abstracted from problematic foundations or implications, it is not worth reconsideration or reclamation. Likewise, evidence that an ethical imperative has proven emancipatory in the past is inadequate proof that it can continue to do so.

Hence, feminist ethics are not feminine ethics. Feminist ethics help uncover and eradicate the devaluation and mistreatment of women. Because nearly all women are influenced by conceptual and material frameworks that are oppressive to women, efforts to eradicate oppression involve criticizing concepts and *institutions* including femininity and motherhood. Furthermore, since the oppression of women includes oppression based on race, class, sexuality, physical ability, caste, and other factors, so all of these are feminist issues. None the less, the focus of this approach is on female humans – is feminist – for several reasons:

(a) Women's oppression is nearly universal, and therefore almost always visible and instructive in exposing various frameworks and mechanisms of oppression at work in any given context. The oppression of women is therefore a paradigm for the consideration of oppression and exploitation in general.[4]

4 Please note that I claim that oppression based on gender is *a* paradigm – not *the* paradigm. There are certainly other paradigmatic forms of oppression as well. It does not follow that any 'one form' of oppression is original, basic, or foundational, or more important than any other. It also does not follow that pure forms of oppression ever exist, or can be observable.

(b) The history of feminist thought provides a specific cluster of analyses of oppression, exploitation, and resistance. Thinkers and actors who call themselves 'feminist,' including ecological feminists, place themselves in agreement with some aspect of this history, though of course they may also disagree with other aspects.

(c) Many of the most influential representatives in the 'history of thought' including most of the builders of Western modern science and technology and capitalism, have included, as a central ideological and practical component, the systematic, direct devaluation and/or oppression of women and whatever else comes to be, or to be considered 'feminine.'

(d) Feminists are aware that when the focus is not on women, their needs, interests, and perspectives tend to be severely neglected.

2

FEMINIST ETHICS AND THE VALUE OF NATURE

> The survival of the species necessitates a renewed understanding of our relationship to nature, of our own bodily nature, and of nonhuman nature around us; it necessitates a challenging of the nature–culture dualism and a corresponding radical restructuring of human society according to feminist and ecological principles.
>
> Ynestra King

The inquiry at hand is largely about ethics: 'norms and values, the right and the good, as these enter into or support . . . well-being' (Card 1995: 66). For environmental ethics, the first question is *whose* well-being is available for and worthy of consideration, a question born from the sense that considering only the interests of rational human beings does not attend to everything valuable in the world. But given that such a 'sense' might be acted on in any number of ways, environmental ethics seeks 'to understand better, for example, the scope of moral respect, the sorts of entities that can and should receive moral attention, and the nature of the 'good' which morality . . . is supposed to promote' (Goodpaster 1978: 309). Thus part of the work of environmental philosophy is to assess carefully the justifications and reasons behind a moral sensibility, to test its applicability, to explore consistent rules and practices, and to discuss the possibilities for *living* a moral sensibility in particular contexts and situations. But before discussing the particulars of ecological feminist ethics – what ethics requires of moral agents who are members of both social and ecological communities – it will be helpful to get a sense of how ecological feminists conceive of ethics, moral agents, and nature.

ETHICS AND CONCEPTIONS OF NATURE

Despite the implications of historical and sociological inquiries concerning the treatment and meanings of nature, the relationship between scholarly work in environmental ethics and nonphilosophical studies has not been as intimate as one might expect. While work in environmental ethics has consistently, if unconsciously, pointed out the extent to which firm moral boundaries between 'nature' and 'humans' are fallacious and dangerous, the ontological and discursive dimensions of shifting moral boundaries, or the truths about matter and meaning that must hold for such shifts to be imaginable or achievable, are less aggressively explored by environmental philosophers. Moral attitudes and ontological understandings can shift, unintentionally, in response to each other, and ethical arguments always have hidden ontological assumptions. Given the project of feminist environmental ethics, it becomes increasingly necessary to enunciate clearly the ontologies within our ethics, and the ethical implications of our beliefs about being.

Writing in the 1940s, Aldo Leopold interpreted the history of ethical thought as evolutionary, emphasizing how conceptions of ethical agents have expanded beyond mere egoism to include also societies and social goods. Leopold, considered by many to be the father of contemporary environmental ethics, argued that (then) current needs and values demanded further extension of the 'moral community' to include the *biotic* community – the ecosystem – and its members (Leopold 1966). Contemporary animal rights theorists Peter Singer and Tom Regan presuppose a liberal notion of progress, though they also question the notion that individual rights-holders must be human (Singer 1975; Regan 1983). They argue not that a focus on individuals ought to be abandoned, but that the ethical boundary distinguishing humans from other sentient, or conscious, beings can be held in place only through prejudicial preference for our own species. Legal theorist Christopher Stone attempts to make room in judicial discourse for considering the interests of nonhuman organic beings, unsettling the comfortable separation between the realms of nature and culture exemplified by legislative institutions (Stone 1974). Because modern legal discourses consider the sphere of life that is not generated or necessarily controlled by humans to be a mere resource, Stone's suggestions amount to a radical questioning of institutionalized instrumentalist conceptions of nature.

The above approaches to environmental ethics effectively point out the arbitrariness or unjustifiability of typical human-centered judgments and values, including most notably those based in Kantian, utilitarian, and egoist ethics. Still, they vary in the extent to which they aim to unsettle our ideas about what nature is. Some ethicists wish merely to reconfigure the boundaries marking what 'counts' ethically from what does not by applying given criteria for inclusion in the ethical universe more broadly. So, for example, Singer, Regan, Donald VanDeVeer (1995), and other advocates for animals argue that some of the benefits of 'culture' ought to be extended to various nonhuman animals, because those animals have the same relevant qualities (sentience, consciousness, and other psychological capacities) that make humans morally valuable. They reject *speciesism*, the unjustified belief that being human renders one superior to any other form of life, and the accompanying belief that only humans have moral value. But in the end, the nature/culture distinction remains. Like Leopold, environmental holists and Deep Ecologists, whose arguments extend beyond sentient or self-conscious beings to include all of nature in the moral universe, tend to point toward more radical conclusions about conceptions of nature. They argue that human-centered presuppositions lead most of us to ignore completely the inherent value of the nonhuman natural world. Unfortunately, there is also a tendency among radical ecologists to betray a loyalty to nature/culture dualisms by characterizing humans as a monolithic, telos-bound species, and nature as the remainder of earthly organic reality, and to fail to recognize the moral value of human individuals and the ecological significance of social injustice.

Paul Taylor grounds his treatise on environmental ethics, *Respect for Nature*, on the fact that 'unlike other creatures, we must decide how to live . . . there is simply no escape from the ultimate necessity to make choices' (1986: 48). Although ambitious in scope and noteworthy in its attempt to undermine the history of human centered, or *anthropocentric* philosophy on its own terms, like the work of other theorists who fail to address the social and political dimensions of ecological problems, Taylor's discussion of 'nature' relies on a firm distinction between the universe in which humans see themselves as interacting primarily with other humans, and the sphere in which humans think of themselves as interacting with or impacting 'nature' (nonhuman individuals or species, bioregions, land masses, the atmosphere, aquatic communities). Certainly this distinction is rhetorically and practically useful in so far as it maps onto choices and actions that appear to be significantly different, in both material and historical terms. Deciding whether to kill a deer for food is different from deciding whether to kill another human being for food, because of the differences in the capacities and features of the beings (which will in part vary from case to case) and because of the meanings and histories of the relevant beings, practices, and relationships. But to leave the distinction between 'human ethics' and 'environmental ethics,' or between culture and nature, completely unquestioned is to miss the relevant *similarities* between them, and therefore to miss the common or related ethical and metaphysical assumptions that contribute to the kinds of things ethicists think of as 'problems' and 'solutions.' Seeing decisions about hunting deer as unrelated to questions about how to treat other human beings is equally problematic.

For ecological feminists, ethically important similarities have been cast primarily in terms of conceptual connections between the devaluation of women and other subjugated groups, interwoven histories of oppression and exploitation, and the relationships among these oppressive systems and institutions and the degradation of nature. Conceiving of nature as 'out there,' or of human interactions with nature as a completely distinct ethical sphere, ignores a crucial question at the heart of ecological feminism: how are human interactions with each other related to, affected by, and contributors to our interactions with nature, and how ought we to respond to and within these relationships? Feminist philosophy offers models of how to construct and clarify ethics that assertively protest histories of male-centered and otherwise unjustly biased thought and practice, and argue creatively for the good of human and nonhuman entities, while remaining ever-mindful and critical of attachment to overdetermined concepts like 'woman,' 'nature,' and 'persons.' The history and function of relevant concepts, like 'nature,' 'rationality,' 'personhood,' and 'rights,' as well as their efficacy in framing, evaluating, and guiding us through ethical matters, are central feminist philosophical concerns.

On the whole, even when it pushes forcefully against anthropocentric values and ontologies, work in environmental ethics varies in the ways and the extent to which it undermines dualistic discourses concerning nature and culture. An expansion of the field of moral considerability does not necessarily entail questioning background assumptions. Just as feminist theory and practice firmly rooted in liberal, individualist assumptions about the agents and subjects of social change may never rattle the norms and meanings of gender, environmental philosophies that argue for unconsidered extensions of accepted ethical norms can leave other assumptions surprisingly intact. For example, seminal thinkers in environmental ethics have not argued for, or incorporated, the unsettling notion that 'nature' is a *constructed* concept, not a self-evident or absolute referent, and that the meanings of 'human' are no less multifarious and shifting. Many of their conclusions reify other ethical norms by relying exclusively on the central tenets of modern Western culture, including beliefs in atomistic selves and rights, and by attempting to stretch their deployment beyond the boundaries of human interests.

While offering these criticisms, and others that I will develop more fully in Chapter 4, it is important to acknowledge that any prolonged, critical preoccupation with our values concerning 'nature,' and with human interactions with nonhuman organic reality, is likely to lead to some recognition of the strange conceptual genesis, history, and force of 'nature.' Pursuing traces of Marx and Engels' reflections on nature, Frankfurt school critical theorists were among the first academics to discuss explicitly the links between cultural conceptions of 'nature' and dangerous, destructive cultural practices. Anticipating more specific treatments by ecofeminists as well as historians of science and technology, Horkheimer and Adorno discussed how 'nature' becomes stripped of mythic relevance in classic and modernist thought, thereby enabling its exploitation by men: the possessors of reason. In fact, meanings of 'nature' and the stuff of nature have undergone innumerable transformations. As historian William Cronon recently asserted:

'Nature' is not nearly so natural as it seems. Instead, it is a profoundly human construction. This is not to say that the nonhuman world is somehow unreal or a mere figment of our imagination – far from it. But the way we describe and understand that world is so entangled with our own values and assumptions that the two can never be fully separated. What we mean when we use the word 'nature' says as much about ourselves as about the things we label with that word.

(1995: 25)

If solid, fixed, eternal, self-evident 'nature,' and hence 'culture' are fictions, then why and how environmental ethics? Feminists will note the familiarity of the philosophical and political problem: if gender is socially constructed, if one is not born, but *made* a woman, and the process of becoming one is largely determined by patriarchal and racist norms, whither a feminism that takes as its starting point the goal of promoting the well-being of 'women'? If race is but a social construct, how ought we to frame attempts to tackle and combat racism? These analogies are significant not only in elucidating the problem, but also in seeking answers.

Feminist and other models of critical, reconstructive theoretical and polit-ical projects might prove helpful to those of us who seek environmentalisms that do not 'fix' nature. For example, in *Racist Culture: Philosophy and the Politics of Meaning*, David Theo Goldberg attempts a theory critical of both race and racism which avoids the reduction of one to the other (Goldberg 1993). He thereby illustrates the usefulness, even for social groups whose race identification is used by others to their detriment, of racial categorization in contemporary racist contexts, and of preserving the current explanatory, identificatory and descriptive power of the concept 'race,' while furthering a strongly deconstructive agenda. Turning decon-structive attention toward 'nature' does not necessarily entail its demise as a useful concept or as a category that helps us make sense of reality. Nor does it relieve us from the responsibility of figuring out how to conceive of nonhuman organic beings and groups, and interact with the entities, com-munities, and networks to which 'nature' refers.

LAYING OUT

Drawing on Wittgenstein's conception of a foundation as 'like an axis, held in place by what revolves or spins around it,' Sarah Hoagland argues that the foundation of traditional Anglo-European ethics is dominance and sub-ordination (Hoagland 1988: 14). In contrast, she constructs ethics from the 'foundation' of lesbian lives and communities. Of course, any ethic has value-laden starting points, and in the end an ethicist must simply either lay out or assume her own. In this sense, circularity is endemic to ethical thought. To assume that ethics matter, or that normative matters are and ought to remain meaningful in discourses, political communities, and material practices, is to commit oneself already to some basis upon which it is arguable that something is better than something else. In 'The Subjectivity of Values,' J. L. Mackie argued that though moral views are subjective conventions held by people, and things can have no objective value, there can still be good reasons for holding them. Ethics can provide normative, justifiable standards without an objective basis, but

> somewhere in the input to this argument – perhaps in one or more of the premisses, perhaps in some part of the form of the argument – there will be something which cannot be objectively validated – some premiss which is not capable of being simply true, or some form of argument which is not valid as a matter of general logic, whose authority or cogency is not objective, but is constituted by our choosing or deciding to think in a certain way.
>
> (1987: 187)

Like the fabrications that keep some of us dry and secure, these subjective foundations are designed and crafted by humans. Though the construction of value systems is rarely as intentional as the pouring of concrete, it is no less human-generated and socially dependent. The most an ethicist can do for her audience is frankly to lay out her motivations and starting points, even if they seem to be points in a circle, in their most compelling light.

It would seem ridiculous to any ecologist, and most biologists, to take some idiosyncratic nonhuman species behavior and analyze it without regard to the species' relationships with other species which share its home terrains. For example, when female lions, who determine the size and constitution of their prides, permanently cast off certain members, likely explanations include individual personalities, group dynamics, and environmental pressures. And we humans have our own strange and useful practices. For example, within most systems of meaning, we place special value on persons, certain interactions, and ways of being in the world – a value that constrains and motivates in ways not reducible to self-regard.[1] Like lioness' actions, human moral agency only makes sense in the rich varieties of our communities, and human community only exists as part of the 'natural' world. While they do not *determine* our ethics, our dependencies on and relationships with nature, and our physical needs and predispositions, shape and limit what ethics can be, or what ethics can mean, in any given context.

---

1 I leave open the question of whether other species have ethics; if they do, their 'ethical' systems are extremely different from ours, though some of the biological/ecosystemic factors shaping them may be similar. For fascinating discussions on the topic of nonhuman ethics, see de Waal 1989, and Masson and McCarthy 1995.

Historically, even when discouraging pure egoism, ethical rules and systems – especially as they commingle with social mores and values – have tended to maintain social power and the ability to control others in the hands of the privileged, though they sometimes enable radical shifts in social power. Finding such relationships between morals and power key to understanding human nature, Nietzsche's genealogy of morals characterizes the history of modern Western ethics as a carefully orchestrated attempt by the physically impotent to exert control over those whose physical strength, cunning, and fearlessness endangers the weak. But despite the negative potential of ethics, if normative evaluations are at all useful or inevitable, and if some aspects of our ethical lives involve choice regarding behavior, character, or what we value, questions arise about how, and regarding what, ethics should be applied. Feminists and environmentalists are critical of common failures regarding ethics, and some might think of themselves as rejecting the normative process altogether, but the simple designations of 'feminist' and 'environmentalist' implicitly endorse some practices over others, and denote normative evaluations about what *should* be, not just descriptions of what is.

I've already established that in feminist ethics, a primary starting point is rejection of oppression and exploitation. But such a rejection is based on the belief that oppressive practices and ideologies harm, or do wrong unto, something of value. Perhaps the most basic ecological feminist starting point for an exploration of ethical alternatives is the assertion of the value of women, not only individually and categorically, but also as persons who possess and inhabit particular, social, political, and historically-loaded identities which can only be possible and meaningful in the context of other persons and 'natural' communities and environments. In what we hope to be our transformative dissections of a uniquely human practice – ethics – those of us who stand at the crossroads of feminism and environmentalism conceive of foundations of ethics as beginning with an assertion of the value of our lives, our communities, and nature. Should we try to prove this value?

Sarah Hoagland argues that to debate the value of women's lives is to admit that it is possible that women's lives are not valuable (Hoagland 1988). Perhaps the best we can do in communicating the justification for a premise of basic moral value is try to evoke a feeling – to draw attention to narratives, poems, experiences, and observations of what we take to be valuable.[2] In pointing out that the foundations for ethics are *felt*, we should keep in mind that feelings are neither irrational nor nonrational. David Hume located the genesis of morality in human sentiment. Hume believed that reason and morality are rightfully 'slaves of the passions,' that society is

2 Thank you to Sheila Jasanoff for reminding me of this point.

necessary for the development of morality, and that goodness does not inhere in objects. For Hume, introducing a discussion of sentiment into ethical philosophy does not amount to conceiving of morality as natural (given) or asocial. In fact, he wrote, 'nothing can be more unphilosophical than those systems which assert that virtue is the same with what is natural, and vice with what is unnatural' (1978: 475). Likewise, ecological feminist ethics do not take any fixed understandings of nature or 'natural' human qualities to be ethical starting points. What they do begin with is the sense that women, humans, communities, and natural objects and systems have noninstrumental value, and we should avoid harming them.

Moral value must begin with human valuers, or valuers whose valuing has ethical meaning. These moral agents are persons who make decisions based on, among other things, notions of right and wrong, good and bad. For a thing to have meaningful moral value, some moral agent must value it as a member of the ethical universe, and it must be the kind of thing to which moral concepts and considerations can refer. It must therefore be somehow connected to or appreciable by moral agents, and must therefore be human, necessary for human life, something which makes human life better than it would be without it, or something that humans can appreciate and respect – even from a distance. An ethically valuable entity must be capable of having interests or doing well, or the consequences of valuing it would be indistinguishable from not valuing it, and moral value would be utterly inconsequential. Moral objects, or morally valuable entities, include whatever is capable, categorically, of being harmed, exploited, oppressed, degraded, pained, and mistreated by those agents. None the less, moral agents must use some kinds of living beings for food, shelter, technology, and science. 'Being alive' or even being worthy of moral consideration, is not sufficient to disallow the use and even the death of a thing. Some death and manipulation is necessary for human life and ethics to be at all possible, but if *abuse* is understood as mistreatment, or harm without justification, it is never necessary to abuse other living beings.

Lori Gruen argues that because the interests and well-being of all those who have such things are inevitably connected to the interests and well-being of others, it is difficult to argue that any one entity is valuable in itself (unpublished). But human interests can include the importance of valuing things for reasons not reducible to their instrumentality, or use value for humans. That is, we might assert that it is important for humans to value each other, and nonhuman entities and communities 'for their own sake,' though this value also ultimately serves the valuers' interests, and always has extrinsic origins. In J. Baird Callicott's words, moral value is created by humans,

> but it by no means follows that the locus of all value is consciousness itself or a mode of consciousness like reason, pleasure, or knowledge. In other words something may be valuable only because someone val-

ues it, but it may also be valued for itself, not for the sake of any subjective experience it may afford the valuer.

(1986: 40)

Though values come from humans, they need not be human-centered, or
based only on the interests and well-being of humans. We can see, appreciate, and care about the interests and well-being of other persons, species,
systems and communities. This valuing might be for aesthetic reasons. It
might stem from the nature and quality of our biological, cultural, or affectionate relationships. It might also be for epistemological reasons. As we
glean new knowledge from science and other spheres of inquiry, we might
notice new sources of respect and value.

Many philosophers use the concept of 'anthropocentrism' to denote ideologies and practices that are human-centered in ways that are ethically suspect. The view of ethics I put forth here is anthropocentric only in a trivial
sense. That is, ethical perspectives are human, only humans use ethics as we
know them, and ethics have to be based on human-generated valuations and
responses. But since more than human interests are 'at the center' of an ecological feminist ethical scheme, it is not anthropocentric in the sense of
being unjustifiably or prejudicially biased toward human goods and interests. Indeed, we cannot truly separate human from nonhuman well-being
without dramatically changing our conception of human physical, emotional, and social well-being, and the false belief that we *can* separate these
has severely disrupted the physical thriving of both humans and nature.
Though an ecological feminist ethical scheme might be conceptually bound,
or limited, by human capacities, our biases can vary significantly according
to the degree of information and inclination we have concerning the interests, goods, and preferences of nonhuman entities. Rachel Carson hoped
that knowledge of our own epistemic limitations would inspire caution and
humility when we make decisions concerning relatively mysterious entities.
At the same time, affective prejudices toward members of our own species
need not be seen as always unfair or unjustified. Again quoting Callicott,
describing what he calls 'species-love,'

> Our social affections are extended to our fellow members and to the
> social whole of which we are part. The intrinsic value we attribute to
> individual human beings and to humanity expresses only our feelings
> for co-members of our global village and for our human community.
>
> (1986: 65)

Social affections felt and extended toward members of our own species,
or others with whom we share systems of meaning, or feelings, of commonality, kinship and understanding can be 'foundations' for our ethical
motivation. That is, emotional, symbolic, and cultural connections with
others help move us beyond simple egoism and generate concern for and

motivation toward the interests of others. Feminists and others have pointed out how partiality toward intimates is a significant and valuable aspect of ethical life. At the same time, we cannot lose sight of the ways in which feelings of special affection – and special moral motivation – toward intimate or familiar others is also a potential problem spot in worlds in which our actions affect those beyond our affectionate and cultural spheres, in which fear of difference has become pathological, and in which our well-being is fundamentally tied to the well-being of persons, communities, species and ecosystems with whom we don't necessarily share fellow-feeling and about whom we may know next to nothing.

A good number of ecological feminist thoughts and actions begin with feelings of special attachment to persons, companion animals, or biotic communities.[3] In 'Am I Blue?' Alice Walker's delight in an acquaintance with a horse, and her witnessing of the horse's despair after his equine companion is taken from him, leads her to consider the similarities between the emotional life of that horse, and the emotional lives of African-American domestic workers who raise white children. Certainly many ecological feminists are motivated by their own experiences as women, and their fellow-feelings with other women around the world. Emotional ties based on commonality are insignificant in ethics. The challenge for ethics is to capitalize on the fruitfulness of given, obvious connections within our species and communities without representing these connections as the summation of moral life.

ETHICS AS LAW

In 1958, Elizabeth Anscombe argued that in the absence of a lawgiving god, a morality based on rule-following, and motivated by an inclination to do one's duty, is completely useless. Modern affinity for ethics based on rules, she concluded, is merely a vestige of an earlier age. Anscombe thereby set the stage for the more recent critiques of Kantian and consequentialist ethics and theoretical turns toward ethics based on virtue, character, and context. Nearly thirty years later, following Anscombe's sentiment, Alisdair MacIntyre located the problems of Enlightenment moral theorists in the 'ineradicable discrepancy between their shared conception of moral rules and precepts on the one hand and . . . their conception of human nature on the other,' and argued that they therefore cannot help guide or motivate contemporary ethical actors (1984: 52). These and other historical accounts against rule-based ethics typically argue in favor of Aristotelian virtue

---

3 In 'The Personal is Political Revisited,' Lori Gruen and I argue that intimate relations with companion animals is a good source of moral motivation toward nonhumans in general (Cuomo and Gruen 1997).

ethics. Though there are discrepancies regarding the supposed attractions of classical notions of the good, they all rely on the observation that socially-embedded notions of the good life, or human well-being, that shape working understandings of what it means to be a good person are more representative of moral life, and more promising as places for philosophers to turn their attention.

Sitting firmly within what some feminists refer to as the 'justice tradition,' the work of nonfeminist philosophers such as ethicist Paul Taylor exemplifies the need for Anscombe's critique as well as other criticisms raised by feminist philosophers. He sets out to create a Kantian theory of environmental ethics, analogous in many ways to human-centered ethical arguments based on respect for rational agents. Taylor's foundation is the 'ultimate attitude' that 'Nature' is something worthy of respect because its individual living members have inherent worth, a perspective he calls the 'biocentric outlook' (1986: 13). That is, each thing has a 'good' that is identifiable and distinguishable, each strives toward its good when it has the freedom to, and that good ought to be valued and respected for its own sake. Any rational moral agent possessing the biocentric outlook, and the attitude of respect for nature, will follow the rules logically dictated by the inherent value of individual living things.

But the ethical norms, rules, and values recommended by Taylor originate in the realm of the ideal, not in actual moral relationships and situations. Feminist philosophers have shown how the justice tradition overvalues rationality and autonomy, conceives of moral agents too individualistically, posits a few rigid rules not readily applicable in ethical life, and misconstrues the role of emotions and emotional bonds in moral life. As Val Plumwood says of Taylor's work,

> The account draws on the familiar view of reason and emotion as sharply separated and opposed, and of 'desire', caring and love as merely 'personal' and 'particular' as opposed to the universality and impartiality of understanding, of 'feminine' emotions as essentially unreliable, untrustworthy and morally irrelevant, an inferior domain to be dominated by a superior, disinterested (and of course masculine) reason.
>
> (1993: 167–168)

Though emerging more directly from reflection on real moral dilemmas, I will argue in Chapter 4 that the animal rights theories of Peter Singer and Tom Regan are also derived from the assumption that ethics is reducible to justice for individuals.

If part of the project of environmental ethics is to recommend criteria for choosing and changing values and behavior, these accounts of the failures of what Anscombe called 'a law conception of ethics' cannot be ignored. Although Taylor admits that conceptions of and desire for well-being are aspects of the ultimate attitude of respect for nature, the attitude is actually enacted in dutiful rule-following, and the bulk of his project is dedicated to articulating and justifying general rules that logically follow from a basic valuing of life. The most interesting and enlightening aspect of his theory is therefore the hidden background, an attitude that in fact might motivate a myriad of practices, systems of rules, and desires, but that is not reducible to rules or motivated by duty. While the importance of an attitude of respect for nature is clear, Taylor's route of exploration is stale.

ETHICAL STARTING POINTS

One way of distinguishing ecological feminism from other movements and theories is in terms of its ethical assumptions and goals. Ecological feminist challenges to other systems of ethics depend not only on feminist and ecological revisions of conceptions of nature, or revisions of what 'counts' as moral objects and agents, and why, but also on feminist and environmentally-minded questions and insights regarding the very meanings and significance of ethics. The extent to which ecological feminism differs from other environmental and feminist perspectives (be they liberal, radical, conservationist, utilitarian, or postmodern) lies largely in differences in what Lorraine Code calls their 'ethical starting points' (Code 1991). These philosophical points of departure provide differing sources of justification for the moral considerability of nonhuman natural entities, lead to different recommendations about how to put values into practice, and have various implications for issues of human social justice. Certainly, because ecological feminism aims toward some version or versions of 'the good,' and rejects practices, values, and dispositions in so far as they detract from good outcomes, it is decisively driven by normative premises. Thus its foundational assumptions and assertions about who and what is valuable, and what aspects of life and reality are significant in determining courses of action, will be an important point of contrast and comparison with other projects. Other noteworthy starting points include presupposition about what kinds of problems or dilemmas count as ethical problems, what goodness requires, and what sort of information is considered necessary to make a thorough moral decision.

Ecological feminists agree with Kenneth Goodpaster, who claims that 'nothing short of the condition of being alive,' is 'a plausible and nonarbitrary criterion' for moral considerability (1978: 310). At first glance, this wide net of consideration may appear overly broad. Indeed, because life requires death, and because what many of us think of as an achievably good human life (including adequate housing, transportation, good food, education, and both meaningful and mindless leisure) requires quite a bit of death and destruction, an ethic that begins with the moral considerability of all living things might seem wildly implausible. But Goodpaster is quick to point out that universal moral considerability does not rule out there being differences of moral *significance* among life forms, by which we might ethically adjudicate when the interests of living things compete. The regulative, or ideal nature of the claim that all living things are morally considerable asks 'for sensitivity and awareness, not for suicide (psychic or otherwise). But it is not vacuous, in that it does provide a *ceteris paribus* encouragement in the direction of nutritional, scientific, and medical practices of a genuinely life-respecting sort' (Goodpaster 1978: 324). Similarly, while ecological feminism values the flourishing of all living beings and communities, I will argue in the following chapter that this basic point of departure does not rule out the possibility that some ethical hierarchies are justifiable.

Ecological feminists follow Anscombe's tradition in endorsing ethics that begin with, yet are not reducible to, a conception of human well-being. This ethical ideal follows directly from the normative implications of feminism, which aspires to promote the flourishing of women and Others, though for ecological feminists women's well-being and human flourishing are always necessarily ecological. The most central philosophical commitments that ground ecological feminism are its feminist ethical starting points – what it values, and how it conceives of moral agents. It is clear in the literature that ecological feminists take the commitments of feminism, developed in various areas of feminist scholarship and practice, as far less problematic than the histories of environmental thought and science created by men, even when feminism neglects to take seriously the interests of nature and nonhuman beings. That is, some version of feminism acts as a given for ecological feminists, as does the notion that nonhuman beings and communities have moral value. Rarely do ecological feminists find nonfeminist environmentalisms constructed by white men to be adequate. Rather, these perspectives are always texts for feminist deconstruction. Any feminist failures to look beyond our own species are problematic, but the ethical starting points endorsed by ecological feminists are first and foremost feminist.

Feminist ethics are also central to ecological feminism because theories of moral agency developed by feminists reflect the complexity and multiplicity of women's lives and interests. This attention to the social nature of the moral agent – the self – is useful for thinking about moral agency as ecological and as formed within and responsive to both human and biotic communities. It is difficult not to notice that feminist philosophers have spent quite a lot of energy on questions about moral agency and goodness within oppressive contexts. We might even venture that these questions comprise the heart of feminist ethical inquiry. Environmental philosophers, on the other hand, tend to take moral agency at face value, and do not consider the ways in which moral agency is compromised by oppression and shaped in specific social locations. One explanation for this difference is the supposed tendency for white and other middle-class women (a description covering the majority of feminist philosophers in the US) to be terribly concerned with being, or at least appearing, good (Frye 1991). In any case, if we can't benefit from the particular psychosocial obsessions of people with the privilege to write their ideas down, we probably shouldn't read any philosophy at all. And, if Hegel, Marx, and feminists like Sandra Harding are at all correct, there is always potentially something to learn from the musings of the subordinated on their own conditions and the character of oppressors.

I also discuss feminist ethics as a source of wisdom for ecological feminism because I believe that feminist ethics *should* be such a source. Central problems confronted by ecological feminism involve values, decisions, conceptions of self and community, relationships and hopes of better tomorrows. Not only is feminist ethics a well-developed area of inquiry concerning these issues, it also promotes political and practical agendas that are widely consistent with the goals of ecological feminism as they've been articulated thus far. Ecological feminism ought to rely on careful, consistent, methodologically-sound inquiries that are interested in the well-being of women and nature.[4] Feminist philosophical studies concerning ethics are an example of such an inquiry.

Feminist ethics is not an isolated sphere of inquiry. Although the field of feminist ethics represents a large amount of the academic work currently done under the banner of 'feminist philosophy,' it intersects at various levels work in feminist epistemology and social and political philosophy, and with feminist political and literary theory. In some of its best forms, work in feminist ethics is also informed by nonacademic practices and activisms.[5] Needless to say, it is impossible to explicate all of the points of debate and argument that have arisen among feminists regarding ethics and moral agency in the last two decades. Still, I hope it will be helpful to give a sketch of the feminist ethics that provide some of the starting points for ecological feminism.

FEMINIST ETHICS

'Feminist' has multiple meanings, ranging from the view that women are entitled to everything men currently enjoy to the view that institutions of gender ought to be eliminated. In this book, I take it to refer to at least the following foundational beliefs, and their manifold, conflicting implications:

---

4 Readers uncomfortable with the notion that interested methodologies can be sound or accurate should consider the work of feminist epistemologists, including Sandra Harding, Lorraine Code, Lynn Hankinson Nelson, Helen Longino, and Naomi Scheman. In *The Science Question in Feminism*, Harding reminds us that scientific inquiry is often *better* – more accurate in representing the world and reliable in predicting future outcomes – when it is shamelessly committed to certain interests. Examples include feminist scientific studies on domestic abuse, breast cancer, and moral development.

5 Some of the feminist philosophers whose work is explicitly informed by activisms include Sarah Hoagland, María Lugones, Iris Young, and Alison Jaggar.

(a) Women are oppressed and mistreated.

(b) The oppression and mistreatment of women is wrong.

(c) The analysis and reduction of the oppression and mistreatment of women are necessary (but not sufficient) for the creation and maintenance of the kind of individual and communal lives that should be promoted within good societies.

(d) Because different forms of oppression are intermeshed, the analysis and reduction of any form of oppression, mistreatment, or unjustified domination is necessary for the creation and maintenance of the kind of individual and communal lives that should be promoted within good societies.[6]

The feminism I have in mind does not assume that women's oppression is reducible to oppression based on gender (that is, the oppression of women *includes* racism, and other forms of oppression, *de facto*), though attention to women is an important (not exclusive) starting point for feminists. These four beliefs, along with analytic attention to women's interests and experiences, have created a number of 'fundamentals' in the work of feminist ethics. Although we might enumerate aspects of feminist ethics, these features are best represented not as a hierarchically structured system of principles and rules of action, but rather as facets of perspectives that ground criticism of phallocentric philosophical and political systems and the creation of woman-friendly alternatives.

If we look at feminist philosophical writing over the last two and a half decades, we find multiple and overlapping agendas in feminist ethics: to respond to and criticize historical philosophical and practical work in ethics; to attend to special problems in women's lives, or in areas of life typically characterized as women's, or private, spheres; to articulate the details of ethical life – including the meanings and importance of choice, responsibility, integrity, autonomy, and honesty – given histories and circumstances of oppression; and to explore and create alternative ethics, values, and projects for contexts in which oppression and domination are not the most significant factors determining the texture of interactions. In projects shaped by these agendas (which, of course, rarely occur as isolated and distinct), several themes emerge, corresponding to these agendas.[7]

---

6 I would argue that a *good* feminist would hold this premise, but it is certainly obvious that not all self-proclaimed feminists have done, or do. There is good reason to believe that this fact is the major drawback of feminism. Still, for many feminists this premise is central.

7 See Moutlon 1977; Jaggar 1983; Pearsall 1986; Hoagland 1988; Cannon 1988; Lugones 1987, 1990, 1994; Young 1990; Card 1991, 1996; Addelson 1991; Held 1993; Meyers 1994; Baier 1994.

GLANCING BACKWARDS

Ethics, values, and moralities, are always political – they express, influence, and respond to power that is economic, governmental, discursive, symbolic, and born in social relations. Values, practices, and conceptions of moral agency derived in oppressive institutions or practices are likely to promote, enable, or allow for oppression and mistreatment. In so far as they contribute to the domination, silencing, and devaluation of those defined as Others, feminists believe that ethics must be rejected or revised. For example, feminism begins with the belief that women and other Others have full moral value, as both moral agents and objects, so the interests of oppressed people, as individuals, and as members of groups, are ethically significant. Historically and philosophically, in overlapping yet distinct ways, people of color, women, and other 'outsiders' to the public sphere have been considered less than full, or fully significant, moral beings, and this fact is fundamental to their subordination. Feminists begin with a critique of this undervaluation, and its connection with other systems and logics of domination, exploitation, and oppression. In some sense this is the starting point for any feminist ethical criticism and the creation of feminist ethical possibilities.

As is common among theorizing born from liberation movements, much of the earliest 'rejecting and revising' work in feminist ethics took the form of responses to the tradition, uncovering the sexism and criticizing the male-centeredness of influential work in the field of ethics. Some feminist scholars pointed out the outright misogyny expressed by Kant, Locke, Nietzsche, Aristotle, and Schopenhauer, and traced the effects of misogyny on respective theories of selves, rational moral agents, good persons, and good societies. Some investigated the ways in which traditional ethical theory has provided justifications for the mistreatment of women and other inferiors. Other theorists analyzed the ways in which a failure to pay attention to women's lives and practices results in ethical schemes that render women invisible, or that are completely unhelpful in providing guidance or explanation for women's moral lives.

In addition to critically evaluating phallocentric traditions, feminist scholars aimed to correct them and fill in the gaps by incorporating more accurate assumptions about the value of women and the ethical significance of their lives. Projects along this line include a veritable library of essays and books on questions in 'applied ethics,' including abortion, surrogate motherhood, pornography, and rape, in which women's autonomy over their bodies and reproductive roles are a central issue. But this sort of attention to the tradition also inevitably resulted in debates about whether nonfeminist philosophy was at all salvageable. If 'adding women and stirring' resulted in dramatic changes in theoretical frameworks and even shifts in grounding presuppositions about the nature of persons and moral problems, then the corrective project could only lead to bigger and better things.

ATTENDING TO WOMEN'S LIVES

A different sort of corrective project in moral theory was begun by psychologist Carol Gilligan in the early 1980s. In her studies of moral development of mostly white, middle-class children, adolescents, and adults, Gilligan found that the females in her study exhibited a form of moral reasoning, which she labeled a 'care perspective,' that differs significantly from the 'justice perspective' typically expressed by male subjects, and identified with most ethical theory in the history of Western male thought (Gilligan 1982). While the justice perspective relies on rights, rules, autonomy and objectivity in making moral decisions, subjects voicing the care perspective were motivated by a sense of responsibility and caring for intimate connections, and they based their moral decisions on contextual factors and relevant relationships. Gilligan's empirical studies, however limited, were considered by many to provide evidence for feminist theories about the effects of exclusively female mothering on gender and 'ego boundaries.' A plethora of feminist philosophical inquiries concerning 'care ethics' followed – some reclamatory, some more critical of Gilligan's work and the tendency to draw hasty conclusions about 'women's moral voice.' In any case, there was widespread interest in the notion that women's moral reasoning (be it natural or 'constructed') may prove fruitful for theorists seeking sources for moral guidance beyond traditional male-identified inquiries. Sarah Ruddick, for example, articulated a whole system of 'maternal thinking,' or peace politics and ethics based on generalizations concerning women's experiences and talents as caretakers. The 'ethic of care' developed by Nel Noddings turned the female moral voice observed by Carol Gilligan in her clinical studies into a moral model for all (Noddings 1984).

Building theory from this sort of special attention to women's lives, as both sites of inquiry and sources of insight, raises (at least) two potential problems. One is that it is almost impossible to talk about something like 'women's lives' without overgeneralizing in ways that erase the differences among women, and that render some women as paradigmatic, and their experiences as definitive. Historically, it is the particularities of the lives and experiences of women who stand at the crossroads of multiple systems of oppression – women of color, poor women, lesbians, and women in postcolonial societies, to name a few – that are not accommodated by the resulting theory. The second problem, which I will discuss in greater detail in Chapter 6, is that in their efforts to construct theories *for* women, writers sometimes failed to be adequately critical of whatever gets associated with women, or is identified as feminine. Michele M. Moody-Adams reminds us that, 'women's allegedly superior moral capacities have been associated historically with the claim that these capacities best suit women for domestic pursuits,' and 'the vision of morality that Gilligan believes to be dominant in women's thinking is bound up with rather limiting stereotypes' (1991:

201). Even more thorough in her rejection of an ethic of caring, Sarah Hoagland argues that no positive philosophy of care can proceed without analyses of oppression and a program for change (1991: 261).

Yet these problems do not render futile all attempts to pay attention to women's experiences and interests. Because the designator 'women' covers an incredibly large and diverse set of people, women's interests stretch over an immense range of possibilities. While feminist ethics must have a critical component regarding what counts as women's interests (*being* interested in something, for example, would be insufficient grounds for designating that thing morally valuable) they must also recognize that various, multiple moral perspectives can be valid and useful in analyzing and constructing ethical practices and norms and constructing 'new' ethics. Generally, perspectives that are sources of innovative or particularly useful moral insights are rooted not in anything necessary or essential about identity, but in practices and in critical responses to systems of power and meaning. These perspectives are determined within real social relations and consequently associated with, adopted by or relegated to members of subjugated groups. Thus practices can help create identities, or subject locations, that are epistemically rich, though they are seldom acknowledged as being rich in knowledge by those with political and economic power.

Examples of epistemically rich perspectives, constructed within subjugated positions, that have been relevant to ecological feminism include Third World women farmers' development of useful and unique attitudes of respect and partnership with the land, lesbians' creation of sexual relationships that transgress heteropatriarchal norms, and groups of mothers who challenge scientifically determined toxic thresholds based on their caretaking of sick children. Though these ethical insights are not biologically or culturally determined, they none the less are closely related to specific experiences of gender identity, and positions within social relations. And though they may not be expressible as rules of behavior, they can serve as helpful moral guidelines and models. Hence many feminists emphasize that conceptions of moral behavior that are inclusive of emotional responses and affective connections, often expressed by women in cultures where male dominance is associated with disaffected rationality, might fruitfully augment ethics based on principled rule-following (Card 1990).

In addition, the morally damaging effects of oppression and mistreatment on agency are not limited to 'oppressors,' or those who benefit from oppressive and exploitative practices. Feminist ethics do not accept or endorse women's practices or values merely because they are enacted or created by women, or associated with traditional constructions of woman and femininity, because these are inextricably bound up with the domination and exploitation of women and anyone or anything else associated with femininity. It follows that, as Victoria Davion has argued, any environmental ethic that is feminist must critically analyze how constructions of femininity are detrimental to women (Davion 1994).

ETHICAL AGENCY UNDER OPPRESSION

In the Introduction to the collection *Feminist Ethics*, Claudia Card has the following to say in response to ethics based on glorifications of women's traditional caretaking roles:

> Feminist ethics interests me especially in relation to problems of agency under oppression: If oppressive institutions stifle and stunt the moral development of the oppressed, how is it possible, what does it *mean*, for the oppressed to be liberated? What is *there* to liberate? What does it mean to resist, to make morally responsible choices, to become moral agents, to develop character?
>
> (1991: 25)

She goes on to list the 'needs' of a feminist ethic concerned with such questions regarding agency:

> One, we need to identify our possibilities for agency in oppressive contexts. Two, we need to distinguish modes of resistance that would make our survival and our deeds worthwhile from those that would not. Three, we need to articulate ideals of the person and community that can acknowledge our histories and yet provide bases for pride in ourselves and each other. And four, we need to be alert to the dangers of becoming what we despise.
>
> (1991: 26)

Consistent with these needs, feminist ethicists have investigated the ethical meanings of trust, anger, integrity, self-esteem, and empathy in moral life, and women's lives in particular.[8] Others have considered feminist responses to violence (Bar-on 1991; Card 1991). Angela Davis, Katie G. Cannon, and Patricia Hill Collins theorize specific ethical tools and methods developed by African-American women in response to multiple oppressions, and as a way of creating community and value (Cannon 1988; Davis 1983; Hill Collins 1991).

A number of writers have directed their energies toward questions about ethical life in more liberatory contexts. While some philosophers put this project in terms of a search for ethical possibilities 'outside of patriarchy,' others stress the resilient nature of damaged and damaging patterns of interaction. Joyce Trebilcot developed 'Dyke Methods,' a list of guiding

8 On these topics see Baier 1985, 1994; Addelson 1991; Davion 1991; Dillon 1992; Myers 1994; Jones 1996.

principles, for herself, that are for use only when men and/or patriarchal values are not present. In her book *Lesbian Ethics*, Sarah Lucia Hoagland conceives of lesbian community as spaces where we act as 'agents under oppression,' yet she theorizes the ways in which lesbian relationships and communities have been the sources of values promoting resistance of male domination and compulsory heterosexuality, and healthy agency for lesbians and other females. Less optimistic about the possibilities for nonoppressive spaces, but none the less using feminist connection as a point of departure for innovative ethics, María Lugones' 'Playfulness, "World"-Travelling, and Loving Perception' is an attempt to describe resistant modes of interaction and agency that creatively maneuver beyond the options presented within oppressive regimes. These more forward-looking and creative subprojects of feminist ethics are of particular interest to ecological feminists whose priorities include the creation of new or revised ethical possibilities.

FROM FEMINIST ETHICS TO ECOLOGICAL FEMINISM

Feminist ethical insights radically question, amend, and refigure traditional ethical foundations, and provide necessary criticism of traditional ethical systems. These systems, or values, have allowed for, and sometimes even encouraged, the oppression of subordinates and the exploitation of nonhuman entities and communities. None the less, nonfeminist innovations in environmental ethics tend to leave unexamined their indebtedness to traditional assumptions, and nonecological feminist theory and practice fails to take seriously the exploitation and degradation of nature, or whatever gets labelled 'natural.'

The emphasis in ecological feminist literature thus far has been on critiques of influential Western ethics and metaphysics that are thought to underlie historical and cultural patterns of domination and exploitation. This criticism exposes Platonic idealism, Cartesian dualisms, Baconian science, and their intellectual and political progeny as important contributors to the intermingled histories of the oppression of women, the plundering of whatever is categorized as 'natural,' colonialism, racism, and capitalism. In *Feminism and the Mastery of Nature*, Val Plumwood synthesizes this common ecological feminist criticism of the oppressive threads in the history of Western thought and practice. Though much of this analysis of the history of ideas serves as my background, I am interested here in a more fundamental, normative level of ecological feminist thinking. That is, I want to explore the grounds for ecofeminist rejection of oppressive and exploitative practices, institutions, and values, and to draw out the more creative implications of the assumed starting points of ecological feminist ethics. Some assumptions about ethics that foreground my exploration include the belief that many different values are embedded in moral reasoning, and that there are a number of legitimate ways to answer questions such as, 'Why is oppression wrong?' 'Why are nonhuman entities morally relevant?' and 'How should one respond to situation x in accord with feminist and ecological values?' What I am after is a tentative sketch of the kinds of values that positively ground environmental ethics consistent with and sensitive to the insights of ecological and feminist critique.

Like Paul Taylor, ecological feminists are centrally concerned with something like 'attitudes' that ethical agents have toward the universe of entities upon which they depend for existence and sustenance. But rather than leaping immediately from abstract attitudes to rules via a sanitary stream of logic, ecological feminists begin with an interpretation of phenomena, explore the relationships among phenomena and social rules, ethics, and values, and suggest alternatives to destructive relationships, attitudes, and practices. The goal of ecological feminist ethics, while varying according to context, is to construct, uncover and articulate ethics that address the patterns and particularities of human agency that create a world riddled with, among other things, an incredible degree of environmental destruction and human oppression. Such ethics consider the ideological and material sources and manifestations of problematic attitudes, and offer plausible alternatives.

3

SO AS TO FLOURISH
The goals of ecological feminism

Miranda kind of blooms when the evening air hits her skin. She stands for a moment watching what the last of the sunlight does to the sky down by the Sound . . . It seems like God reached way down into his box of paints, found the purest reds, the deepest purples, and a dab of midnight blue, then just kinda trailed His fingers along the curve of the horizon and let 'em all bleed down. And when them streaks of color hit the hush-a-by green of the marsh grass with the blue of The Sound behind 'em, you ain't never had to set foot in a church to know you looking at a living prayer . . . A bramble scratches her on the face, and a few feet on she trips over a creeper from a sweet bay. *No point in cussing*, she hears her daddy's voice. *Little Mama, these woods been here before you and me, so why should they get out your way – learn to move around 'em.*

Gloria Naylor, Mama Day

There is not a place in the world that does not reveal the touch and bear the consequences of human hands and minds – not Antarctica, not the deepest equatorial jungle, and certainly not Tokyo or New York City. At the same time, there are not people who have not been shaped by the effects of landscape and water, the climate and natural features of the area in which they live.

Stephanie Lahar

In this chapter I discuss the values and ethical goals at the heart of ecological feminism. In addition to the feminist ethical starting points discussed in the previous chapter, a defining feature of ecological feminist thought is its commitment to the *flourishing*, or well-being, of individuals, species, and communities. Despite the absence of explicit discussions of flourishing, commitment to the well-being of moral objects is the basis upon which oppression, degradation, and other forms of harm and manipulation are rejected by feminism and ecofeminism. This chapter is an attempt to articulate an ecological feminist conception of flourishing in more positive terms, and to discuss its usefulness as an ethical starting point which can avoid reliance on fixed or dualistic understandings of nature and culture.

WHY FLOURISHING?

Ecological feminism rests on the claims that women and other Others are full moral agents, that oppression and its correlates ought to be eliminated, and that minimal moral consideration ought to be given to all living things and systems.[1] Acceptance of these premises requires the revision of values, practices, ontologies, and institutions that deny women's full agency and the moral considerability of nonhuman life, and that promote domination and oppression. This, of course, is no small task. But rather than become bogged down considering only the innumerable, deeply entrenched, debilitating practices and values that ecological feminists reject, it might be helpful to consider also the positive goals that lie beneath what sometimes appears to be a paralyzingly pervasive critique.

Ecological feminism demands much from a basic ethical conception of the good. It should be applicable, at least in a very basic way, to a variety of sorts of entities, including human individuals, human groups and communities, nonhuman sentient individuals, species, and ecological communities. It should be useful for thinking about the interests of technologically and linguistically advanced beings, as well as plant life and systems of organic and inorganic matter. It should be *naturalistic* – grounded in (though not necessarily identical with) facts about people, societies, animals, and ecosystemic processes – but should not be *teleological* – based on the assumption that there exists a determinate final end to which things and processes inevitably aim. If we begin with these criteria, and the fundamental claims stated above, it begins to become clear why flourishing is a primary focus of the ethics described here.

Given present sets of political and ecological circumstances, if we are to consider anything morally valuable, or if ethics is to get off the ground at all, some amount of human flourishing is necessary. So ethics implies human flourishing, both logically and practically. Also, ethics that assert the value of all people, and reject hierarchies that have led to the unjustifiable, categorical devaluation of women and others, assume that a preferred states of affairs is one in which, *prima facie*, as much human flourishing as possible occurs. Since nonhuman communities and entities are necessarily, intrinsically bound up with human life and interests, the well-being of nature is implied, to at least a minimal degree, in human flourishing. Some degree of nonhuman flourishing is instrumentally necessary for human flourishing. In addition to the necessity of nature for human life (and hence

---

1 If it is impossible to *eliminate* oppression or exploitation, they ought to be reduced as much as possible.

human moral life), ecological feminists hold that all living beings and systems are appreciable within ethical systems and values – as members of the moral universe, whose interests ought to be taken seriously by moral agents, and as entities that ought to flourish in their own right whenever possible. That is, even when we are unable to accommodate the interests of every relevant entity, the 'greatest good' that is sought by ethics includes the interests of all living beings and systems. Ethics that begin with flourishing capture the sense in which instrumental and noninstrumental value are often enmeshed.

If valuing something morally does not mean promoting *its* good, ethical valuing is either ineffectual, or reducible to something like economic value. A thing might be valued because it is the kind of thing that does not fit into systems of economic value, because its undisturbed presence contributes to the kind of world that is valued, or because its uniqueness, beauty, or complexity evokes humility and respect. In some instances, rational reasons elude us, and we simply *find* ourselves valuing someone or some thing that in no meaningful sense can be said to have use value for us. Regardless of the source, noninstrumental valuing *pays attention* to the interests of the thing apart from the interests of the valuer, though these might coincide. Consider: I may value the marsh on the edge of the city because it is a pleasant place to walk in the fall, and because I believe that escapes from concrete improve the lives of urban dwellers. I may also, at the same time, encounter 'the marsh' as a thriving community with a life and logic of its own, as a home to critters for whom I have compassion, and for beings and populations about which I know very little. In much the same way that I value loved ones because of what they bring to my life *and* because I appreciate the ways they move in the world completely apart from me, I may value the marsh for instrumental reasons, and for reasons that hinge on the fact that it *just is* something independent, beautiful, and complex. Certainly, instances of instrumental valuing often provide the knowledge and motivation that lead us to value noninstrumentally, and to value things and beings with whom we are not intimately, or not at all acquainted. One might say there is every reason to believe that, developmentally and otherwise, ethics begin with partiality. Still, the very fact that we are able to value species, ecosystems, and communities whom we might never encounter is a clue to the commonness of noninstrumental valuing. When we value things for noninstrumental reasons, we attempt to include the interests of another at the center of our decision-making. It is when our values and decisions do not center *solely* on our own interests that our thinking is ethical.

This view of moral value agrees with Kant's claim that to be morally valuable is to be valued as an 'end,' and not merely as a means to someone else's well-being. When we meaningfully designate decisions, issues, or aspects of human life 'ethical,' we claim that part of what is involved in determining better actions or modes of being is something not fully represented by self-interest. None the less, self-interest may be closely related to – even implied in – the interests of others. It follows that valuing something beyond its usefulness, or aiming toward the flourishing of others, does not necessarily require forgoing one's own flourishing. The flourishing of others may ultimately serve one's flourishing, or the flourishing of one's own community or species. It may also happen that caring about the flourishing of others results in alterations or compromises on given conceptions of what one's own flourishing requires.

Even valuing a human community can be based on the belief that it is best to promote its flourishing, apart from its immediate benefit for the valuers. Why, for example, should the existence of healthy native communities be actively promoted by nonnative members of postcolonial societies? It might be the case that nonnative Americans rightly believe that promoting the well-being of Native American communities is in the long-term interest of all Americans, all people, or of their own individual and communal well-being. None the less, valuing Native American communities beyond their 'use value' also requires allowing the flourishing of these communities and the individuals who comprise them. Noninstrumental valuing would therefore inspire a strong desire respectfully to uphold treaties that grant Native Americans the right to engage in traditional practices without interference from the US government. When Anglo-Americans claim to 'value' Native American communities – or the lessons to be learned from them – without promoting their well-being apart from Anglo interests, the valuing is instrumental. Although valuing people and communities for instrumental reasons is not bad in and of itself, this sort of valuing is not sufficient to prevent exploitation, or to disrupt a one-dimensional understanding of other persons and communities.

If an ethic does not aim toward and prioritize the flourishing of moral agents and the entities that they value deeply for noninstrumental reasons; and entities upon which they rely for life itself; and entities that are irreplaceable, can feel pain, and are friend and kin to humans – what good is it? According to the critique at hand, power associated with privilege of race, wealth, gender, sexuality, ethnicity, and species is exercised, consciously or not, in ways that exploit the use value and undermine the well-being of morally considerable beings. Ecological feminists propose ethics that attend to the reasons *why* so much that is capable is not able to flourish, and how more flourishing might be made possible. Assessing actions, practices, institutions, attitudes, and values in terms of their impact on ecological and human flourishing is not the only fruitful starting point for ethics, but it is certainly promising.

FLOURISHING IN ARISTOTLE'S ETHICS

For most philosophers, any discussion of flourishing will evoke thoughts of *eudaimonia*, Aristotle's description of the subject matter of ethics. Aristotle begins his inquiry in *The Nicomachean Ethics* with questions about the optimal result of human action, and the ultimate goal of all human striving, as a way to introduce questions about what it means to live ethically. On Aristotle's view, human well-being requires something more than the satisfaction of desires, as utilitarians typically characterize happiness. Rather, the ancient Greek concept *eudaimonia*, translated as 'happiness,' 'the good life,' 'living well,''excellence,' and 'flourishing,' refers to the achievment of the best of what it means to be human. For Aristotle, *eudaimonia* describes a virtuous life as dictated by reason, enabled by education and necessary external goods, and achievable in a community or *polis* – an actively excellent life.

So far it is clear that this ancient conception of flourishing describes an ideal for humans – what it means to be the best possible ethical *agent*. Although I do not intend to offer an argument in favor of an Aristotelian conception of human virtue or flourishing, I find some aspects of his query incredibly useful for thinking about the moral value of nonhumans, and for articulating ethics that begin with questions about what flourishing is, and how we might promote it. Consider, for example, the reasoning used to justify defining human excellence as a life of reason and virtue. Any form of excellence, it is asserted, corresponds with a characteristic function, 'For just as for a flute-player, a sculptor, or any artist, and, in general, for all things that have a function or activity, the good and the 'well' is thought to reside in the function, so it would seem to be for man [sic], if he has a function' (1980: 12–13). Certain kinds of people have functions; body parts have functions – and good ones perform their functions well. It follows that, as a general claim, a good person will excel at the human function. This is what follows when Aristotle asks about the human function:

> What then can this be? Life seems to be common even to plants, but *we are seeking what is peculiar to man*. Let us exclude, therefore, the life of nutrition and growth. Next there would be a life of perception, but it also seems to be common even to the horse, the ox, and every animal. There remains, then, *an active life of the element that has a rational principle* . . . If this is the case, [and we state the function of man to be a certain kind of life, and this to be an activity or actions of the soul implying a rational principle, and *the function of a good man to be the good and noble performance of these*, and if any action is well performed when it is performed in accordance with the appropriate excellence: if this is the case,] human good turns out to be activity of soul in accordance with virtue, and if there are more than one virtue, in accordance with the best and most complete.
>
> (1980: 13–14)

Of course, Aristotle assumes that human goodness – which only certain humans (not women or slaves) are capable of – is the purpose of ethics. But given even these prejudices, note the other questionable assumptions in Aristotle's conception of human flourishing:

(a) Being a good person entails actualizing the highest potential of the social and biological type 'human.'

(b) 'Goodness' is therefore generalizable over the entire category of moral agents, so there is one true description of human excellence.

(c) The features which define a good human are identical to the features that define and distinguish 'human.' Put formally, harmonica player : harmonica-playing:: human : x, where 'x' is a quality that is as *unique* and *definitive* of 'human' as harmonica-playing is of harmonica player. A good harmonica player might be an awesome cook or a terrible lover, but because these qualities are not unique and definitive of 'harmonica player,' they are insignificant in determining whether a harmonica player is an excellent harmonica player. Likewise, qualities such as growth, possessed by humans but shared by nonhumans, cannot be definitive of humans, and cannot therefore be equated with the good for humans.

(d) The feature which defines 'human' is rationality, which for Aristotle implies having a soul and being capable of specific forms of excellence, or virtue.

Aspects of Aristotle's ethics will be helpful for ecological feminists only in so far as anything survives the revision or rejection of at least the preceding assumptions. According to ecological feminists, ethics do not necessarily exist only in the service of human goods. In fact, any environmental ethic extends the moral universe to include living beings and systems, as well as human individuals and communities. When human virtues, or interests, are the issue, feminist and multicultural ethical insights find standard universalizing conceptions of moral agents, including Aristotle's, to be misrepresentative, male-centered, and based on analyses of human life that render women, slaves, outsiders, and nonhuman life invisible – as moral agents or objects. Philosophical definitions of human nature, or human moral goodness, as one thing are falsely universalizing, and typically rest on the belief that there is an immutable essence to human nature and goodness, but 'moral agent' is not a singular biological type – neither is 'moral object.'

Regarding the musician analogy, Aristotle assumes that characteristic qualities are essential and singular. But, of course, a good harmonica player shares qualities with a good conductor (such as good pitch and a sense of rhythm), and promoting the harmonica player's good harmonica-playing requires encouraging some aspects of good musicianship. Likewise, human flourishing requires growth, nutrition, sentiment, dependence, and things that are also sources of well-being for nonhumans. A good harmonica player is a good musician, just as human well-being is an example of flourishing life. Although ethics might be mindful of the specific requirements of various forms of flourishing, it need not be limited to promoting only human flourishing, or to conceiving of human well-being as completely unrelated and dissimilar to the flourishing of nonhuman life. Finally, although ecological feminists may agree that rationality is a significant aspect of much human experience, and that rationality is important in shaping and enacting morality, they reject the notion that what it means to be human is to be rational – and that goodness is just the best expression of rational selves.

Given these fundamental disagreements with the Aristotelian conception of 'the good life,' what remains that might be of interest in shaping feminist environmental ethics? This discussion of Aristotle's ethics is motivated by my belief that, given the above critique, his outline of *eudaimonia* invites a much broader discussion of various sorts of flourishing, and what the flourishing of beings who are not moral agents might entail. For although it is *human* well-being that most interests Aristotle (and most thinkers in the history of Western philosophy), his comments about well-being, the relationship between flourishing and function, and the externalities necessary for *eudaimonia*, point toward some fruitful lines of inquiry for ecological feminism.

Aristotle's conception of good persons clearly applies only to full, adult moral agents:

> It is natural, then, that we call neither ox nor horse nor any other of the animals happy; for none of them is capable of sharing in such activity. For this reason also a boy is not happy; for he is not yet capable of such acts, owing to his age; and boys who are called happy are being congratulated by reason of the hopes we have for them.
>
> (1980: 19)

Because moral agents and their rational virtues are the focus of his ethics, this view is not likely directly to provide the building blocks for an argument that nonhuman entities are moral objects. Happiness is the subject of ethics, and horses, birds and other nonhumans cannot be happy – if happiness is *eudaimonia*, and *eudaimonia* is human flourishing, defined in terms of uniquely human rational activities in which animals do not participate – by definition. But does this circular logic imply that animals and other living things do not possess their own capacities for well-being, or flourishing? Certainly not.[2] What Aristotle's ethical system provides is a way to describe

---

2 As a biologist, Aristotle based his conception of human well-being on a foundational analysis of how it is that plants and animals flourish, physically and involuntarily. For a thorough discussion of how anthropocentrism is none the less fundamental to Aristotle's ethics, see Nussbaum 1986.

what it is that we should pay attention to when we wonder how to take nonhuman beings seriously as members of the moral universe. Anything that possesses characteristic activities or qualities has the theoretical capacity to exist with health and integrity (at least as much as every human has the capacity to be virtuous). Promoting the good of a nonhuman entity amounts to promoting what is good for it, given its typical and special life cycles, modes of interaction, biological and ecological functions – 'everything without which the life would be incomplete and lacking in value' (Nussbaum 1986: 297). But before thoroughly investigating this provocative point, there is one more aspect of Aristotle's ethics that might be of interest to ecological feminists.

Again: the thing which we desire for its own sake, and for the sake of which we desire all other things, is *eudaimonia*. Yet Aristotle's ethics begin and end with acknowledgements that selves are social. Human flourishing is itself a social concept, as it requires education, friendship, adequate wealth and goods, and a healthy social and political context. 'Man is born for citizenship,' and the aim of politics, which for Aristotle includes social, ethical, and formal political relations, is to promote 'the good for man' (1980: 12, 2). The basic claim is that we are political as surely as we are human, and so our social units ought to promote our flourishing as social selves, which in turn creates a stronger *polis*. What would follow from the observation that we are *ecological* beings – 'mere citizens of the biotic community,' in Aldo Leopold's words – as surely as we are human? Perhaps our social units ought to promote our flourishing as ecological selves, and therefore some degree of flourishing of nonhuman life, in order to create a stronger ecological community.

FLOURISHING AND DYNAMIC CHARM

In order to be at all practically useful, ecological feminist ethics need a number of working conceptions of flourishing, including the flourishing of human individuals and groups, and the related flourishing of species, ecosystems and some nonhuman individuals. Before making sense of how a conception of flourishing, and human flourishing in particular, might capture an ecological feminist sensibility, it will be helpful to get a more detailed picture of what it means for something to flourish. Though I am not arguing for an Aristotelian ethic, some aspects of human and ecological (nonhuman) flourishing discussed below are informed by the rich, social, contextualized and biological notion of the good found in Aristotle. Perhaps his views are helpful because, in the words of Julia Annas, 'Ancient ethics gets its grip on the individual at this point of reflection: Am I satisfied with my life as a whole, with the way it has developed and promises to continue?' (1993: 28). Ecological feminists engage in similar types of navel-gazing, yet also wonder about the developments and promise of 'our' cultures, and what promise holds for other forms of life. It is in the texture of their search for goodness that the work of ecological feminists resembles that of ancient male thinkers.[3]

In the *Physics*, Aristotle defines a natural thing as something that possesses internal sources of change and resistance to outside forces – sources that are not 'implanted' or created by external forces, but that require much external support for their development.[4] Taking something like this definition of natural living things as a point of departure, it is possible to generate a conception of flourishing, and of what is capable of flourishing in an ethical sense, that is sensitive to real biological and physical needs and potentialities, but that takes change, malleability, and uncertainty as fundamental determinants of reality. A number of theorists in environmental ethics have used criteria similar to Aristotle's to demarcate members of the moral universe. In 'The Schopenhauerian Challenge in Environmental Ethics,' Gary E. Varner argues that Schopenhauer's metaethics provides a moral ontology that recognizes the moral 'patiency' (what I refer to as moral considerability) of both individual members of the ecological whole, and the ecosphere, or world, itself (Varner 1985). According to Schopenhauer, 'individual will corresponds to the set of things which exhibit an irreducible pattern of contingently ordered behavior,' or irreducible patterns of 'formative nature' (1985: 215). So members of the category of *genuine* individuals (moral objects) possess unique, intelligible characters, or unique causal and motivational patterns not explained by descriptions of empirical character or external circumstances. This category includes all organic species, the world as a whole, and individual members of higher organic species possessing their own identifiable character or motivational patterns. Among morally considerable individuals, there is a justified hierarchy of value, based on degrees of individuality, which are determined by levels of 'clarity,' or sophistication of knowledge. For Schopenhauer, the justification is based on his belief that the most ethics can provide is some avoidance of

---

3 Perhaps this is also because of ancient ontologies, and the close proximity between ancient philosophy and myth. It should not be surprising that a philosopher who was also a biologist might shed some light on how to characterize and determine the good for nonhuman beings – despite the fact that his work was a human-centred response to the less human-centered philosophy of Plato and his predecessors. I am not committed to the view that ecological feminists are most like ancient philosophers – certainly, even in the limited history of Western philosophy, resemblances also exist with Process philosophy, Spinoza, and Merleau-Ponty. Even more profound similarities exist between some examples of ecofeminist or ecological feminist thought, and nonwestern philosophies, including Buddhism, Taoism, Gandhism.

4 Except in so far as anything living is 'created' through others' reproductive activity and nutritive assistance in early stages of development, all in the context of an adequately abundant and safe environment.

suffering through compassion. The more one can know and feel, the more one is able to suffer, and so the more one matters ethically.

Jon Moline attempts to reconcile holistic and individual interests in environmental ethics by arguing that Leopold's ethics draws an even wider circle around the class of moral objects, including human individuals and communities, biotic communities, and all organic populations describable as units with internal mechanisms enabling characteristic responses *to environmental changes* (Moline 1986). This criteria gives us reason to 'count' some individuals in the moral universe, without committing ethics to promoting the individual interests of protozoa or plants, while still appreciating the value of plants and other members of biotic communities: individual members of 'higher' (sentient, conscious) species are capable of response in ways not exhibited by individual plants, for example, so some sentient animals might be morally valuable as individuals, while plants are only valuable as members of species, populations, or communities. Like Varner, Moline believes that this criterion only determines basic moral considerability. Although we ought to expand the moral universe to include whatever is capable of unique and characteristic response to its surroundings, we should maintain preexisting ethical commitments to human rights and interests – so some hierarchies of value are justified in environmental ethics.

These conceptions of moral considerability illustrate ways of determining not only what kinds of entities 'count' in ethics, but also what is at stake when something is thought to be morally considerable. In these views, and in ecological feminism, it is an entity's *dynamic charm* – its diffuse, 'internal' ability to adapt to or resist change, and its unique causal and motivational patterns and character – that renders it morally considerable, and that serves as a primary site for determining what is good for that being or thing. I use the concept of 'dynamic charm' to denote these clusters of real transmutable qualities, in order to avoid the implications of fixedness and invariability that follow when 'core' qualities are mentioned, and also to evoke a concept with compelling medieval and contemporary associations. In its earliest meanings, 'charm' referred to magical spells or incantations, or to things with magical powers. But in contemporary physics, 'charm' is one of the terms used to characterize quarks – the energetic 'building blocks' of protons and neutrons. Quarks exist in pairs, called flavors, and charm quarks are always coupled with strange quarks. In common use, 'charm' refers to a quality that attracts and delights, or an amulet that inexplicably provides protection. Whatever it is that living things and systems have – what evokes our awe, respect, and what draws us into relationship, and what enables us to change and adapt – *is* magical, mysterious, and fundamental, regardless of our ability to explain things scientifically and poetically. Yet science and other empirical inquiries can, in theory, give us the kind of information we need to proceed with as much respect as possible with regard to living systems – as physics creates meaningful models that allow us to proceed when 'matter' becomes mysterious (think: *energetic building blocks?*). And although something's charm is real, we might not be able to grasp or identify the boundaries of that charm. Indeed, charm is context-dependent, and so a being might have many different, even conflicting sets of charms. What counts as charm in one world might appear unattractive in another context. Yet we might say that charm is evident when something is thriving, in terms of its own capacities or physical requirements, in terms of '*its* charms.'

Dynamic charm is not an immutable Aristotelian essence, but an active capacity for response and change. It is most apparent in instances of alteration, adjustment, and resistance to environmental and internal fluctuations. It is not a set of natural traits through which something responds to the 'outside' environment, but a socially and/or ecologically determined capacity to respond and adjust to unpredictable externalities (climate changes, predation or hostility, pollution, scarcity) and unpredictable changes that seem more internal (disease, changes in preference, aging). Dynamic charm is 'internal' in that it is a manifestation of the biological potential of a specific sort of entity, is physically locatable in a specific body or group of bodies, and because its failure results in the demise of that body or group. Yet it is dependent on externalities to develop, and the very nature of an entity's dynamic charm can shift dramatically as a result of forces and events originating ouside the body or community.

The fact of an entity's dynamic charm is ethically significant for at least three reasons. First, the entities that could be said to exhibit dynamic charm are the same entities upon which moral agents depend (socially and biologically) for their own flourishing and survival – thus they help enable ethical life. Second, because an entity with dynamic charm can be described as having an active well-being associated with its capacities for change and response, those concepts and orientations that comprise 'ethics' can be meaningfully applied to it – it can be 'harmed,' not just damaged, 'dominated,' not just controlled, 'respected,' not just fancied. Third, ecological feminists find that living entities and systems *evoke* moral responses such as respect, attending,[5] responsibility, commitment, and duty, and these responses, though less common, are as basic to their ethical lives as moral sentiment regarding other humans is to most moral agents.[6]

---

5 'Attending' is the concept introduced by Sarah Hoagland in *Lesbian Ethics*, to capture what is good about caring, without importing the aspects tied to oppressive gender roles.

6 It is certainly possible, on this view, to develop ethics that also hold nonliving systems to be the objects of moral value, although is difficult to imagine how nonliving entities could have noninstrumental value. For this reason, the ethics that I describe as ecological feminism do not apply to nonliving systems, although they could conceivably 'count' mixed systems or beings as moral objects. It is likely that the difficulty of drawing distinctions

Perhaps the most well-known sentence that Aldo Leopold ever wrote is his claim that, 'A thing is right when it tends to preserve the integrity, stability, and beauty of the biotic community,' and many commentators have worried, justifiably, about the lack of attention to the needs or interests of humans and other sentient individuals in this foundational principle of Leopold's land ethic (1966: 262). But what if we put the emphasis of Leopold's claim not on the object, 'the biotic community,' but on what he believes should be encouraged by ethics: integrity, stability, and beauty? Are these criteria of health and flourishing not applicable to individuals, groups, and species as well as biota? Generally speaking, an entity is able to flourish when its dynamic charm, through change and readjustments, remains sufficiently integrated and stable – not static – to persevere and thrive. If we understand 'beauty' to refer to those perceptible (if often unnameable) qualities that evoke our moral sentiments – its dynamic charm – we can see Leopold's triumvirate as capturing a significant part of what ecological feminists care about, and the reasons why they promote the flourishing of all living beings and communities.

Below I describe some aspects of an ecological feminist conception of flourishing in a way that is general enough to apply to various and varied sorts of entities. I do not mean to imply that human flourishing and non-human flourishing necessarily share more than structural similarities, or that human communities necessarily resemble nonhuman 'communities.'[7] The relevant common feature for ecological feminist ethics is the capacity of living things and systems to flourish in the sense outlined here, and the fact that their flourishing – whatever it actually entails (and it will entail vastly different things for different entities) – depends on the flourishing of others.

Flourishing occurs in bodies

While a conception of flourishing should not reduce the goals of ethics to biological goods, flourishing entails some degree of physical health. Knowledge about what flourishing requires thus needs thorough, reliable conceptions of what is in the interest of individuals, species, and communities. Although the concept of 'health' is always relative, and can certainly be misused (as in eugenics), it is possible to develop and assess specific prescriptions for bodily well-being that *aim* to promote well-being, and that are

between nonliving and cyborg systems will become increasingly clear – and ethicists will need to articulate more carefully these murky matters concerning being, agency, and value as technological changes occur. Of course, which technological changes are good ones – and how money should be spent to encourage technologies – is always and already a matter of ethics.

7 I use the concept of 'community' to refer to ecosystems, populations, and bioregions. I do not mean to imply that these communities, or groupings, function at all like human communities.

assumed to be best-answers-for-now. If we ought to interact with moral objects in ways that promote their flourishing, as well as our own, ethical responsibility will sometimes require scientific inquiries that *intend* to discover what various beings and systems require to thrive, physically and otherwise, and the integrity and stability of a living thing or system 'from the perspective of' that entity, or with its interest in mind. Needless to say, when we are talking about the flourishing of human individuals and communities (and the flourishing of at least some other sentient beings – certainly primates and cetaceans), 'physical' well-being cannot be clearly distinguished from 'emotional' well-being, or other forms of health and happiness that are not easily reducible to somatic matters.

Flourishing occurs in process

Because it requires periods of development and enactment, 'flourishing' is a designation that can only be applied to something over a span of time. It entails change, and some degree of overall improvement (though not every moment must be improving), and can only be determined 'on average,' or 'over the long haul.' If we want to know if something or someone is flourishing, we must look at their history, and investigate what is likely for their future, from their perspective. Thus, adaptability, flexibility, and responses to history and context are morally relevant.

Flourishing is achievable by individuals only in communities

Ecological feminism begins from the biological and social facts that individuals are not atoms, and that we are social as well as distinct. Humans cannot flourish without other humans, ecosystems, and species, and nothing in a biotic community can flourish on its own. Likewise, communities (both social and ecological) depend on the existence of other communities. Ethical objects therefore flourish as both social and ecological entities. To be extracted from community, human or otherwise, is to lack relationships and contexts that provide the meaning, substance and material for various sorts of lives.

Knowledge about flourishing is no less social and ecological. Conceptions of flourishing should ultimately be generated and revised by a community of knowers and ethical agents in social and ecological contexts. The kinds of moral deliberations and choices that result in notions of flourishing, and decisions about actions and states of being that promote flourishing, are enabled by social institutions that encourage flourishing and autonomy.

Flourishing is achievable by individuals as well as aggregates

The concept of flourishing is something that can be applied to individuals and to communities, and individual and communal flourishing contribute to each other dialectically. They are not, however, reducible to each other, and it is possible that aggregates can flourish without each member flourishing, and for individuals to flourish in contexts in which their flourishing appears impossible. Strangely, it does not make sense to say that an individual is flourishing in a community that is not flourishing – in which its members' health is not promoted, in which conduits of exchange and the import and export of energy or goods have ceased to function, and in which the mechanisms whereby the community tends to adjust or resist change and adversity have broken down. In such instances, it is likely that such a flourishing individual is a member of a flourishing sub-community that feeds or strengthens it. On the other hand, a community cannot flourish unless a significant number of its members are flourishing. A community's 'flourishing' cannot depend on oppressing or instrumentalizing the members of the community (so, on this view, an economically prosperous society built on slavery cannot flourish, in an ethical sense).

Flourishing requires good consequences and good persons

Flourishing is not a mere ideal notion, but one that can be pursued in varieties of personal choices, local activities, and the creation and development of social institutions. Considerations regarding flourishing should therefore include attention to consequences, and assessments of which actions and institutions are likely to produce and contribute to flourishing. None the less, in so far as they value the flourishing of life, ecological feminist ethics are not fully representable in consequentialist or distributive terms. Flourishing requires more than experiences of satisfaction and a maximum of positive outcomes, and flourishing is not easily represented quantitatively. In fact, some forms of flourishing may be more valuable than others, and hierarchies of different forms of flourishing are based not on consequences, but on kinds of moral values attached to different forms of life.

For example, I argued in Chapter 2 that any ethics must be attached to humans or human goods and interests.[8] If this view is plausible, we can imagine an ecological feminist ethic that considers the flourishing of human individuals to be more important than the flourishing of other nonhuman individuals. In instances when these two forms of flourishing are in conflict, given that some effort has been made to avoid the conflict, human interests might ethically outweigh the interests of an individual dog or snake – if serving the well-being of the nonhuman would significantly detract from a human's flourishing.

---

8 Given this, a misanthropic perspective that argues for the elimination of humanity in the interests of wilderness is not an ethic (perhaps it is an anti-ethic).

Flourishing requires integrity and 'self'-directedness

Moral agents who are capable of deliberating and making choices require a high degree of integrity and liberty to flourish. In fact, feminist philosophers from Mary Wollstonecraft to Emma Goldman to Annette Baier have argued that limitations on women's autonomy are a significant aspect of their oppression, and many feminists agree that increased autonomy and self-determination for women is a universal feminist goal. Although feminists need not aspire to purity, or assume that appropriately self-directed agents are not also socially and ecologically determined, we might be able to capture what is valuable in the concept of autonomy with an ethical concept that is less tied to traditional liberal, atomistic 'selves,' and accompanying obsessions with individual liberty. Recently, Claudia Card has argued that the worries about lost autonomy are actually about the need to maintain or achieve moral integrity. Card notes that, 'integrity – literally, wholeness, completeness, undividedness – involves considerations of consistency, coherence, and commitment, whereas autonomy involves considerations of dependence and independence' (1996: 32).

Because common conceptions of autonomy and self-determination assume liberal selves, ecological feminists also stress the ethical value of integrity and self-*directedness* for nonhuman entities, including communities. While individuals and communities are never self-constituted or determined, there is an extent to which self-directedness is possible in any situation in which feasible options exist. When possible, ecological feminists therefore promote the unhindered unfolding of nonhuman life through policies of (human) nonintervention. They also acknowledge that 'wilderness' is somewhat social – or rarely free of human-generated effects – and that all populations always change and evolve in the midst of influential environments and other beings. Still, if ecological 'self'-directedness is valuable, and is suggested by the very notion of flourishing, examples of nonhuman flourishing that do not require human intervention are superior to flourishing brought about by human interference in nonhuman processes and lives, other things being equal.

The flourishing of moral agents requires the flourishing of moral objects

Like Aristotle, ecological feminists believe individual human flourishing has ethical, as well as cultural and material requirements. Moral agency as we know it at the end of the twentieth century requires a thriving universe of living things and systems. While it is certainly logically possible to develop ethics that do not require flourishing organic and social worlds, such ethics cannot be consistent with ecological feminism, or any view that values the flourishing of human life in ecological contexts.

This ecological feminist notion of flourishing is superficially similar to the philosophy of self-realization put forth by Deep Ecologist Arne Naess (Naess 1989). However, though in many instances ecological flourishing is likely to be consistent with human flourishing, the particularities of human existence, and the fact that we are, after all, humans, make it worthwhile to mark out specific notions of human flourishing. These will not in every instance be the same as ecological flourishing and, furthermore, the fact that our judgments are shaped by human lenses means that we can probably say more about the varieties of human flourishing. Of course, it is not inconceivable that a 'human lens' would decide that the best decision in a given situation is simply to let someone or something *be*, regardless of what humans stand to gain from manipulating the entity in question. Furthermore the philosophical force of the concept of flourishing in ecofeminist ethics is significant partially because ecological feminism takes off from facts of oppression, and the specific insights drawn from its critical project motivate the more positive project of articulating alternative values and practices. Naess and other Deep Ecologists' failure to give adequate attention to human interactions with each other prevents their ecological philosophies from adequately addressing the multiplicity and importance of human needs and goods (that is, human flourishing), the complexities of human histories, and the connections between environmental issues and problems and human social and political reality, or the 'social' sources of 'ecological' realities.

Although much of what is embedded in this concept of flourishing motivates the kinds of critical analyses that many ecofeminists have put forward, its potential for shaping more positive ethical claims and directives has not been adequately examined. Feminists tend to utilize the concept of 'the good life,' though it is clear that women's flourishing, as individuals, and as a class or as groups, has certainly been a universal feminist goal. Iris Young's attempt to delineate 'five faces of oppression' could be characterized as a description of how oppression is more than harm, in that it makes flourishing nearly impossible. I choose to discuss ecofeminist ethical goals in terms of *flourishing* both to avoid the impression that there is just one possible set of criteria (*the* good life), and because I believe flourishing more fluently captures the valuable unfolding of nonhuman life.

POTENTIAL WORRIES

Ecological feminists build ethics on commitments to flourishing, and on other moral investments, in the interests of women, the eradication of oppression and other unnecessary harm, and the development of worldviews that see human life as both uniquely dissimilar from and thoroughly enmeshed in nonhuman communities. Still, a number of points might be brought against a view that takes flourishing to be fundamentally import-ant. I consider a few such points briefly before going on to discuss specific questions about women's flourishing in ecological contexts.

First, it might be argued that, because almost anything can flourish, ethics aiming toward flourishing might promote the flourishing of bad, or unde-sirable, things. For this reason, ecological feminists need to emphasize how flourishing, in an ethical sense, cannot rest on significantly limiting the flourishing of other entities capable of flourishing. On this view, hatemon-gering groups (*as* hatemongerers) should not flourish in so far as they aim to limit the flourishing of other beings and groups. Likewise, hunters should not flourish *as* hunters. Unfortunately, contradictions and conflicts are not always clear – they are often a matter of interpretation. Obviously, an array of ethical tools are needed to distinguish when and how it is justified to dis-rupt someone or something else's flourishing, given that some flourishing must always be sacrificed for the flourishing of others. Sometimes narratives and various other forms and sources of wisdom about the various possibil-ities of flourishing must be thoroughly explored to know how best to pro-mote flourishing. In any case, the sentence, 'Allow entities with dynamic charm to flourish' is not an ultimate principle – it is a value-laden guideline.

Similarly, it might be claimed that the concept of flourishing has no teeth, that it is too imprecise and general to provide any real ethical guidance, or that ethics that aim toward flourishing are too idealistic. Such ethics *are* idealistic – but no more idealistic than most views about how to move toward better lives and societies. Any idea about flourishing should begin with the real world, and compare it to ideals based on the broadest possible notion of beings' capacities and potential. In fact, we might find it useful that the imprecision of a non-teleogical, contextual concept of flourishing prevents perfectionist, or absolutist ethics, and depends on close contextual readings of the requirements of something's well-being. In this sense, ethics of flourishing are dependent on science and other sources of wisdom, including oral traditions, narratives, and practical insight, to tell us what flourishing requires. The result is ethics that are somewhat loose and subjective, yet also rely on empirical and other information to construct specific goals. As far as values go, 'flourishing' could prove to be about as accurate as a concept like 'profitable,' although the knowledge that something is flourishing requires different kinds of scientific observations, and also requires making consid-erations from the 'point of view' of the being in question.

Finally, some ecological thinkers might assert that a view that rests ulti-mately on human well-being is anthropocentric. Ecological feminist con-cerns with flourishing, as I've described them, *do* begin with the interests of women, or *humans*, as I believe any ethic must. But because 'human' neces-sarily includes more than the human, because any human perspective depends on nonhuman reality in myriad ways, and because humans can hold nonhuman entities and interests at the center of their moral purview (as ecofeminists argue they ought), this view transcends the standard dichotomy between anthropocentric and nonanthropocentric ethics. In environmental ethics, thinking that is 'human centered' is problematic because it fails to see humans as necessarily related to nonhuman life, and because, for purely prejudicial reasons, it considers human to be uniquely valuable. But an ethical view can consider human interests to be centrally valuable and find 'the center' of our moral lives to be also populated by non-humans who are thick with interests.

HUMAN FLOURISHING

Val Plumwood argues that in place of rule-based ethics, a social, ecological notion of moral agents gives rise to a relational, virtue-based ethics (Plumwood 1993: 184). Such an ethic need not rely on 'old social forms,' but can promote a 'new human and a new social identity in relation to nature which challenges [the] dominant instrumental conception, and its associated social relations' – in my words, new notions of human flourishing (Plumwood 1993: 186). One way in which the concept of flourishing is relevant to environmental ethics is that it captures what ecological feminists want to bring about in and through our interactions. But 'flourishing' also captures something about how we want to *be* – as persons, and as moral agents.

Questions about human flourishing are particularly tricky, especially from a perspective that eschews the notion that there is some immutable or universal human good, but still locates flourishing in the well-being of bodies. Because human nature is not fixed or universal, and does not necessarily 'aim toward' any one *telos*, or end (as Aristotle thought it aimed toward wisdom and virtue), and because human capacities are expressed in vastly different ways and worlds, the meaning of human, and women's, flourishing is uniquely contingent on contexts, histories, and the stories that shape lives and social realities. As far as the work of ethical theory and practice is concerned, useful and accurate notions of human flourishing can only emerge from richly contextualized, sometimes local, evaluations of what it means to be human, what people want and strive for, and what enables their living in ways they value in specific historical and cultural locations. Also, although physiological considerations must be part of what it means to flourish, human flourishing cannot be understood solely as the fulfillment of biological needs, and when biological criteria are used we must remember that these are always conceived and filtered in and through social and cultural lenses. Even Aristotle believed that what it means to be human, and to thrive as a human, is determined through a variety of cultural considerations, including intellectual, emotional, spiritual, and political well-being. Finally, conceptions of human flourishing that are consistent with ecological feminism must be ecologically sensitive, or built upon an awareness of the fact that all humans are ecological, as well as social and individual beings.

The vast variety of human 'modes of being,' interests, and economic and technological systems makes it impossible to assert many very specific universal aspects of flourishing. Indeed, a contextualist, non-teleological ethic of flourishing calls for a broad and complicated philosophical anthropology (Willet 1995). Truths about humans change and shift, and the discursive volume on certain aspects of well-being rises and falls through history and across cultures while new criteria gain significance and old measures lose their prominence. The challenge for ecological feminism is to employ conceptions of human flourishing that are sufficiently rich to accommodate the variety and complexity of forms of life – especially the lives of women and other Others – without rendering the concept meaningless with specificity. We might, for example, find significant patterns evident in instances of human flourishing, or cultural conceptions of flourishing that do not depend on oppression. Likely examples might include the fact that human individuals require a high degree of nurturance to thrive, or that human flourishing increases with greater amounts of 'free expression.' Also, despite wide contextual and constitutional variety, human individuals require connection and community, and in fact *only make sense* in terms of social and ecological surroundings which constantly call us forth to adapt and change.

Human flourishing is not any one thing, but there are patterns to the sorts of human flourishing implied by ecological feminist ethics. As in Aristotle's view, conceptions of flourishing provide models for moral agents, and indicate what we ought to enable for the objects of our ethical attentions. As an activism and a practice, ecological feminism needs to develop suitable, compelling, and context-sensitive models of ecological, human flourishing.

Interlude
ON ETHICS WITHOUT PURITY

As much as I love the forest, I am less drawn to its embrace
than I am to other, more inhospitable environments: the rocky
shores of the North Atlantic, the arid deserts of the
Southwest, the rugged summits of the Appalachians and the
Rockies . . . Lately I have come to recognize what compels me
to this wilder nature, this inaccessible or dangerous or remote
nature, is indeed its wildness, its disobedience, its rowdiness,
its resistance to the domination of men. This nature, this sister nature, is where I gain my courage and patience. It is the
model for what I want all my sisters to be able to choose to be,
without fear or retaliation: useless, unyielding, and free.

                                                    Linda Vance

We are the women of daylight; of clocks and steel
foundries, of drugstores and streetlights,
of superhighways that slice our days in two.
Wrapped around in glass and steel we ride
our lives; behind dark glasses we hide our eyes,
our thoughts, shaded, seem obscure, smoke
fills our minds, whisky husks our songs,
polyester cuts our bodies from our breath,
our feet from the welcoming stones of earth.

                                            Paula Gunn Allen

'San Francisco felt like home. I found a lot of different sorts of
attractive people there. And I knew everyone minded their
own business and didn't care about what I was doing.' . . .
Many women also came to big cities in order to work in factories during the war and they, like ex-military women, stayed
because they found the anonymity of a big city to be more
compatible with what became their life choices.
(Lillian Faderman, *Odd Girls and Twilight Lovers: A History of
Lesbian Life in Twentieth-Century America*)

Ethics is as much about our character as our actions. Living feminist environmental ethics entails (for some of us) a radical shift in how one sees
and interacts with the world. It also requires attention to who we *are* in the
world. In this sense any ethic contains a latent ideal – not just of the best
actions or decisions, but of good persons. In the language of the last

chapter, ethics is concerned not only with how to promote flourishing in our social and ecological interactions. What it means for us to flourish – as moral agents, as women, as ecological feminists – is also a fundamental ethical issue. There are countless conceptions of human flourishing that might be helpful for ecological feminists as we attempt to increase the flourishing of others, and our own flourishing. In this interlude I explore some conceptions that are helpful to me.

I am not content with an ecological feminism that does not have anything to say to me as a lover of women, cities and machines, a creature of comforts, and a political being whose moral imagination is currently obsessed with questions about sexual freedom and racial responsibilities. I do not want to be fixed, or limited, by common notions of what ecological feminist lives are.

But I also need inspiration. With all of the limitations of politics based in identity, I still crave images of flourishing that will help me ponder the possibility of ecological feminist identity – life – in the US and at the beginning of the twenty-first century. Images to encourage stretching into an ethic that both challenges and melds with my sense of myself here and now: body and mind, cultural product and mainstream outsider, intellectual and naked giggler. Images and ideas that help figure the look and the feel of inhabiting spaces in between nature/culture, gender, racial formations, animal bodies. Ways of figuring out how to make this inhabitation visible, identifiable, meaningful.

CYBORGS AND MYTHIC FLOURISHING

> Contrary to what people say, myths are neither univocal nor timeless.
>
> Luce Irigaray

Women: Some believe we are estranged from primordial harmonies. Some detest harmonious wails. Some feel comfortable only if there's carpeting. Some won't forego their windowboxes of herbs and clover. Some know nature as a golfcourse. Some have never encountered concrete. Some spend their days in factories and rarely see the sun. Some work under the sun and dream of a place that's clean and cool and shiny. Some know their own fingers only as stiff with earth and pain. Some hate themselves naked. Some love the smell of sweat. Some would rather climb six flights of stairs to a windowless room in a city than sleep on the ground under the stars.

In her vastly popular essay, 'A Cyborg Manifesto: Science, Technology, and Socialist-Feminism in the Late Twentieth Century,' Donna Haraway takes an image likely to evoke horror in thinkers with ecological and feminist sensibilities, and shows its surprising and ironic potential as the center of an instructive, motivating myth and the symbolic embodiment of a renegade feminist perspective that deconstructs domination. As a point of contrast to Universal Natural Woman, Haraway employs the image of the Cyborg. The cyborg is

> a cybernetic organism, a hybrid of machine and organism, a creature of social reality as well as a creature of fiction, that illustrates the possibilities of feminist epistemology, science, and politics that do not strengthen problematic dualisms that have been cast as the ultimate feminist foil – nature/culture, human/animal, man/woman, scientific knowledge/'embodied' or 'intuitive' knowing – but which instead playfully traverse and inhabit the boundaries between these constructed, incredibly durable categories.
>
> (1991a: 149)

Because these dualisms have been 'techno-digested,' their effects and manifestations are not so easily identified, subverted, or deconstructed by contemporary politics (1991a: 163). Instead, our transgressions of patterns, practices, and institutions of domination, what Haraway calls the Informatics of Domination, require new political identities and myths. Her feminist postmodern myth is built on her belief that members of cultures driven by the technologies of the late twentieth century *are* cyborg – our dependence on and identification with machines is hardly less significant than the fact that we are flesh. Like Mary Shelley's monster, the cyborg is a powerful symbol because she is a surprising amalgam of elements, and because it is surprising that we identify with her. But Haraway also intends the cyborg to function as a plausible ideal:

> A cyborg world might be about lived social and bodily realities in which people are not afraid of their joint kinship with animals and machines, not afraid of permanently partial identities and contradictory standpoints. The political struggle is to see from both perspectives at once because each reveals both dominations and possibilities unimaginable from the other vantage point.
>
> (1991a: 154)

When I first read the Cyborg Manifesto, Haraway's assertion of the power to be found in the inevitable conjoining of organic and mechanistic systems both frightened and excited me. Imagine rendering dualisms meaningless by breaking the very taboos that maintain them – by highlighting the ways in which our lives already render stark splits utterly ridiculous. If the line between machine and life is becoming obsolete, or its obsolescence makes visible the untruths beneath the separation of nature and culture (and whatever else), then there are reasons to be hopeful, and modes of being that do not depend on impossible either/or decisions between technology and life. But, I also wondered, shouldn't we be worried about the increased infusion of our lives with hard wire and electronics? And if we let down our guard to celebrate the potential of cyber being, who will protect the interests of organic being, and the extinction of irreplaceable forms of human and nonhuman life? And, most importantly, why should we suddenly trust anything about contemporary technologies when we know exactly who is getting more rich and powerful from them, and when we know exactly who has access to them: people who already hold the power of racial, economic, and gender privilege in the center of their big tight fists. Now, pondering the cyborg's image through the lens of this book, I want to hang on to the thrill and investigate the threat, and see what they offer to a conception of flourishing.

Haraway considers this incarnation of her own socialist-feminist politics, and, we might conjecture, her own scientific training, a blasphemy which both seriously and irreverently uses what it reveres. Like many theorists, Haraway is concerned with feminist and socialist tendencies actually, if unintentionally, to deepen the dualisms they want to question or eliminate. From Marcuse to Merchant, she finds, these traditions 'insisted on the necessary domination of technics and recalled us to an imagined organic body to integrate our resistance' (1991a: 154). But the pure, natural, inherently wise and good organic body is a modernist myth. In addition to rejecting this myth, Haraway also intends to dismantle 'totalizing' theory, including feminist taxonomies and socialist and Marxist feminisms which erase differences through universalizing conceptions of 'women's activity.' So Haraway's project is as much a response to feminist and ecofeminist glorifications of nature and femininity as it is an indictment of the destructive histories of capitalism, militarism, colonialism, racism, and totalizing, monocular Marxist critiques.

> Feminisms and Marxisms have run aground on Western epistemological imperatives to construct a revolutionary subject from the perspective of a hierarchy of oppressions and/or a latent position of moral superiority, innocence and greater closeness to nature.
>
> (1991a: 176)

The Cyborg Manifesto challenges ecological feminism to generate more satisfying 'revolutionary subjects.' Can Haraway's cyborg be such a subject, or nonabsolute ideal, for ecological feminism? Can she help us figure out what it means to flourish?

I find the cyborg to be an instructive muse for explorations of ecological, feminist ethics precisely because her flourishing does not rest on purity: of nature and culture, human and animal, organic unity or technological salvation. Rather, she is the product of 'fruitful couplings' of disparate universes of meaning (1991a: 150). As a result the cyborg offers a picture of flourishing that fits the impossible rubric of twenty-first century postindustrial life, and such a rich, messy notion of flourishing can help ground ecological feminist values and guidelines. And, I must add, this mythical image appeals to me because of *my* politics, my identities, my aesthetic sensibilities. And because she is not nice.

Part of the attraction lies in how the cyborg occupies a life at the intersections of nature and culture, and how she flourishes and thrives in her context. As an integrated system, a cyborg has dynamic charm. Indeed, 'flourishing,' and 'thriving' better describe her than does a thin term like 'happiness,' although the cyborg definitely revels in pleasure. She is 'completely without innocence,' and pleasure without innocence is not simple happiness or satisfaction (1991a: 151). Pleasure without innocence includes the knowledge that imagination, connection, and the order of the world are complicated and that perfection is impossible. In addition, although Haraway avoids moralism in ways typical of postmodernist feminist writers, the cyborg certainly embodies values, takes (some) responsibility within her environments and relationships, and rejects domination (her slogan: Cyborgs For Life on Earth). None the less, because we don't know exactly what the cyborg's connections to others are, we cannot know the bases for her evaluations and decisions. Probably most tellingly, her 'liberation rests on the construction of the consciousness, the imaginative apprehension of oppression, and so of possibility' (1991a: 149).

For ecological feminists who cut our teeth (and bled) on the denials demanded by mother-earth-goddess ecofeminism, the cyborg can be a helpful and provocative model of transgressive, insubordinate nature- and culture-loving relationships and identities. But even if the borders are exactly where we want to be – even if we feel playful, ironic, and charged with possibility – aren't our occupations of between-places more *troubled* than this? I am worried about what the cyborg lacks. An edge. A history. A fierce sense of loyalty based on connections. Vulnerability. The legacy of her multiplicity. Tears from laughter (as Teresa De Lauretis notes, whatever her connections are, they seem rather *dry*).

Without dismissing these worries, I want to keep in mind that the cyborg is best read as a creative response to an unacceptable, impossible dichotomy of choices: between the worlds of the Wanderground and Blade Runner. Those of us who are content with neither because of their practical, ethical, and political deficiencies or impossibilities – or because we don't see ourselves present, or comfortable, in them – need to articulate other options as we lay out grounds for rejecting various ethical and political theories. My concerns echo questions raised by other feminist theorists. Historian Joan Scott argues that the cyborg betrays scientific and technological determinism (Scott 1989). De Lauretis aptly notes the cyborg's lack of sexuality and desire, and wonders therefore where embodied sparks of transgression and change – body politics – originate (De Lauretis 1994). These writers remind us of the dangers of optimism, especially concerning the integrity of female bodies under the rule of technology and capitalism. And De Lauretis' critique makes me notice how the mechanistic qualities of the cyborg evoke a lack of trust. There is, in fact, a sense in which she fits too well, or makes too much sense, in sterile worlds – like the worlds of science and technology – which have been so toxic for women and nature, and in which so much of what we (all) are is incomprehensible. Where are the 'parts,' of the cyborg that do not fit into *any* discourses of power? What is her sense of the meanings of *her own* body (whatever it may be), and its place within social and ecological relations? What does it mean for liberation to rest on *construction* of *consciousness*, for oppression to be apprehended *imaginatively*? Cyborgs dwell on any number of discursive and ontological borders – human/animal/machine is only one possible hybridity. It follows that, for Haraway, 'women of colour might be understood as a cyborg identity, a potent subjectivity synthesized from fusions of outsider identities and in . . . complex political-historical layerings'(1991a: 174). But Paula Moya argues that Haraway's reading of 'women of color' as an example of an empowering cyborg identity both idealizes the social identities of women of color and also stretches its meaning so far from its material basis that 'anyone can be a woman of color' (1996: 134). Furthermore, she criticizes Haraway's use of latinas to breathe life into a theory that does not do justice to their lives:

> Ironically, Moraga and other women of color are often called upon in postmodernist feminist accounts of identity to delegitimize any theoretical project that attends to the linkages between identity (with its experiential and cognitive components) and social location (the particular nexus of gender, race, class, and sexuality in which a given individual exists in the world).
>
> (1996: 129)

By privileging Chicanas as an embodiment of cyborg identities, Haraway, 'instead of liberating them from a historically determined discursive position, ironically traps them – as well as their living counterparts in the real world – within a specific *signifying* function'(1996: 131). Following Chela Sandoval's explication of 'oppositional consciousness,' Haraway describes the cyborg as birthed entirely from marginality and survival, and Moya finds this origin story to be both an inaccurate description of the construction of latina identities, and an insufficient source of feminist creativity and resistance. Rather, real historical identities, and their bases in social and material relations, motivate and direct being and action in the world. The requisite consciousness for liberation rests on responses to real conditions – *in* the linkages between identities and social locations, from which agency and imagination inevitably percolate.

The power of the cyborg lies in the fact that she is an example of a border-dweller who *flourishes* on the borders. But is that enough to resist and disenable the forces that attempt to annihilate difference? Is that enough for ethics?

FLOURISHING AND CURDLED SELVES

Like Haraway, María Lugones desires alternatives to purity. But where the cyborg renounces identity (her identity is an anti-identity), Lugones argues for a complex, embedded, historical yet visionary version of identity politics, 'from within a hybrid imagination, within a recently articulate tradition of latina writers who emphasize mestizaje and multiplicity as tied to resistant and liberatory possibilities' (1994: 458). To ensure that the differences between her project and projects like Haraway's are not lost on her readers, Lugones opens her piece with a caveat: 'All resemblances between this tradition and postmodern literature and philosophy are coincidental, though the conditions that underlie both may well be significantly tied. The implications of each are very different from one another' (1994: 458).

Lugones' 'Purity, Impurity, and Separation' is an exploration of the relationships between ethical and ontological purity, and oppression and control. The logic of purity constructs and maintains a world that is 'unified and fragmented, homogenous, hierarchically ordered,' and peopled by subjects who are unified, abstracting, pure, and rational (1994: 463). But because all selves are actually multiplicitous, messy, and embodied, the pure, unified subject is a ruse. The maintenance of its existence, however illusory, depends on the labor of others, and the illusion of purely separate nature and culture, public and private, mind and body:

The modern subject must be masked as standing separate from his own multiplicity and what commits him to multiplicity. So, his own purification into someone who can step squarely onto the vantage point of unity requires that *his remainder* become of no consequence to his own sense of himself as someone who justifiably exercises control over multiplicity. So his needs must be taken care of by others hidden in spaces relegated outside of public view, where he parades himself as pure. And it is important to his own sense of things and of himself that he pay little attention to the satisfaction of the requirements of his sensuality, affectivity, and embodiment . . . If women, the poor, the colored, the queer, the ones with cultures (whose cultures are denied and rendered invisible as they are seen as our mark) are deemed unfit for the public, it is because we are tainted by need, emotion, the body. This tainting is relative to the modern subject's urge for control through unity and the production and maintenance of himself as unified . . . Thus we exist only as incomplete, unfit beings, and they exist as complete only to the extent that what we are, and what is absolutely necessary for them, is declared worthless.

(1994: 466–467).

Lugones proposes a *logic of curdling* as a resistant response to the logic of unity. In curdled logic, the world is seen as complex and heterogeneous. Identities, while multiplicitous and embodied, are not mere collections of unconnected fragments (463). Located in the 'world of the impure' *mestizaje*, curdled identities embody 'either/or, ambiguity . . . breaching and abandoning dichotomies . . . resistance to a world of purity, of domination, of control over our possibilities' (1994: 459). Impure identities begin with separation – from limiting identities, from domination and fragmentation – similar to the curdled emulsion of a failed mayonnaise. The different aspects are separated but impure: like yolky oil and oily yolk.

For Lugones, not all forms of impurity are transgressive, although impurity and multiplicity contain the potential for resistance to unifying logic. Acquiescence to the logic of unity allows fragmentation: 'parts that do not fit well together, parts taken for wholes . . . composed of imagined parts . . . composed of parts produced by subordinates enacting their dominators' fantasies' (1994: 463). But, in avoidance of fragmentation, the logic of curdling enables a subject who 'in its multiplicity perceives, understands, grasps its worlds as multiple sensuously, passionately as well as rationally' (1994: 465). Such a *mestizaje* subject is able to engage in impure resistance to interlocked oppressions. The difference between fragmentation and curdled multiplicity lies in the ability to create resistance from heterogeneous identities that are meaningful and liberatory without being unified or pure.

FLOURISHING WITHOUT PURITY

The distinction between fragmented and curdled, multiplicitous identities helps me grasp the necessity of resistance in ethics. Resistance to the maintenance of difference-obliterating worlds of meaning. Resistance to purity-obsessed logics. Resistance that begins from within connectednesss. A cyborg might be curdled – but without *her own* knowledge of her own bottom-up connections with others, nothing prevents her from being fragmented. This knowledge is partially about identity, which in turn is a matter of history, ethnicity, social location, and agency. It is our responses to fallacious and morbific origin stories that enable agency for the oppressed, but transgressive and liberatory ethical agency requires more than a great big, dislocated 'fuck you.' Like cyborg being, ecological feminism entails resistance to most given conceptions of what human selves are or can be – as gendered, as racialized, as members of a species which, more often than not, characterizes itself as disconnected from nature. However, flourishing on the boundaries of nature/culture is not just a matter of

dwelling on the overlapping borders of identities, practices and characteristics which are not supposed to occur within the same body – it requires
claiming a space there: cultured animal, mutt, anti-feminine woman, race
traitor, computer-enhanced forest-dweller. It also requires active opposition
to unifying logics that aim to fix us, and that have aimed, variously, to fix
Others since time immemorial.

Having said that, I want also to remember that resisting purity implies let-
ting go of dreams of a purity of resistance. How do we transgress boundaries while maintaining, and acting from connectedness, as complex and
contradictory social, ecological beings? How do we act from connectedness
and resistance without striving for new forms of purity? How do we even
begin? By seeing the world as multiplicitous and complex. By naming and
performing identities and ways of being that are in between the spaces of
species, gender, and race. By rabidly protecting whatever provides us with
the strength to resist and to thrive. By refusing to let those who reside com-
fortably within logics of unity, and their institutions, get away with murder.

SISTERWOMANCHAINSAW

We (you and I) are walking in the woods. The air is cold and damp, but the
combination of our protective layers of wool and gore-tex, and our pace,
prevents us from feeling the chill. When it begins to snow we feel lucky to be
outside, on this trail in Kentucky, in the first snow of fall. The leaves are
gold, red, yellow, and brown. There is still some green, too, and the damp
has soaked the tree bark black. The white snow, against these colors, is perfect – or it so approximates my mind's stereotypes of 'picture perfect' that I
want to savor it like a painting. Clean white against crisp color. A rare combination.

We're hiking up the hill, boots gripping and sliding in damp chocolatey
earth. Leaves are already decomposing like muddy lace beneath our feet.
Your nose is red, ice against my cheek, your breath a contrast of steam and
sweetness. The air is still, and because the season has driven the critters out
of sight, in search of warmth, it almost seems like we are alone on this hill-
side, where life has slowed in anticipation of winter.

Then, as unexpected as thunder on a sunny day – gunshots – too close –
and my heart like lead drops through my chest, into a pit of terror.

A wave of knowledge comes in an instant. It's Hunting Season.

We stop. We confer with glances. And in less than a minute we begin
walking, now as fast as we can, back to the trailhead. The colors blur and
earth becomes hard as we fill the air with chatter about wolves and other
predators. About poverty and hunger. To soften the intensity of my unyielding desire to put nothing but distance between myself and men with guns, I
tell you about the time I learned to shoot a forty-five. I also tell you about
the guy in Wisconsin who shot his brother, who was sitting in a tree, because

he mistook him for a deer. We recall movie images of black men being chased by the Klan through dense, humid forests. And when we're near the end of the trail we remember the chainsaw in the back of the truck.

We (you and I) want to scare the deer. We want to sabotage the hunt.

The pull-cord is tight, but after about twenty tries the damn chainsaw finally starts. Its loud metal whine cuts into the cold stillness, harsher and more sustained than any gunshot. I think: run away. I think: this is a warning. I think: I could take this chainsaw and rip right through their truck as though it were a cartoon image. My face is burning and zinc-colored smoke is engulfing us, but the urgent vibration of the resonant machine swells my pounding heart. I'm afraid the hunters will come and get us, and I fear their guns, but we let the chainsaw roar for as long as we can stand it. We want to scare the animals. We want them to run to safety.

No one emerges angrily, or frightened, from out of the woods. You kill the engine, and the silence rings across our small universe. On the way home you seem to savour the lack of noise, but I am preoccupied with worry because I cannot find the words to describe my sense of failure, and of jubilation. Then we (you, then I) begin to talk. About how when deer flee in fright, they are more vulnerable to hunters. About how the flesh of one deer can feed a family for weeks. About what it means when a practice turns into a sport in a racist patriarchy. About women hunters and about the purposes of national forests.

We agree that we don't know if we helped the deer, or if there was anything we could have done to make good on our compassion for the deer who live in those Kentucky woods. Yet we don't want to let go of our sense that we did something to disrupt an institution that we disdain. That we tried to stand in solidarity. That in discussing the story, we might figure out how more effectively to enact compassion and rage. That in my sense of myself, and in our sense of us, it matters that we were not content to let it be.

90

4

SELVES, SYSTEMS AND CHAOS

> Mankind has generally put property ahead of life. Men care
> little about living matter or its cultural economy. Men's so-
> ciety is built upon ownership of property. Life itself is treated
> like a commodity, productive capital, and possessed as a tool
> of labor, but not as the basis of an identity to be cultivated.
> Patriarchy cares little about spiritualizing sexually differen-
> tiated nature. This perverts its relationship to matter and its
> cultural organization.
>
> Luce Irigaray

> An ecofeminist perspective about both women and nature
> involves this shift in attitude from 'arrogant perception' to
> 'loving perception' of the nonhuman world. Arrogant percep-
> tion of nonhumans by humans presupposes and maintains
> sameness in such a way that it expands the moral community
> to those beings who are thought to resemble (be like, similar
> to, or the same as) humans in some morally significant way . . .
> In contrast, 'loving perception' presupposes and maintains
> difference – a distinction between the self and other, between
> human and at least some nonhumans – in such a way that per-
> ception of the other as other is an expression of love for one
> who/which is recognized at the outset as independent, dissim-
> ilar, different.
>
> Karen Warren (with the help of Marilyn Frye)

Feminist ethical starting points provide points of entry for ecological feminist arguments against nonfeminist ethical perspectives which merely extend
traditional philosophical concepts to include nonhuman animals, or
'nature.' Although an important feature of ecological feminist ethics and
activisms is their inability to be fixed neatly within debates between 'red'
and 'green' environmentalists, the conceptions of selves and communities
employed in the ecofeminist project challenge liberal positions, nonfeminist
radical ecologies, and anthropocentric feminisms. This chapter is an
attempt to make clear the depth to which ecological feminism challenges
some other influential approaches to animal rights and environmental
ethics. Central to my belief that ecological feminism is vitally theoretically
and politically challenging is the superiority of its ethical starting points.

Although other radical conservationist and environmental thinkers have emphasized conceptual and practical connections between social justice and ecological problems, ecological feminism is vastly different from extensionist positions in that it does not assume human social problems have been solved, or that traditional approaches to those problems are adequate to assess and address the nexus of current ecological/social disasters. In addition, ecological feminisms do not find radical positions that treat humans as a unified, undifferentiated species, or nature as a self-evident, manipulable given, to be helpful or accurate. Rather, the existence and intersections of difference, and the ways in which some differences are constructed as possibilities for oppression, domination, and exploitation, are key points of inquiry in unpacking any specific set of relations of domination. For all of their particularities, both liberal and radical ethics concerning nonhumans are lacking a crucial element if they ignore the social depths of human nature. It is not logically impossible that attempts to address social and environmental problems which are not mindful of the depth of the interrelatedness of oppressions, might result in *improved* practices and institutions. These practices cannot, however, result in sufficiently significant, long-term shifts away from underlying oppressive and exploitative ideologies and modes of interaction. Worse, they may even strengthen them. If underlying premises about the nature of the agents, objects, and subject matter of ethics are so influential, a good way to discuss significant disagreements among ethical theories and perspectives is to compare their grounding assumptions and motivations. Comparing ecological feminism with other approaches to environmental ethics, the starting points of interest to us are ethical, in that they include assumptions about what comprises the ethical universe, or the category of ethically significant entities and relationships, and on what grounds membership into the realm of ethical considerability is granted.

Many well-known attempts to construct new environmental ethics, or 'ecological perspectives,' including popular representations of the need to Save the Planet, come directly, unmediatedly, from the same foundations as egalitarian, rights-oriented, democratic values. Many conservationist perspectives are traditionally liberal, and use democratic rights-based arguments to defend the view that the environment ought to be preserved for the good of humans. These views rely on the maintenance of a clear distinction between nature and culture, and of an understanding of ethics as being only about human persons. They are therefore fundamentally, philosophically contrary to environmental ethics that value nonhumans beyond their usefulness, though in specific instances human-interested environmentalists and those who 'speak for the trees' may agree on environmental policy and practices.

Although some feminists may argue that we should protect nonhuman species and environments for human interests alone, from within ecological feminism, perspectives that do not look beyond the value of humans do not pose interesting challenges. Far more illuminating in the contrasts they provide, are movements and theories based on arguments that nonhuman entities have moral value. While other examples of environmental ethics might be strikingly contrasted with ecological feminism, I focus in this chapter on nonfeminist approaches to animal rights, primarily because so many feminists have fought for humane treatment of nonhuman animals, and have made explicit philosophical and practical connections between feminism, vegetarianism, and anti-vivisectionism. This is not surprising, given the applicability of anti-cruelty rhetoric in making the case for both women's and animals' rights, the raw similarities between the worst examples of ill-treatment of women and animals, and cultural associations of contemporary Western femininity with a tendency toward affectionate relationships with nonhuman animals. The contrast between 'animal rights' arguments and ecological feminist approaches to the suffering of animals is noteworthy because of the agreement between them: that our moral attention should be directed toward nonhuman animals. But ecological feminist analyses of the sources of the problem, and arguments for the moral considerability of nonhuman animals, differ deeply from the philosophical, ethical, and political commitments of liberal animal rights approaches.

LIBERAL FOUNDATIONS IN ENVIRONMENTAL ETHICS

Animal rights theorists extend traditional conceptions of who 'counts' ethically, as something that should be given ethical consideration as itself, beyond its use value for others, with the following argument: since humans are morally considerable because they possess (or could possess) the capacity to suffer or to have other fundamentally important cognitive experiences, so nonhuman animals with those capacities ought to be considerable as well.[1] Utilitarian arguments for animal rights, echoed in 'cruelty-free' labels, and popularized by People for the Ethical Treatment of Animals, are based on an insight voiced by Jeremy Bentham in 1789, that any being capable of suffering is morally considerable. Nearly two hundred years later, this claim found full philosophical articulation in Peter Singer's 'Animal Liberation,' in which he argued that only unjustified prejudice toward our own species, or 'speciesism,' prevents us from acknowledging the suffering of nonhuman animals and taking their interests into account, morally. Like our ethical interactions with other humans, Singer believes our interactions with

---

1 Strictly speaking, Peter Singer is not an 'animal rights theorist.' In 'Animal Liberation or Animal Rights?' (1987) he distinguishes his view from Regan's arguments for the rights of animals, and claims that a utilitarian focus on *interests* is superior to the rights approach. None the less, common liberal assumptions, and the common uses of both sorts of arguments by animal rights activists, lead me to consider them under a common label.

nonhuman animals are ethically relevant because animals are sentient – they possess the capacity for sense experience. His position is based on a utilitarian understanding of the goal of ethics as maximizing satisfactory consequences for all those affected by an action, and preventing suffering. Anti-speciesist utilitarians believe that these moral goals – and the implication that we must grant moral consideration to all sentient beings – stem directly from reason.

Tom Regan's work follows Singer's intuition that the similarities between humans and other animals render speciesism unjustified (Regan 1983; Regan and Singer 1976). However, Regan relies on a Kantian, duty-based ethical scheme to argue for the rights of animals. Kant's ethics, also based in a metaphysics that identifies reason as the inevitable and appropriate basis for ethical principles, establishes rational beings as ends in themselves, not mere means to the ends – purposes, goals, goods – of others. By arguing that nonhuman animals should be respected as ends in themselves, Regan reduces the Kantian emphasis on rationality, but his final position is built on the Kantian belief that there are some beings who have special value, or dignity, which moral agents have a duty to respect. Moral agency requires rationality, but dignity, or inherent value, 'belongs equally to those who are the experiencing subject of a life.' So, reason, possessed by human moral agents, demands that we recognize the value, and hence the rights, of all conscious beings.

Animal rights theories, which include some of the earliest self-identified philosophical work in environmental ethics, often begin with analogical arguments in favor of extending rights to nonhuman animals, and claiming that prejudice against animals is ethically equivalent to racism and sexism. The extensionist claim is that as 'we' (rights holders) have extended moral and legal consideration to blacks and women, on the basis of some fundamental equality with previously-accepted rights holders, so ought we to extend such consideration to sentient, nonhuman animals. Again, the proposed grounds for positing the moral equality of humans and other animals is their ability to suffer or their possession of conscious experience. A guiding assumption of this approach is that liberal, individualistic, rights-based ethical responses to histories of oppressive treatment are philosophically and practically adequate and have been somewhat successful.

How should feminists, African-Americans, gay men, and lesbians read the opening of Peter Singer's groundbreaking book *Animal Liberation*, first published in 1975?

A liberation movement is a demand for an end to prejudice and discrimination based on an arbitrary characteristic like race or sex. The classic instance is the Black Liberation movement. The immediate appeal of this movement, and its initial, if limited success, made it a model for other oppressed groups. When a majority group – women –

began their campaign some thought we had come to the end of the road. Discrimination on the basis of sex, it has been said, was the last form of discrimination that is universally accepted and practiced without pretense, even in those liberal circles which have long prided themselves on their freedom from prejudice against racial minorities . . . If we have learned anything from the liberation movements, we should have learned how difficult it is to be aware of the ways in which we discriminate until they are forcefully pointed out to us. A liberation movement demands an expansion of our moral horizons, so that practices that were previously regarded as natural and inevitable are now seen as intolerable.

(1975: iv)

Singer's observations about continental drifts in acceptability of liberation discourses remind us that sometimes ideas which are initially the object of ridicule eventually come to gain wide acceptance. But those of us who identify with those discourses will inevitably ask for the assumptions behind Singer's 'we,' especially if *we* are among those who are never assured a permanent place within the authoritative first person plural. Feminists are aware of the ever-present possibilities of backlash, resurgent fundamentalism, and the potential for dramatic misrepresentation of a dissatisfied woman's words and deeds. Many of us are also aware of the sometimes minuscule impact of liberatory talk on material conditions, and the fact that the visibility of a form of discrimination can have surprisingly little to do with the speediness of its eradication. The model struggles for rights which Singer describes as successful have not resulted in liberation because the problems they meant to address are not reducible to 'discrimination,' 'inequality,' or anything that a liberal approach can adequately address. In fact, the masculinist, individualist, rationality-revering assumptions about human selves embedded in Singer's 'we' are not only unhelpful – they are instrumental in male and masculinist control of nature, women, and other disempowered people.

Liberalism is problematic for feminist environmental ethics both in its conception of moral agents – human selves – and in its criteria for considering someone a moral object. Despite their philosophical differences, both Singer and Regan inherit the liberal image of human selves as discrete, solitary knowers whose individual experiences and capacities are of utmost importance in ethical decision-making. They take these qualities of human persons to be the source of ethical *agency*, and find animals ethically valuable – define them as significant ethical *objects* – in so far as they resemble individual human knowers and experiencers. Ultimately, their starting point is the human individual who possesses natural qualities (sentience or rationality) and therefore rights, and who is able reasonably to discern these qualities in others. Ethical truths emerge from facts about such individuals, and human societies are aggregates of such individuals.

95

AGAINST LIBERAL INDIVIDUALISM

In opposition to human-centered ethics that only consider the interests of rational human persons, both utilitarian and deontological animal rights theorists intend to demote rationality as the only basis for considering something morally valuable or including it as an object of moral consideration. Yet they maintain a liberal, individualist conception of ethical agents. Note that 'individual' here refers not just to a specific historical body, uniquely located in space and time. The liberal view of the individual, exemplified in the views of Singer and Regan, is of individual selves who are fundamentally self-sufficient and self-contained, like 'atoms.' Society is therefore 'constituted by individuals for the fulfilment of ends which were primarily individual' (Taylor 1986: 29). We are individuals first, and the fact of our membership in societies or other groups is secondary to understanding what, and who, one is. In the corresponding conception of rationality, which we might think of as a *hyper*-rationality, rationality is the essence of humanity – all persons possess it, and it is bound by the same norms wherever it occurs. Although exercised through interaction with the world, hyper-rationality is thought to be a function and product of individual cognition. It is inborn, and isolatable from the body, sensation, emotions, and other 'environmental' influences. Such rational agents are assumed to be self-interested egoists whose natural propensities are best expressed and encouraged in market economies (Plumwood 1993). It follows that morality is necessary 'to provide a framework of legal and moral rules which will insure that the whole system does not break down through the untrammelled egoism of self-seeking' (Grimshaw 1986: 197).

The difference for animal rights theorists is that ethics, generally concerned with determining the correct reasonable, justified rules that individuals ought to follow when interacting with other rational (read: human) individuals, is *extended* to include questions about how rational individuals ought to interact with other sentient or conscious nonhuman individuals. But the rational, utility-maximizing, atomistic human self is the ethical starting point, still serving as the model for what 'counts' morally. Individualism underlies arguments for animal rights: although one doesn't have to be rational to count as a valuable member of the moral universe, one counts as a member because human rationality (hyper-rationality) requires it and because one (sentient individual) is significantly similar to a rational person. Because they rely on individualistic understandings of social and political reality, recommendations made by liberals depend on a limited view of how rational individuals conceive of problems, and a false belief that attention to individuals, through the granting of rights, can solve problems like racism, sexism, and speciesism.

Current debates between liberals and communitarians (both feminist and nonfeminist) indicate both the attractiveness and limitations of liberal, rights-based approaches to ethics in general, and ethics concerning non-humans, in particular. A view that pays utmost attention to the interests of individuals *as* individuals, and that considers concern for liberty and personal freedom to be the central work of ethical values and state institutions has much appeal to those who have experienced the privileges available in liberal, democratic societies. It also is appealing to those of us who have not experienced those privileges, and hence sometimes seem to crave self-directedness above all else. If we experience ourselves as individuated persons, however complex, as well as community members, we want ethical and political systems that value self-direction and protect individual liberties, and that hesitate to sacrifice individual interests to the goods of communities. But must individual interests and liberties be sacrificed by ethics that are not built on hyper-rational, individualist assumptions about moral agents and objects?

While it is true that *this* kind of body, within *this* material and historical context sees itself as a clearly bounded individual (as did the bodies of most of the prominent thinkers in the history of Western philosophy), the experience of such a high degree of individuation is not universal in the human species. Describing moral agency in strictly individualist terms, or using atomistic individuals as an ethical starting point, neglects the extent to which our selfhood is social, and misrepresents individualism as a natural fact. Refuting atomistic conceptions of human moral agents and the 'delusion of self-sufficiency,' communitarian philosopher Charles Taylor argues that without a certain form of social flourishing, there would be no possibility of individuals who are capable of possessing and respecting rights in the first place (Taylor 1992).[2] Moral agents – selves – as isolated as we sometimes seem, are necessarily relational, and our relations are neither atomistic nor linear. Communitarian feminist philosophers also believe that human individuals necessarily shape and are shaped through our interactions with other persons, and within communities and groups.

> In its identity, character, interests, and preferences, [the self] is *constituted by*, and in the course of, relationships to particular others, including the networks of relationships that locate it as a member of certain communities or social groups. . . Relationships to others are *intrinsic* to identity, preferences, and so on, and the self can *only* reason as the social being she is [emphasis mine].
>
> (Friedman 1991: 164–165)

But feminists conceive of selves as social without losing sight of the great ethical and political significance of individual intentions and volition

---

2 Unfortunately, Taylor tends to conflate 'flourishing society' with 'Western democratic society.'

(Benhabib 1992). Though they emphasize the social nature of human individuality, feminists remain critical of the ways in which social relations and formations are damaging – producing and reproducing prejudice as well as connectedness, oppression as well as resistance, confining norms as well as identity. María Lugones' work is largely an effort to articulate the significance of the fact that selves are typically constituted in and by several different communities. Because different communities produce different meanings, or are different 'worlds,' selves formed in the context of divergent, conflicting worlds are not unified but multiplicitous:

> Sometimes the 'world'-traveller has a double image of herself and each self includes as important ingredients of itself one or more attributes that are *incompatible* with one or more of the attributes of the other self: for example being playful and being unplayful.
>
> (Lugones 1990: 173)

Even if we accept a more complicated theory of selves, questions remain about how and how much we ought to value individual persons, especially when those persons have both unique, definitive, seemingly self-initiated motivations and interests *and* interests and capacities that are only accurately described as socially and ecologically determined. But tensions between individual and group interests are not new to philosophy. While many nonfeminist moral philosophers emphasize worries about autonomy in the face of communal interests, feminist and environmental ethicists also remain concerned about the well-being of groups, communities, and networks of biological interdependence. The both/and approach of ecological feminism, in which individuals are considered valuable as necessary, beneficial, members of communities *and* as unique persons or sentient beings, draws from the insights of feminist ethics, communitarianism, and ecology.

SOCIAL AND ECOLOGICAL SELVES

Revised conceptions of human selves allow feminist philosophers to dispel paranoia about threats to individual autonomy through an accompanying revision of what it means to choose freely. For example, Marilyn Friedman shows how a feminist social conception of the self actually unsettles assumptions in debates among philosophers concerning the justifiability of partiality. If 'relationships to others are intrinsic to identity,' then 'the self can only reason *as* the social being she is,'and what might otherwise be conceived as partiality is actually a justified concern for a nexus of interests held by both the individual self, and others necessarily, intrinsically related to oneself (Friedman 1991: 165). This point about partiality should not be lost on those with concerns about autonomy: given that selves are social, self-interestedness is not necessarily egoistic. For social selves, being self-directed entails and requires more than respect for individual liberties and rights.

Friedman is careful to distinguish a feminist social conception of the self from nonfeminist theories, in that feminists do not take constitutive communities and relationships at face value. Where nonfeminist communitarians such as Alisdair MacIntyre and Michael Sandel assume a conventional, conservative stance toward traditional familial and communal ties, Friedman finds that a sufficiently critical and complex conception of gendered selves illuminates the need for and possibility of resistance to oppressive norms governing conventional relationships. Certainly, any ecological feminism would want to reject *aspects* of many traditional loyalties – to family, species, race, nation, and culture – in so far as they found and fuel oppression and domination within their own systems, and also foster unwillingness to take 'outsiders' seriously as morally significant beings.[3]

Human individuals need not be seen as atomistic, self-determining, independent or hyper-rational to be ethically significant as the possessors of moral responsibility, duties, or rights, and freedoms. Rationality itself has been theorized by feminists and others as social, embodied, emotional, and varied. Ethicists who begin with the presumption that individual human autonomy is an ethical ideal or ontological fact generally consider arguments in favor of communal interests or community-based values to be threatening to individual liberty. Instead, ethics might *begin* with recognitions of the necessity of human and biotic interdependence, and the valuing of good relationships and communities. In starting here, we need not abandon commitments to some forms of autonomy and individuality:

> Often theorists who see autonomy as a primary, fundamental trait posit a contradiction between self-sufficiency and interdependence, on the assumption that a person has to buy interdependence at the cost of some measure of autonomy. Theorists who start from community and interdependence can accommodate the requirements of autonomy better than theorists for whom autonomous existence is the 'original position' can accommodate the requirements of community.
>
> (Code 1991: 79)

Autonomy does not necessarily entail the existence of free, isolated atoms. As Charles Taylor points out, the kind of freedom 'we' crave or need is achievable only within certain societies, and makes sense only within communities.

---

3 María Lugones, in a lecture presented at the University of Cincinnati in November, 1995, argued that for people of color (especially) even communities of origin that are places of incredible discomfort can be sources of strength and identity. Indeed, many communities to which women belong are sources of both strength and pain. The clear dichotomy introduced elsewhere by Marilyn Friedman, between communities of choice and origin, is therefore problematic (Friedman and Wise 1995).

By setting up a contradiction between freedom and dependence, autonomy-obsessed theorists make it logically difficult for their theories to account adequately for the realities of human interdependence with each other, and with nature. Deborah Slicer argues that such an oppositional approach is typical of animal rights liberalism (Slicer 1991). In contrast, if we begin with the awareness that ethical agents and objects are fundamentally interdependent individuals, the stage is set to discuss community and individuality fully without falling into a problematic and inaccurate individualism. As many philosophers have argued, communitarian starting points more accurately reflect human biological and social reality and so are better able to represent issues of individuality and autonomy as they occur in the fabric of our lives.

This feminist line of argument against liberal individualism might be extended to reflect ecological realities – ecological flourishing is certainly necessary for some degree of social and individual development and flourishing. Our very selfhood and moral capacities are formed within and by social and ecological networks of dependence, interaction, meaning, material exchange, opposition, affection, and power. Ecological feminists see human ethical and political agents as primarily, necessarily, and intrinsically social, in a broad, ecological sense. In addition, ecological feminists conceive of human selves as social and as ecological, as necessarily and significantly participating in/as nature as well as human social reality. Feminist critiques of liberal individualist ontology, epistemology, and politics, along with ecocentric insights about the ways in which conceptions of human nature have glorified *Homo sapiens* and downplayed our stunningly interdependent relationships with nonhuman nature, contribute to ecological feminist conceptions of human selves as socially and ecologically constituted and embedded (Plumwood 1993). This complexity of connection recommends an attitude of humility as well as recognition of human ignorance concerning biotic interdependencies and long-range consequences (a point also stressed by Aldo Leopold and Rachel Carson).

Ecological feminist desire to incorporate factors such as gender, race, economic status, sexuality, historical and geographical location, into a loose, critical, multiplicitous conception of human selves renders uncritical, universalizing accounts of isolated selves inadequate. Liberal conceptions of the self misconstrue the extent to which we are socially and culturally constituted as at once natural and 'more than' natural. A view of isolated selves makes sense only in so far as nature and the social aspects of human life (reproduction, the body, the labor of women and colonized peoples) are backgrounded as invisible inputs into the public aspects of life. A purely rule-based, rationalist ethics, against which feminist philosophers have been arguing for years, is tied to such notions of what human selves are, how they make decisions, and how they interact with each other. Liberal emphasis on hyper-rationality in defining persons and ethics stands in stark contrast to feminist revisionings of selfhood, epistemology, emotion, and mind/body dualisms. Though we need not deny the value of human rationality and reason, the glorification of a hyper-rational self is inconsistent with an environmental philosophy that aims to demote rationality from its position as the basis for ethical value, and to recognize the value of nonrational entities.

THE OBJECTS OF ETHICS

The importance of liberal, individualist animal rights theories rests in their call for greater consistency in applications of the central tenets of influential ethical traditions. This call results in the enlargement of the ethical universe considered by the liberal view, because the category of moral objects is extended to include beings other than humans. Singer and Regan emphasize the hypocrisy in prejudicial applications of liberal ethics: if the aim is to prevent suffering, there is no reason to discount the suffering of nonhuman animals; if the aim is to respect beings with dignity, we ought to respect all living, experiencing subjects. Though groundbreaking in their counter-hegemonic attention to nonhuman individuals, and their commitments to ethics of compassion, most animal liberationists fail to question the conceptions of the ethical self, and of moral agency, embedded in their own liberal background. Because they fail to dissect their own dependence on problematic ethical starting points, including assumptions about the nature of moral agents, liberal arguments for animal rights inadequately address the depth of the causes of the domestication, torture, murder, and mistreatment of nonhuman animals. Feminist ethics, and ecological feminisms in particular, entail a deeper questioning of the universal, rational, egoist, atomistic, human moral agent than liberal ethics can offer (Plumwood 1993).

Thus far in this chapter, I've focused primarily on the problems for environmental and feminist ethics with liberal conceptions of moral agents, or selves. But animal rights perspectives are equally problematic in their individualist characterizations of moral *objects* – or those beings who have moral value that ought to be recognized by moral agents. Although there is a worthwhile distinction to be made between deontological and utilitarian ethics in terms of their justifications for extending moral considerability to nonhuman animals, both make liberal, individualist assumptions about the nature of objects of ethics, that are inconsistent with feminist, ecologically-minded ethics.

Ethical positions that focus on animal rights can only conceive of nonhuman animals as significant in so far as they are sentient or conscious individuals – not as members of communities, not as repositories of human conceptualizations, not as individual agents fundamentally shaped and determined by their social or ecological immersions. But mistreatment of animals is not merely, or always, a failure to respect the rights of individuals.

101

It also involves a failure to take seriously whole classes of ecologically embedded beings – some sentient, some extremely psychologically complex, some hardly identifiable as individuals –and a failure to take seriously their relationships with each other. It is also a failure to question the false boundary around humans and their interests. Projects that truly re-value nonhuman animals pay attention to the ways in which they are categorized and constructed as natural, and will also see sentient individuals as ecological beings.

An oft-repeated criticism of Regan and Singer's work is that liberal egalitarianism leads each to the absurd view that any sentient or self-conscious being has moral value equal to human persons, captured most infamously in Singer's claim that urban rats who bite 'slum children' have moral rights equal to the children.[4] In fact, this problematic egalitarianism is a result of their telescopic focus on individual moral objects. If suffering or sentience are the only significant aspects of morally valuable beings, those beings cannot not be taken seriously, in an ethical sense, as parts of communities, embedded in social and/or ecological networks of interdependence. The *differences* between them – between a child and a rat, between an endangered manatee and a fisherman, between a domesticated, beloved dog and an endangered wolf, and between a wild pig and a pig on a farm – are irrelevant. Additionally, conflicts are mistakenly characterized as between isolated individuals, when they are actually between richly enmeshed sets of interests and meaning. Given the existence of powerful social institutions like factory farming and animal experimentation, the claim that the suffering of sentient beings ought to be prevented is most useful in the context of other obligations, such as the obligation to promote broader ecological values.

FEMINISM AND THE PREVENTION OF SUFFERING

My remarks here have been directed mostly at the liberal assumptions that both Regan and Singer share. But Singer's utilitarianism, or the notion that preventing suffering is a suitable goal for environmental ethics, deserves some special attention. The irony of my remarks on utilitarianism and environmental ethics is that its focus on suffering is both too much and too little (too late). In other words, a utilitarian focus on preventing suffering will result in too much concern with preventing pain, and with insufficient regard for other kinds of harm.

---

4 In fact, self-defense should provide adequate justification for transgressing any rights the rats might have. The point of objections to Singer's claim seems to be directed at the notion that the interests of rats should even be considered at all.

Nietzsche railed against utilitarianism as an ethic for the weak, who fear pain, risk, and confrontation. Similarly, some environmental ethicists argue that animal liberation's focus on preventing suffering stems from a domesticated fear of the realities of natural life, including pain, suffering, violence, and death. It is impossible not to agree that suffering is inevitable, and especially inevitable in ecosystemic communities. Furthermore, pain and dissatisfaction can be useful, instructive, and necessary aspects of any healthy life and community. But the kinds of suffering that motivate the work of Regan, Singer, and other advocates for the rights of animals are neither inevitable nor necessary for flourishing. Factory farming, the meat industry and experimentation on animals cause unnecessary suffering and ruin the lives of countless intelligent, sentient beings. To claim that the ethical problems involved are not reducible to pain and suffering is not to claim that suffering is ethically irrelevant. 'Suffering' is certainly a large part of what is ethically problematic about the following example of animal torture, but oppressive institutions of gender, the exploitation of workers, and the categorical devaluation of nonhuman beings (whether or not they are eaten by humans) are enmeshed factors preventing both human and nonhuman well-being:

> Life for the day-old Perdue chicken begins with painful dismemberment as its beak is burned off with a hot knife ... At about eight weeks of age the roughly five-pound birds are taken to one of Perdue's slaughter plants. Here, before their throats are slit, they are pinned upside down on a conveyer line and their heads are dragged through an electrified trough ... Up to thirty percent of Perdue workers (most of whom are women of color) are afflicted with a crippling condition of the hands and wrists caused by having to butcher up to seventy-five chickens per minute ... Donna Bazemore, a former Perdue employee, told NPR she saw women urinating and vomiting on the work line because they were not allowed to leave it to go to the bathroom.
>
> (Sequoia 1990: 51)

Ecofeminist perspectives sometimes incorporate the kinds of analogies made by animal rights activists between different forms of victimization, and recommend the logical extension of some aspects of interpersonal (human) moral life, such as caring, friendship, and respect, to nonhuman entities. None the less, individuals are not the sole agents or objects of domination and mistreatment. As Iris Young argues, our multiple group identifications most strongly determine where we sit within systems of oppression. While it is true that ecological feminists seek to minimize needless suffering and other unjustified violence perpetrated by humans, not all ethically relevant harm is reducible to individual pain, dissatisfaction, or suffering. Specifically, ecological feminism is also concerned with aspects of oppression and mistreatment that do not always cause pain, that are not always experienced negatively by their victims, and that are not only perpetrated on individuals. Consider, for example, the ethics of domestication. To *domesticate* means 'to tame to domestic use or uses,' or 'to accustom to household life and affairs,' and *domestic* means 'of the home, the household, or the family,' or 'devoted to home life' (Random House Dictionary 1980). Within ethics of domestication, a 'good' woman is a woman well-suited to and contented with life in the home, who obeys the master of the house as a 'good' horse obeys the wielder of the whip. In fact, as Susan Griffin illustrates poetically in *Woman and Nature*, both domesticated women and domesticated animals love their masters. Some measure of domestication is required of all humans, and men as well as women must adapt to 'human living conditions' if they are to count as full moral agents, as citizens, as livers of good lives. None the less, domestication entails far more stringent ethical requirements for females in most societies, and many species of nonhuman animals are reduced to mere instruments through domestication. Domestication often occurs within systems or institutions, and for humans, it often depends upon and reproduces meaningful social identities such as 'wife.' Domestication is logically and practically related to oppression, but because it entails changes in desire and affection, the degree of pain or suffering caused is not a good indicator of the extent to which domestication is harmful. Shifting the focus away from suffering also leaves room for respecting forms of agency that necessarily result in violence and pain, including the lives of animals in the wild, and some revolutionary social movements.

The prevention of individual suffering is relevant to ecological feminism, as it is relevant to feminism, though it is not the foundational requirement of ethics. This is not to say that the unique qualities of sentient individuals should not be valued and protected, or that the unique qualities of humans are not ethically important, or that partiality to certain individuals, or certain sorts of individuals is never justified. Differing from nonfeminist proponents of partiality, feminists tend not to minimize the importance of ethics beyond our constitutive or intimate communities. That is, feminist arguments in favor of certain forms of partiality toward intimates, associates, or comrades, generally support the view that ethics should also include concern for those with whom we are not immediately or apparently connected. Sarah Ruddick even argues that a nurturing, caring attitude toward intimates should be the basis for a global peace politics. Similarly, relationships with individual nonhuman animals can provide uniquely important emotional and ethical entry points for thinking about environmental ethics, and for taking seriously the interests of nonhuman entities. Lori Gruen and I have argued that intimate relationships with nonhuman animals are important sites for developing more ecologically sensitive moral orientations (Cuomo and Gruen 1997).

Finally, feminist critiques of liberal theory and politics should not be taken as claims that rights bestowed by political and legal institutions are unimportant, or that fighting for institutional recognition and protection is completely wrong-headed. Rather, such struggles are necessary in liberal societies – they are perhaps necessary right now in any society, and this fact will continue to provide typical dilemmas for people with radical political goals. But these struggles, even when successful, are not adequate. Without radical shifts in concepts, values, institutions, and practices (both discursive and material), social and environmental exploitation will continue to escalate.

HOLISMS

The communitarian starting points recommended by Friedman, Code, and others echo ecofeminist ontologies of connectedness.

> There is no end to any act. The rock thrown in the water is followed by waves of water, and these waves of water make waves in the air, and these waves travel outward infinitely, setting particles in motion, leading to other motion and motion upon motion endlessly.
>
> (Rich 1978: 172)

In chronicling the legacies of patriarchal thought, ecofeminists want to inspire questions about how the oppression of one group, one class, one species, can affect others beyond that group. Griffin illustrates the symbiosis of images of untouched soil and myths and practices concerning the bodies of women; how misogynist attitudes about female sexuality manifest themselves in cruel treatment of domesticated nonhuman animals; how desire to squelch the uncontrollable nature of the wild contributes to racist and imperialistic beliefs and practices. Beings cannot be completely isolated. Nor can practices.

This emphasis on connection, and a corresponding ethic that values connections and interdependencies is reminiscent of Aldo Leopold's 'Land Ethic.' Leopold recommends a shift in ethical starting points – from thinking of ourselves as members of human society and conquerors of the land to 'plain member and citizen of it' (1966: 240). Throughout Leopold's writings, he emphasizes the subtle intransigence of biotic interdependence and the far-reaching, if incomprehensible effects of even minute manipulations of the biotic community and its members. In contrast to movements and philosophies arguing for the recognition of the rights of sentient animals, holistic ecological philosophies, including recent work influenced by the writings of Leopold and John Muir, as well as proponents of Deep Ecology and the Gaia principle, reject many aspects of human-centered culture, and deride the animal rights movement as a mere extension of humanism. Instead of focusing on individual capacities and the rights of sentient individuals, their ethical starting point is nature as a whole system. This inherently valuable system of ecosystems, biotic communities, or bioregions, is composed of species, individuals, and relationships, which are valuable as necessary parts of the whole:

> An environmental ethic which takes as its summum bonum the integrity, stability, and beauty of the biotic community is not conferring moral standing on something else besides plants, animals, soils, and waters. Rather, the former, the good of the community as a whole, serves as a standard for the assessment of the relative value and relative ordering of its constitutive parts and therefore provides a means of adjudicating the often mutually contradictory demands of the parts considered separately for equal consideration.
>
> (Callicott 1989: 25)

The value of ecological communities is not reducible to use value for humans. Like human beings in the eyes of traditional ethics, biotic communities are inherently valuable. Unamended calls for the rights of all sentient beings are ethically inadequate because a focus on pain or cognitive experience comes out of the assumption that human beings are paradigmatic ethical objects, and that other life forms are valuable only in so far as they are seen as similar to humans. Instead, though the views of holists differ with regard to suffering, they believe the primary goal of ethics to be the recognition of the value of biotic communities, wilderness, 'untouched nature,' and consequently its lesser members, as morally valuable apart from their instrumental value for humans.

Because they tend to view humanity as a monolith, nonfeminist holists often assert the existence of an identifiable, singular cause behind human mistreatment of nature. Typically, anthropocentrism, or human-centered values and ontologies, are believed to be the root of environmental degradation and exploitation. Ecological holists believe that the majority of humans, especially those in postindustrial, technological societies, ignore the extent to which we are dependent members of biotic communities and ecosystems, and that in order to halt the degradation of nature, radical ontological and ethical shifts toward a more humble 'citizen' perspective are necessary. Human placement *within*, as opposed to above biotic communities, calls for humility and a reconceptualization of our relations to nature. But while holistic thinkers like J. Baird Callicott and Arne Naess want to include 'human' in 'nature,' by refusing to consider the particulars of human cultures, they leave unexplored the permeability of the boundaries between nature and culture, the specific ways these boundaries are maintained and transgressed, and the fact that the concept of nature is a product of culture. Flattening the meanings of 'human' and 'culture' implies an equally flat, undifferentiated, self-evident 'nature.' That is, while there is an acknowledgement that aspects of the human/nature divide are false, holism does not critically engage the arbitrariness and flexibility of the divide, or its shifting location, in part because it sees the 'human' side uncritically.

Though ecological feminist philosophy more closely resembles Leopold's holism than animal rights liberalism, its disagreements with deep ecology and other ecological holisms are no less challenging.[5] Because holistic perspectives consider humans most commonly as a species, they cannot accommodate inquiries concerning the relationships between the harm humans do to each other and the harm we do to the nonhuman world. Consider: to what extent are most people and groups who misuse political or economic power exclusively *human*-centered? Is first-world megaconsumption and toxic dumping really allowed or encouraged with the interests of the human species in mind? Surely self-centeredness, corporate greed, ethnocentrism, militarism and nationalism result more directly in questionable environmental ethical practices than does anthropocentrism. If so, the most pressing ethical questions concern the relationships among these various prejudices. But proponents of Deep Ecology and other holistic environmental ethics pay little attention to social justice issues, and focus instead on how and why humans, as a species, tend to devalue and destroy the biotic community and its members.

Holistic conceptions of natural systems, and what it means to promote the well-being of these systems, are often based on scientific models, especially those inspired by ecological sciences. Followers of Leopold, Deep Ecologists, and other holistic environmental thinkers, often rely on conceptions of natural communities as harmonious and balanced. Aldo Leopold's famous claim that biotic communities possess or aim toward beauty, stability, and integrity, and that this natural teleology ought to guide our ethical actions, is a perfect example of the belief that nature's strivings indicate what we *ought* to promote, thereby creating ethical norms. Though the historical and theoretical associations of contemporary environmentalism and the science of ecology are important, the relationship between 'ecology' and 'environmental ethics' must be teased apart somewhat.

Despite the attractions of the notion that a natural teleology of ecosystemic harmony can dictate our ethics, ethical norms can only be created and justified by humans in social contexts. We can acquire ideas and models from nature, or from science, but there is a degree to which the normative use we make of them is a matter of choice. As Paul Taylor argues,

> How humans should live with other species, and even whether humans should live at all, are matters that require the making of normative and evaluative judgments. The biological sciences can give us the relevant factual knowledge, but those sciences cannot provide the

5 For discussion see Salleh 1984, 1993; Plumwood 1993; Cuomo 1994.

standards on which our normative and evaluative judgments are grounded. As long as humans in their role of moral agents have the capacity to use biological knowledge for purposes of their own choosing, the question of how they *should* use it and *for what purposes* is an ethical question, not a scientific one.

(1986: 50).

Furthermore, much ecological science relies on metaphors to describe interactions among species, individuals, and systems. Scientific models and metaphors, such as the views that nature is comprised of either webs of competition, or diverse interdependent populations and communities striving toward harmonious equilibrium, make poor ethical starting points. Metaphors are chosen and constructed by scientists, and should not be taken uncritically as accurate, ultimate givens about the world. In the words of Max Black, metaphors have 'cognitive implications whose nature is a proper subject of philosophical discussion' (quoted in Hesse 1966: 158). Metaphors also have normative implications, as they encourage us to conceive and hence interact with the world in ways dictated by common understandings of whatever serves as a model. Anticipating Carolyn Merchant's description of how modern science's mechanistic conception of nature helped create values that turn nature into an instrument, Mary Hesse describes how this metaphor conceptually reduces understandings of both 'nature' and 'machine':

> The two systems are seen as more like each other; they seem to interact and adapt to one another, even to the point of invalidating their original literal descriptions . . . Nature becomes more like a machine in the mechanical philosophy, and actual concrete machines themselves are seen as if stripped down to their essential qualities of mass in motion.
>
> (1966: 163)

Environmental philosophy must be critical of the scientific models and metaphors it inherits or assumes. Making a broader argument against defenses of science that believe it self-evident that science is valuable because it 'works,' Evelyn Fox Keller states,

> As equally routinely as the effectiveness of science is invoked, equally routine is the failure to go on to say what it is that science works *at*, to note that 'working' is a necessary but not sufficient constraint. Science gives us models/representations that permit us to manipulate parts of the world in particular ways . . . neither instruments themselves, nor the values, interests or efficacy associated with them are devoid of aim. To be sure, instrumental knowledge has force in the world, but force, as we learned in freshman physics, is a vector. It has not only magnitude but directionality as well. And if we grant directionality to

the force of scientific knowledge, then the obvious question arises: In
what other directions might science work? Toward what other aims?
(1992: 74–75)

Science can inform ethics by providing data, models, feedback, and projec-
tions of risk and impact. All the while, ethics must question science's models, methods, goals, and assumptions.

Addressing the relationship between ecology and environmental ethics
more specifically, in 'The Ecology of Order and Chaos,' Don Worster points
out that recent controversies within the science of ecology, a specific
instance of related debates about foundations and models in science in general, make it an inadequate, and inappropriate, basis for an ethic (Worster
1993). The demotion of the conception of ecosystems popularized by
Eugene Odum entails a shift from seeing ecosystems as harmonious communities striving toward equilibrium through cooperation, to instead thinking of ecosystems as overlapping populations coexisting and competing
amidst chaotic relationships and disturbances (Taylor 1988). Even without
anthropomorphizing, it is not difficult to see parallels in conceptions of
human communities in which interdependence can be seen a number of
ways, including as natural and teleological, or as a necessary burden for
individuals who otherwise face existences that are 'nasty, brutish, and
short.' But a metaphorical conception of nature, communities, and ecosystems as teleologically bound toward harmony is not necessary for environmental ethics, as a teleological conception of human community is not
necessary for interpersonal or social ethics. Powerful metaphors encourage
us to think that only two options are available: chaos or harmony; nature as
pure machine, or imbued with full intentionality; human beings as selfish,
atomistic utility-maximizers, or as wishy-washy group-thinkers with no
autonomy. In fact, options exist beyond the cognitive universe evoked by any
powerful metaphor and its opposite.

Moral agents can decide how to negotiate the world without hopes of
reaching a predetermined, necessary state of harmony or static equilibrium,
or any ultimate state. Indeed, the abandonment of such a teleology also
entails abandoning hopes that our decisions and actions will result in perfect harmony or order, and such non-teleological ethics can't be motivated
by a desire to actualize a preestablished end or enact given roles. We can,
however, value the somewhat ordered/somewhat chaotic universe in which
we inevitably dwell, and we can also decide that it is good and worthwhile
to prevent significant destruction to other valuable members of the universe
through the agency and choice that also seem inevitable.

A provocative picture of how to negotiate chaos as meaningful agents, or
why we should bother trying, is provided by Sartre in 'Existentialism is a
Humanism,' in which he confronts the question of ethics in the face of
inescapable subjectivity. Contrary to the abysmal consequences that some

believed follow what Nietzsche called the Death of God, or the demise of widespread belief in an ultimate arbiter or determinant of moral responsibility, Sartre felt that in an age (or, I'd add, in a *life*) without gods, our ethical uniqueness and responsibility are even more pronounced.

> Man first of all is the being who hurls himself toward a future and who is conscious of imagining himself as being in the future . . . [a person is] at the start a plan which is aware of itself . . . nothing else than a series of undertakings . . . he is the sum, the organization, the ensemble of the relationships which make up these undertakings.
>
> (1987: 475, 481)

Notorious for its flawed characterization of subjectivity as exhausted by the freedom to choose, this existentialist view defines existence as comprised of the results of inevitable choices. But we need not agree with Sartre's conception of agency to be pulled by questions about choice and responsibility in the face of unknowable existence. In response to situations subject to moral luck, Claudia Card argues that the most we can do is take responsibility by 'locating ourselves as morally relevant centers of agency' (Card 1996: 28). Questions of moral responsibility in the face of disorder remain if we have any choice at all about ethical matters. For ecological feminists, this is a core question of environmental ethics: what are we to undertake, here and now, given our social and environmental contexts and locations? Our moral responsibility is to, in so far as we are able, create ourselves, our species, and our roles within contexts that are, among other things, oppressive and chaotic.

Like many environmental philosophers, ecological feminists have in mind a sort of extension of the ethical universe, though the expansions they have in mind are not merely a matter of extending traditional or hegemonic ethical norms and principles to new kids on the 'ethically significant' block (such as women, tribal peoples, or sentient beings). Instead, they emphasize how extension to include anyone but straight white landowning men into the ethical universe entails radical revisions of 'subjects,' 'objects,' 'communities,' and 'value.' Hence, their approaches are not, strictly speaking, extensionist. Feminist ethicists are familiar with how even the 'add women and stir' approach to theory can inevitably stir up given notions of moral agents as impartial, uncaring, unemotional, public, egoist, sprung-like-mushrooms individuals. The history of the philosophical field of feminist ethics could be read as a progression from approaches addressing the absence and/or derision of women in traditional ethical theory, to formal ethical consideration of ethical problems of particular concern to women (including reproductive issues, gender-based discrimination, and sexual autonomy) to queries about the significance of 'woman's voice' for ethical theory, to explorations of specifically feminist ethical norms, guidelines, systems, and approaches. That is, the history of feminist philosophical

110

thought evinces how noticing that women are missing from descriptive and normative claims about the world can lead to analyses of the many ideological and philosophical assumptions and structural social factors that make serious theoretical and political consideration of women's interests so difficult and unlikely. A similar history might be told about work that pointed out and addressed the lack of pluralism and complexity in early feminist conceptions of 'woman,' and subsequent analyses of the implications of the absences of women of color, poor and working-class women, old women, and lesbians, within feminism.

Close attention to the implications of criticizing traditional understandings of the ethical universe, or of broadening it, unearths prescriptions far more radical than liberal and holist environmentalists (and many liberal feminists) are willing to admit. One cannot fully acknowledge the moral value and/or agency of women and other groups of oppressed people, nonhuman animals, ecosystems, and species without fundamentally shaking up the foundations of most traditional ethical systems. Though ecological feminists want to draw upon relationships between the ethics that inform treatment of humans and nonhuman entities, they argue for radical revisions of and alternatives to male- or human-centered traditions, including a demotion of liberal emphases on atomistic individuals. These feminist ecological revisions can be useful, especially in light of the questions raised within the field of environmental ethics concerning the constitution of morally relevant entities and the possibilities for intraspecies relationships, in helping those of us who are interested to alter practices and institutions that are unjustifiably destructive and harmful.

5

NOT SO STATIC AFTER ALL
Ecological feminism and anti-essentialist criticism

Theorists who consider their work both environmentalist and feminist include thinkers from a variety of academic and political locations, so it is not difficult to isolate specific, varied philosophical and stylistic strands within ecofeminist work, some more significant than others. As I've tried to emphasize throughout, there is a fairly wide spectrum of approaches to the ecofeminist project, ranging from uncritical attempts to embrace women's social positions as 'closer' to nature, to poststructuralist analyses of the discursive connections between constructions of woman and nature. In the remaining chapters, I return to a discussion of some of the questions and issues surrounding the ecofeminist project in its broadest interpretations, although I will continue to employ a distinction between ecofeminism and ecological feminism. It is not at all irrelevant that ecofeminism is most often identified by its critics with object-attentive approaches to the connections between feminism and environmentalism, and I believe the reasons for this monocular association are terribly important. Because much ecofeminist work focuses on the objects of oppression - on 'women,' and 'nature,' for example - it is particularly vulnerable to charges of essentialism. Though overall I argue for an ecological feminism that does not take 'women' and 'nature' at face value – that is, one that is not merely object-attentive – in this chapter I want to explore how and why some strands of ecofeminism remain standard targets of dismissive critique despite the significant developments away from strictly object-attentive positions. I argue against what I call simplistic anti-essentialist rejections of ecofeminism, and map out some of the more pressing philosophical and ethical problems that are obfuscated by the delegitimizing barb of simplistic anti-essentialism. I argue for more careful attention to and assessment of the material, social, and discursive impacts of ecofeminism, as well as ecological feminist revisions of some of its problematic features and implications.

Many of the examples of early ecofeminist writing already discussed, like most contemporaneous feminist work of the 1970s and 1980s, did not sufficiently problematize the category 'woman.' This work did not attempt to address the complex and multiplicitous nature of gender, especially as it intersects with race, class, culture, and other identities and political positions, and therefore cast 'woman' in a distortingly limited way. Similarly, a tendency among object-attentive ecofeminists to refer to 'Nature' as a unified given contributes to their writing being interpreted in accord with ideological constructs that keep nature/culture dualisms unchallenged. In discussing women/nature connections, early object-attentive ecofeminists focused both on attitudes about women and nature, and also on what they described as 'real' qualities, such as embodiment and fecundity, possessed by both women and the natural world. Hence it is not surprising that ecofeminism has become a favorite straw-woman for a one-dimensional, anti-essentialist postmodern feminist attack.

Although prominent ecological feminist thinkers, especially philosophers such as Karen Warren and Val Plumwood, have moved explicitly toward more complex, constructivist interpretations of 'woman,' 'nature,' and the connections between them, including their treatment in the history of thought, ecofeminism is still strongly associated with the kind of feminist thinking that is preceded by powerfully negative markers like 'cultural' and 'seventies.' It is therefore dismissed by theorists whose main concern is to reject any thinking that relies on universalizing concepts or gestures toward essentialist notions of 'woman.' Ecofeminism is repeatedly taken to task for relying on dangerous, historically and culturally bound, universal conceptions of 'woman' in arguing for attention to the connections between women and the stuff of nature, and the ecofeminist project is summarily rejected as regressive. As Diana Fuss so clearly points out, such anti-essentialist arguments are often thought to provide 'terms of infallible critique,' stopping further serious inquiry dead in its tracks (Fuss 1989).

Wholesale rejections of the ecofeminist project are characteristically inattentive to differences among examples of ecofeminism, and exhibit a tendency to lump various kinds of theories together under the umbrella of an unnuanced critique (and then press 'reject'). A typical example of this approach occurs in the epilogue of Alice Echols' *Daring to Be Bad*. Echols' lumpen rejection of what she problematically labels and then casts off as 'cultural feminism' includes a misrepresentation of even the minuscule body of ecofeminist work she refers to when she ventures:

Eco-feminists and feminist pacifists have argued that women by virtue of their closeness to nature are in a unique position to avert ecological ruin or nuclear annihilation. This thinking marks a further departure from radical feminism, which maintained that the identification of women with nature was a patriarchal concept . . . radical feminists defined ecology and militarization as human rather than feminist issues.

(1989: 288)

113

In fact, many early ecofeminists were also radical feminists, and most eco-feminists agree that the identification of women with nature is patriarchal.

ANTI-ESSENTIALIST ARGUMENTS

A typical rejection of essentialism, and of ecofeminist essentialism in particular, is often based on an argument that goes something like this:

1 There are no essences (immutable, ahistorical, eternal, universal, and necessary truths) and therefore no truths about women that rely on essences. That is, Woman is a fiction, although the power of the concept is based in our mistaken belief that it represents an essential truth. Gender (some theorists also include sexual difference) and conceptions of Woman are social constructions, not metaphysical truths.
2 Various oppressions, mistreatments, and privileges that affect women are created, enacted and enforced through a definition of Woman as possessing a certain immutable and universal essence, and therefore essentially different from and, by inference, inferior to Man.
3 Feminisms based on notions that there exist essential features of Woman perpetuate the notion that women are necessarily, categorically, naturally different from men - a notion at the root of the problems that feminists aim to redress - and the notion that women's universal similarities supersede their differences from each other.

Therefore:

4 Statements like 'Women are closer to nature than men' attribute essential features to women and, worse, rely on the notion that there is an essential female nature. Hence they replicate exactly those false conceptions of woman's essential nature that have been most damaging (such statements also attribute an essence to Nature, which is also a social construct, and to Man).

It does not seem wrongheaded to ask if ecofeminist claims really are *essentialist*, or otherwise rely on fixed foundations, or notions of 'woman' that ought to be rejected. I agree with anti-essentialist feminists that we ought to reject theories and practices built on false ideas of 'woman' or other distorting, oppressive ontologies. Indeed, we should seek out and create theory and practice that does not fear the philosophical depths of political problems. In so far as we can ever anticipate the dangers of theory, we need to explore just how problematic essentialist and universalist foundations really might be. That is, essentialism is not inherently (essentially) problematic, but when it is problematic, the reasons for its specific rejection need to be articulated and justified. This point is important because, despite the fact that anti-essentialist arguments against ecofeminism are rarely careful and specific, a strange constellation of factors has created an academic feminist discourse in which even simplistic anti-essentialist arguments have a powerful impact on decisions about what gets taken seriously. Attributing the most naive, essentialist meanings (and motivations) to political or activist discourses strikes me as suspect, although the critical project of investigating the implications of any discourse is incredibly important.

Even when anti-essentialist arguments against particular examples of ecofeminism are well-founded, wholesale rejection of the ecofeminist project is an overly dramatic response, especially given the material truths within the conceptual connections and practical relationships articulated by ecofeminists and other ecologically-concerned feminists. The fact that these connections are not immutable or necessary, and are not dependent on the existence of entities with essential features and natures, is a crucial point, and one which has inspired numbers of feminists to attempt carefully to map the social, contingent, contextually-embedded specificities of the relationships among different forms of oppression, different conceptual entities, and different material beings. But the relationships themselves – and the practices, institutions, and philosophical commitments that affect and preserve them – remain compelling. In fact, these relationships are most compelling when they are understood as providing clues about the ways concepts like 'woman,' 'nature,' 'primitive,' and 'body' get written and interwoven, and the ways cultural constructions, practices, and biological matter are formed and reformed.

As scores of feminist theorists are currently working to maintain the feminist subject in the face of the demise of universal Woman, ecological feminists want to claim a space in which to discuss the connections among whatever gets labelled 'natural' and the humans (women, people of color, the poor) who tend to be discursively, practically, and conceptually associated with the natural, and whose association with nature is detrimental to them. Like Aristotle, they want to 'save the appearances' and take seriously the evidence and manifestations of these associations, while creating and recreating feminism and environmentalism. It is impossible to do this without discussing women and nature, without using the concepts that refer to the beings and matter at hand. We are well-advised to note the extent to which defining gestures endanger plurality, but in the end it is concepts which make talk, and hence theory, possible. In the spirit of creating and fostering multiple, multiplicitous discourses, we can *expand* and *loosen* the concepts that were supposedly handed to us as self-evident, unified, and fixed, by Modernity.

When ecofeminists discuss women's nature and aspects of femininity as superior to ruling patriarchal systems of thought, the problem is less a matter of 'committing' essentialism and more a problem of attributing false universals to whoever falls under the category 'woman.' An example is Charlene Spretnak's descriptions of ecofeminist spirituality:

The theme of women's elemental power is a common one, and by that I do not mean 'merely' our power to form people from our very flesh and blood and then to nourish them from our breasts, or the fact that we run on cosmic time, i.e., share the cycles of the moon. I mean that there are many moments in a woman's life wherein she gains experiential knowledge, in a powerful body/mind union, of the holistic truths of spirituality . . . females are predisposed from a very early age to perceive the connectedness in life; for example, females are more empathetic, and they remain more aware of the subtle, contextual 'data' in interpersonal contacts throughout adulthood.

(1991: 35).

Is the problem here that Spretnak is relying on essentialist notions of 'woman'? Clearly, the argument could be made that her reference to women's knowledge, perception, and empathy replays essentialist, patriarchal conceptions of what 'woman' means, in so far as it assumes universal, natural, physical and metaphysical aspects of female experience. Spretnak values aspects of human experience that have been devalued by the traditions currently most powerful in shaping most of the world's economic and political realities, but she is not questioning the truth or validity of the conception of 'woman,' or the necessity of social realities that she wants to reclaim.

None the less, a simplistic anti-essentialist critique that begins and ends there misses what is most problematic in Spretnak's view of 'woman,' and also what is helpful about her discussions of women's experiences. When ecofeminists discuss practices commonly engaged in by women, or qualities supposedly or actually exhibited by many women, especially those which are considered definitive of 'woman' in many cultures (such as the identification of women with mothering), they often misrepresent these practices and qualities as 'woman's ways,' as though all women share them, or women who do not are inadequate. But even stating something as unsavory to some of our sensibilities as 'Women are the Mothers of the Earth,' can have multiple intentions and meanings. It can mean that all women are or should be mothers, that mothering is necessarily connected to being female, and that the female relationship to the planet and its inhabitants ought to be maternal. It can point to the absurdity of the devaluation of mothers and caretaking activities in the face of the facts that many women are mothers, that it is women who give birth to future generations, and that those women, through their practices, have access to information that people who are not mothers (most men) do not have, and this information is uniquely relevant to taking care of life on Earth. It can imply that women are socially constructed to be identified with mothering, that even those women who reject motherhood or who don't care at all about motherhood are affected by the norms of the woman–mother connection prevalent in most cultures,

116

and that this affects female relationships with other things constructed as 'mother,' such as the planet.

Though these possibilities rely on tenuous notions of the connections between gender and practice, drawing attention to the conceptual and practical connections between 'woman' and 'mother' is important philosophical work because of the discursive and physical power of their amazingly prevalent association. These associations shape the economic, reproductive, and political dimensions of lived reality, so even if they are ultimately rejected, understanding them is central to feminism. Instead of categorically discounting any discussion of woman/mother or woman/nature connections as unimportant because they are constructed, *or* assuming the validity of those associations because they appear natural or entrenched, feminist theorists need to continue to interrogate them with care.

As some feminists have tried to make clear through their rejections of essentialist notions of 'woman,' ecological feminists need not be committed to the view that there exists some metaphysical or ontological truths about 'woman' and 'nature' – that there is stuff out there that necessarily fits into the categories, or that the categories are anything other than fictions that fuel our contingent, historically-bound conceptions of reality. Ecological feminists are committed to the view that people, beings, and stuff are defined and made meaningful within discourses which name them as, among other things, 'woman,' and 'nature.' These are powerful discursive and practical categories and constructions that we cannot ignore, because the value and treatment of things and beings depends in part on the ways in which they become associated with them. Still, our theoretical attentions should not amount to appropriating concepts and categorizations that have been historically damaging to exactly what we aim to protect. Nor should efforts to deconstruct influential relationships amount to merely ignoring them theoretically, or leaving them practically untouched.

Anti-essentialist critique is probably the most common argument brought against ecofeminism. But the so-called 'problem of essentialism,' in ecofeminism and elsewhere, is more often actually a matter of false universalization of certain conceptions of 'woman,' and a lack of attention to the diversity of women's experiences and of conceptions of womanhood that results from feminist theorists' racism, solipsism, and tendency to aspire to the (fallacious) objective view from nowhere modeled throughout much of the history of Western philosophy. In fact, *any* object-attentive theoretical approach is likely to run the risk of over-generalizing, or attributing false universals to the given object category, or of stating its case in ways that are easily interpreted as doing so. As Marilyn Frye acknowledges, 'mistaken generalities are to be found in feminist theorizing, and need to be corrected. But they are mundane, discoverable, correctable; they are not profound and usually do not merit passionate or paranoid denunciation' (unpublished: 6). Problematic generalizations are sometimes the result of a theorist situating her self, family, or culture as a paradigm case which structures paradigm-case categorical thinking, à la ethnocentrism, though such thinking does not necessarily entail a commitment to any *essence*. There is an element of self-as-paradigm cognition in early feminist theories, but Frye asserts that, 'condemning these theories as essentialist seems to me to misdirect our attention and to obscure rather than illuminate, and to leave unanalyzed the active constructive ethnocentrism implicit in such theories' (unpublished: 10).

ECOFEMINISM AND CULTURAL CRITICISM

One sphere of inquiry where one might expect to find engagement with the kinds of questions currently discussed by those working at the intersections of feminism and environmentalism is in the study of the meanings, mechanisms, and constructions of culture, especially as such inquiry entails being curious about constructions of not-culture, or nature. Jody Berland and Jennifer Daryl Slack, editors of a special issue on the environment of the journal *Cultural Studies*, remark in their introduction that cultural studies was slow to turn attention to environmental issues, but that this is changing because:

> 'Nature (and by extension, the environment) is semiotic . . . it is a cultural construction.' Hence the coding of culture and of environmental issues, coalitions, movements are understood to have registers in differential relations of power articulating to class, race, gender and ethnicity . . . Cultural studies is, however, rather less prepared to handle the 'problem' of the 'physical substance.' . . . How do we speak of that which is not reducible to the mode in which we speak – both acknowledging the mode in which we speak and that which asserts itself apart from having a 'voice'? There is an earth after all.
>
> (Berland and Slack 1994: 1–2)

Work in cultural studies, they venture, might explore the ways in which concepts and representations affect human placement inside and outside of nature. In 'Communities, Environments and Cultural Studies,' Jennifer Daryl Slack and Laurie Anne Whitt also make a strikingly ecological feminist point:

> The tendency of Western societies to parse out humans as separate from and dominant over nature is a habit of thought and a pattern of action which buttresses the tendency to parse out certain humans as separate from and dominant over others . . . Yet so well-entrenched are these buttressing effects that the nature and extent of their complicity has been overlooked by cultural theorists, whose critiques of the oppressive social formations of late capitalism are resoundingly

silent about the relationship of human communities to the other-than-human world in which they are situated.

(Slack and Whitt 1994: 5).

But much recent work in cultural studies that actually sets out to engage the sets of issues around which ecological feminism is motivated, or ecofeminism and ecological feminism more directly, provides striking examples of simplistic anti-essentialist critiques. I'll briefly discuss some of this work to provide a sense of where I think some critiques go wrong in evaluating, and devaluing, the ecofeminist project in familiar ways. In short, these simplistic anti-essentialist arguments can be characterized as subjecting ecofeminist work to unfair and unjustified comparisons, and mischaracterizing ecofeminism through cursory readings that fail to represent it in its historical and political contexts.

In 'Cyborg and Ecofeminist Interventions: Challenges for an Environmental Feminism,' Stacy Alaimo contrasts ecofeminism with Donna Haraway's approach to 'negotiating a feminist environmentalism,' characterizing ecofeminism as a glorification of nature, problematically similar to 'a patriarchal, capitalist politics that casts the earth as a feminized victim and throws the blame on to housekeeping, nurturing women – leaving capitalist America free to *mind its own business*' [her italics] (1994: 138). This characterization of ecological feminism is based primarily on her readings of *Woman and Nature* (published in 1978). Though she mentions a special issue of *Hypatia* on ecological feminism, Alaimo doesn't consider any of the work within it to be ecofeminist, and characterizes arguments against certain aspects of ecofeminism made by ecological feminists Ariel Salleh and Stephanie Lahar as anti-ecofeminist.

In stating that, 'attempts to valorize women and nature via glorification and mystification may only bind them more securely to narratives of phallic domination,' Alaimo's characterization of the dangers of glorification are familiar, if abstract (1994: 144). She characterizes Merchant and Haraway as different from the derided ecofeminists (despite Merchant's arguments in favor of ecofeminism in her 1992 book *Radical Ecology*) because they characterize nature as a nongendered, active agent by using the analogies of coyote and cyborg. Putting aside the fact that Haraway labels her cyborg a 'bad girl,' what is striking is Alaimo's refusal to notice that most ecofeminists (including Griffin) speak of nature and its myriad constituents as active agents (Penley and Ross 1991). Consider Rebecca Johnson's nonromantic, nongendered depiction of urban land as provider:

Organic gardening is my link with The Land as an idea and a complex corporal system. I garden for sustenance and as a spiritual practice. The annual events of germination, waving green life, fruition, and

119

decay are the only things I really believe in anymore. If I worship at all, it is at the compost pile. It receives my most consistent offerings.

(Johnson 1993: 252)

The opening of Carol Stabile's essay 'A Garden Enclosed is my Sister': Ecofeminism and Eco-Valences,' provides a perfect example of a theorist committing foul ball. She begins with three lengthy quotes: the first two are third-person journalistic accounts of toxic pollution affecting children in urban areas; the third is a first-person description, written by an ecofeminist, of her pastoral cabin home. This nicely sets up Stabile's methodology: she does not look at ecofeminist arguments, and she is not interested in showing them in a light sympathetic to its own stated agendas. She writes,

In this essay, I unpack the ideologies and strategies undertaken by ecofeminists in particular that . . . prevent the formation of powerful coalitions across a wider sector of the left. By analyzing the manner in which certain ecofeminist strategies circulate in regressive fashions, I hope to point toward the possibility of more progressive forms and formats; to point toward, in effect, a feminist and socialist environmentalism that is committed to a global understanding and formulation of the concept of an ecosystem: one that is more cognizant of, and attentive to, the complexities of that term.

(1994: 57)

Though she attributes to ecofeminism enough power to prevent the development of a powerful left, Stabile gives us very little on which to hang her characterization of ecofeminism, stating rather than showing that, for example, 'ecofeminists uncritically invoke the articulation between "woman" and "environment." She relies on cursory, controversial readings of early Griffin, Daly, and Collard, typified by comments like, 'Ecofeminism reassociates the female with the primitive or the premodern . . . both Daly and Griffin accept a stereotypical rendering of femininity' (Stabile 1994: 60).

Now, it could plausibly be argued that Griffin and Daly glorify femaleness, and in so far as that can be semantically represented by 'femininity,' one might be tempted to say that they value femininity. But whatever one's arguments with writers like Griffin and Daly, it is simply not true that they render femininity stereotypically. For Griffin, the ideal female is represented as a lioness who devours the scientists who poke and prod her. And one only has to consult the index of *Gyn/Ecology* to learn that Mary Daly defines femininity as 'roles/stereotypes/sets of characteristics' and social norms that are destructive to women (1978: 26). Both theorists aim to engage and articulate ontological possibilities unimaginable from patriarchal or phallocratic contexts. Though they may be unconsciously informed by them, they are certainly not reducible to the 'primitive' or 'premodern.'

120

Stabile's characterization of ecofeminism as equivalent to Deep Ecological critique of 'anthropocentrism' or 'speciesism,' with 'single-minded attention to the environment,' also betrays a lack of familiarity with the heated philosophical debates that have ensued between ecofeminists and Deep Ecologists, in academic texts and journals, environmentalist newsletters, and environmentalist gatherings, for years (1994: 66). Like Alaimo, she virtually ignores the many examples of ecofeminist thought that do not fit the simplistic, straw-woman characterization encapsulated in unsupported claims like: 'By insisting that women – across race, class and national lines, across history – have a more intimate and stable relationship with nature and the natural, ecofeminism flattens out and ultimately ignores race and class distinctions' (1994: 58-59). She ascribes to all ecofeminists, again without substantiation, the view that women have 'special links with the environment and nature . . . by virtue of their anatomical configuration' (1994: 59), and chooses to ignore ecofeminist attempts to address various points of political alliance and connection across difference, and to create feminist theory that values differences among women.[1]

The important questions Stabile asks, regarding why ecofeminist philosophy isn't meaningful to working-class and poor people in the United States and why ecofeminism and mainstream environmentalism generally do not address urban ecological issues, are inevitably unhelpful because the 'ecofeminism' she is criticizing is misrepresentative. In fact, there are networks of feminist and nonfeminist women working against toxins in their workplaces and communities, and the question of how ecological feminist academics and activists can support these networks is a pressing one. It is certainly the case that environmentalism is perceived as a 'white people's thing,' and that most ecofeminist theory is written by white women. The fact that feminism in general tends to be created by, and attractive to, white and otherwise privileged women is with us still. But instead of providing an analysis of the successes and shortcomings of current versions of ecofeminism – especially those which aim directly to explore race and class, such as the work of Vandana Shiva and Maria Mies, Karen Warren, and Ynestra King – or about whether ecofeminists appropriate Third World women's movements, or about the adequacy of the 'feminism' in ecofeminism for looking at what we are currently calling 'environmental racism' and 'environmental justice,' what we get from Stabile is yet another story about how feminist work by white women in the late 1970s was essentialist.

Finally, and most importantly, Stabile's characterization of anti-essentialist critiques, and her tendency, which unfortunately is not unique, to lump anti-essentialism together with specific political criticisms of feminist

---

1 Examples of ecofeminist work that do not clearly fit Stabile's characterization include King 1989; Shiva 1989; Roach 1991; Warren 1991; Gaard 1993; Riley 1993.

work by women of color, lesbians, poor and working-class women, cannot escape comment. Citing only Audre Lorde's 'Open Letter to Mary Daly' as evidence she states, 'Not only does the belief in a special connection between women and nature feed into sexist and profoundly misogynistic ideologies, it is, as feminists like Audre Lorde have noted, very much a class- and race-based claim' (1994: 68). But as Amber Katherine points out, Lorde's critique of Daly was not anti-essentialist, but anti-universalist (Katherine 1998). In fact, Lorde herself had a few choice words to say about women, nature, and ancient, embodied ways of knowing and she said them in exactly the way that anti-essentialist feminists love to hate *when they are written by white women.* In 'Poetry Is Not a Luxury,' Lorde writes,

> For each of us as women, there is a dark place within, where hidden and growing our true spirit rises, 'beautiful/ and tough as chestnut/ stanchions against (y)our nightmare of weakness/' and of impotence . . . These places of possibility within ourselves are dark because they are ancient and hidden; they have survived and grown strong through that darkness. Within these deep places, each one of us hold an incredible reserve of creativity and power, of unexamined and unrecorded emotion and feeling. The woman's place of power within each of us is neither white nor surface; it is dark, it is ancient, and it is deep . . . But as we come more into touch with our own ancient, non-european consciousness of living as a situation to be experienced and interacted with, we learn more and more to cherish our feelings, and to respect those hidden sources of our power from where true knowledge and, therefore, lasting action comes.
>
> (1984: 36–37)

It is almost amazing that Lorde has not been the subject of much anti-essentialist critique. I find it difficult not to see this omission as a failure to take her seriously as a theorist, though it might also denote a recognition on the part of simplistic anti-essentialists who respect Lorde that to label a thinker 'essentialist' is to issue proclamation that her work is utter and complete nonsense. I cannot also help but wonder if it is more threatening to white theorists to see white women identify with nature, than to see an African-American woman extol a self-conception that is natural and embodied.

To sum up, ecological feminist theorists who discuss women and nature need not conceive of them as Entities with Essences, and even those who do may still have a few valuable things to say. When we consider 'women' and 'nature,' we can assume that no real universals apply, though patterns may be overwhelmingly apparent and determining, that the meanings of the terms are historically bound, and that many features of the meanings we utilize promote mischaracterizations and mistreatment of whatever falls within the space mapped by the terms. Yet we also know that there are real social and ecological beings subsumed under the categories, that the con-

cepts help us negotiate reality, and that they can be most helpful and representative if conceived broadly and pluralistically. We cannot ignore the relationships between 'woman' and women, and 'nature' and the stuff that is
considered natural. Likewise, we cannot ignore the ways in which these and
other subjugating concepts and categories are parasitic and symbiotic upon
each other, make sense because of each other, are enacted upon each other,
and become reified through practices, and the ways they criss-cross in and
through people's lives, conceptual schemas, and political situations.

DISCOURSE AND POLITICAL PRACTICE

Teresa De Lauretis' 'Upping the Anti (sic) in Feminist Theory,' lays out ways
in which anti-essentialist arguments, and the feminist essentialist/anti-
essentialist debates themselves, obfuscate the real issues within feminism,
and the challenges feminism presents to nonfeminist positions and practices
(De Lauretis 1990). In addition to concurring with her characterization of
anti-essentialism's function as a political smokescreen, I agree with her
analysis of the feminist fear of essentialism as homophobic, and particularly anti-lesbian. Feminist and ecofeminist discourses that typically become
labelled essentialist tend to be lesbian, *focused* on women (especially
women's bodies), normative, and optimistic about potentials for change
while pessimistic about so much current and historical cultural product.
The extent to which thorough anti-essentialist purges are carried out on
forthrightly lesbian theory, and on attempts to articulate conceptual, epistemic, and physical possibilities that endeavor to fashion themselves as sep-
arately as possible from heterorelational or phallocratic discourses and
practices, is incredible. More disturbing is how totalizing anti-essentialist
arguments can be, especially at a historical moment seemingly ruled by the
enemies of political innovation, creative knowledge-seeking, and
unbounded sensual curiosity. Even a staunch secularist can see the dis-
course-rattling potential of goddess-talk in the heat of a reactionary right
wing Christian power surge. Citing María Lugones' 'The Logic of Pluralist
Feminism,' Frye argues that simplistic anti-essentialist critiques make it easy
to substitute a 'theoretical anxiety about essence for a political concern
about domination and injury' (unpublished: 1). The lack of political concern in so much simplistically anti-essentialist work is striking and notorious. For example 'in writings denouncing essentialism what is most likely to
be problematized is lesbian 'naturalism' – heterosexualism is rarely noted'
(unpublished: 18n).

Aggressively dissecting discourses and practices that call upon women by
virtue of some traditional identity – as feminine, as mothers, as caretakers
or nurturers, as female-embodied, as destined, natural harborers of ways
and wisdoms that do not fit into paradigmatically male, hyper-rationalist
epistemologies – is important philosophical and political work. These

ontological commitments are politically and epistemologically suspect, if not completely misguided, and resulting characterizations of woman, nature, and femininity are often uncritical and dependent upon ontologies and ethics that contradict ecological feminist aims. But our assessment of these discourses cannot stop there, because these discourses are more than words on paper or in the air. Discourses motivate, describe, fuel, transform, and limit action in the world. Specifically, activisms are related to the discourses that motivate and describe them. So if ecological feminist theories (or other forms of discourse) are closely related to ecofeminist activism, the theory must be evaluated not only in terms of its consistency, logic, and embedded political and ontological commitments, but also in terms of its effectiveness and manifestations within political movements and activities.

Several authors have discussed the merits of 'strategic essentialism' as serving important political functions, such as motivating, identifying, and simplifying social movements, despite its theoretical limitations. For example, although universal 'woman' and 'mother' are myths, political rhetoric that addresses women and mothers by those names can effectively mobilize women who see themselves as having certain interests or qualities in common to gather together and create ways to fight for those interests and foster those qualities. A number of such movements which Ann Snitow describes as 'motherist,' have been the focus of a good deal of ecological feminist thought, and ecofeminist reclamation of certain movements as 'ecofeminist' (Snitow 1990). Often these movements are not described as 'feminist' or 'environmentalist' by participants – they are described as efforts to create a means of survival by women struggling to feed their families and caught in the middle of eco-destructive practices that destroy their traditional sources of subsistence and livelihood. These movements, even when women coalesce as political actors under the umbrella of uncritical 'motherist' rhetoric, can in turn become the sources of questioning presuppositions concerning women's roles and identities. Essentialist discourses do not necessarily essentialize their subjects. In fact, Snitow argues that, instead of rejecting motherist discourses as anti-feminist, taking 'the long view . . . can help feminists include women to whom a rapid political or theoretical movement forward has usually seemed beside the point – poor women, peasant women, and women who for any number of reasons identify themselves not as feminists but as militant mothers' (1990: 20).

Glorification of women's experiences, or of whatever is associated with women, females, or femininity is often the result of a concerted, if shallow, effort to take women's embodied experiences seriously. Glorification is only partially normative – it is also an invitation for women to experience their bodies as beautiful, strong, natural and cultural and something other than 'mother.' This invitation is a justified and risky ecological and feminist response to many aspects of life in a female body – justified because the traditional devaluations are based on misrepresentations, or characterizations of women's bodies that bear little resemblance to the more complex and delightful ways they are often experienced by women themselves, risky because glorifying gendered bodies as gendered easily slips into what looks like false universalisms, and also tends toward celebration of some of the very things that feminists want to question. Glorification can play into stereotypes, and runs the risk of replicating harmful, engrained patterns. Still, its attractions should not be minimized by theorists whose sources of enlightenment are primarily intellectual.

Ecological feminists desire relationships with nature, and with embodiment, that help shift understandings of what nature is. To open up the conceptual space to value a devalued entity, the thing must be seen as something other than what it is supposed to be. Of course it is possible to frame this in essentialist terms: we have been told lies about what this body is, what nature is, when in fact there is some other immutable truth about what it really is, in fact what it was all along. There are many examples of lesbian and ecofeminist thought that point in this direction, that include attempts to carve out fixed, universal definitions. But, I'd like to suggest that the very act of claiming the power to define entails a deconstructive move. Attempts to represent lesbian sexuality, and ecofeminist efforts at recharacterizing nature, are often less fixed and fixing than they may seem at first glance. If we look closely at articulations of these desires we see that they are not motivated so much by essentialist ontologies as by the desire to articulate the power of the somatic and connections among what is supposed to be forever separate. We might think of such attempts, even those we ultimately reject, as *conversational* moves, responses to phallocratic mischaracterizations and lies, demands for alternatives, and for the consideration of our own observations, namings, and evaluations, and the data of experience. Interestingly, whether one intends it or not, calling for attention to one's own voice opens up the possibility of its fallibility, and acts as an invitation to other voices, definitions, conceptual possibilities. When concepts, meanings, definitions are continually exploded, the real dangers of essentialism become minute.

Though there is a growing impatience with simplistic anti-essentialist arguments, as yet there is insufficient attention to feminist work that has been castigated as 'essentialist,' or effort to reframe that work historically, in light of developments within feminist theory and communities, as well as post-structuralist insights. Such a move must be more than a fervent reclamation of ersatz essentialist feminist work and insight, and must begin by critically and cautiously assessing the merit, usefulness, and historical significance of such work. Ecological feminist theory will not sufficiently develop until we are willing to transgress the hesitancy of feminist theorists to take seriously work that has been rejected as essentialist – an ironic statement given the seriousness with which many nonacademic thinkers take the intersections of environmentalism, feminism, and other work for social justice.

6

CONSIDERING THE PROBLEMS
IN ECOFEMINISM

It is crucial to my critique of gender hierarchy that gender
hierarchy restricts the elaboration of the feminine within sexual
difference by its reduction of the feminine to what is not man.
A crucial aspect of ethical feminism is that it enlarges continually the space in which we could both write and speak of the
rich and multi-layered sexuality of a creature that struggles to
achieve individuation from the imposed strictures of gender
hierarchy and rigid gender identity. Such a creature would
remain as other, the *heteros* to a system of gender hierarchy
which thwarts the process and the struggle for individuation.
Drucilla Cornel

Despite the preceding defense of ecofeminism, I certainly believe that some
ecofeminist efforts to build upon connections and articulate feminist environmental ethics *are* problematic, but not merely because they are essentialist. In fact, something like the glorification of motherhood or femininity
is a bad move for feminists, and ecological feminists in particular, for reasons beyond those stemming from a reliance on essentializing concepts. Or,
putting the problem in simple anti-essentialist terms leaves unarticulated
why asserting that woman = mother, woman = feminine, mother = nature,
feminine = caring is not a good idea, theoretically and practically.

One move along these lines that I would like to call more deeply into
question is the widespread acceptance among ecofeminists of a 'care ethic'
as basic to ecofeminist ethics. This unexamined attraction to a care ethic is
related to a general veneration of 'feminine values' that informs much
ecofeminist thought, and such veneration promotes, rather than dismantles
what Karen Warren, echoing Horkheimer and Adorno, has called a 'logic of
domination.' Work that values femininity and 'female nature' can be found
throughout the history of ecofeminist thought, especially in earlier work,
and is prevalent in the two anthologies that were the first published books
specifically on ecofeminism, *Healing the Wounds: The Promise of
Ecofeminism*, edited by Judith Plant, and *Reweaving the World: The
Emergence of Ecofeminism*, edited by Irene Diamond and Gloria Feman
Orenstein. My critique of this work points to more stimulating directions

both for ecological feminist theorizing and for the progeny of essentialist/anti-essentialist debates.

THE CARE ETHIC

In Chapter 2, I outlined the aspects of feminist ethics that ground the perspective I identify as ecological feminism. I return now to a discussion of ethical presuppositions, in order to highlight some problematic ecofeminist ethical assumptions. Because much early ecofeminist writing came from feminist, rather than specifically ecological circles, the influences of feminist theory and the debates raging therein are evident throughout ecofeminist thought. In mapping out specific recommendations for improved societies, institutions, practices, and ecological interactions, many ecofeminists have used feminist ethics as a foundation. But of course, there are many different examples of feminist ethical perspectives, and not all of them are equally sound or useful.

With a few exceptions, ecofeminists seem particularly drawn to the work of feminist moral theorists who have articulated a 'care ethic.' The idea of a care ethic, and the literature that explores the possibilities of such an ethic, originated with Carol Gilligan's studies of gender and moral development (Gilligan 1982; Gilligan *et al.* 1988). A care ethic is based on the values expressed by the girls and women involved in Carol Gilligan's psychological studies – context-laden values which also happen to be those generally associated with women in Western patriarchal cultures – nurturing, care-taking and maintaining relationships. In their efforts to take women's experiences seriously in the development of a feminist ethical theory, feminist and ecofeminist theorists have taken up the care ethic based on the following three supposed facts:

(a) Women and girls in Gilligan's studies express more interest in context, caring, and relationships than in abstract, institutional rights and responsibilities.

(b) In the cultures in which most feminist theorists reside, women are considered more nurturing and caring than men, for either natural or socially constructed reasons.

(c) Ethical considerations about caring, intimacy, and contextuality have been far less prominent in the history of philosophy and the history of political institutions, especially in the West, than considerations of right and wrong action have been.

But even given these points, it is not obvious to all feminists that ethics based on care are adequate.

Some examples of ecofeminist invocations of the care ethic might help illustrate both its appeal and its weaknesses. In the Introduction to *Healing the Wounds*, Judith Plant writes,

Our pain for the death of the forest is simply, and most fundamentally, compassion for the senseless destruction of life. This compassion that we feel is the essence of a new paradigm which ecofeminism describes in detail. Feeling the life of the 'other' – literally experiencing its existence – is becoming the new starting point for human decision-making

(1989: 1)

Plant acknowledges that the traditional female role as caretaker has been undervalued and is fraught with guilt and anxiety. Yet she asserts that 'women must struggle to claim those aspects of our socialization that are of benefit to the species, believe in them even though they have been so under-valued . . . and impress upon men their own responsibility to change' (1989: 3).

The idea that women should reclaim aspects of their experiences and perspectives that have been devalued by patriarchal ethics is certainly worth pursuing as we construct feminist ethics. Reclamation of historically deval-ued ways of being might serve as the basis for an ethic that at once subverts oppressive values and presents alternative paradigms. For example, although female friendships are ignored or devalued by most traditional ethics, important insights into the value of bonds of affection, virtues of friends, and political potential of filial relationships are gained through the analysis and experience of women's friendships and intimate relations. But despite the potential for reclamation, theorists must remain mindful of the fact that these potentially fruitful 'aspects of our socialization' are products of the same oppressive systems that in many sectors promote the devalua-tion of compassion and caring. If we assume that there is some logic to oppressive thinking, then it follows that there are reasons why women are socialized in certain ways (however impossible it may be to determine things like 'reasons' and 'intentions' behind processes like 'socialization'). That is, there are reasons that contribute to the social construction of 'woman' and promote the domination of women. If it is true that female behavior is part of what maintains oppressive systems, then it is also true that aspects of that behavior and the values and presuppositions grounding it must be examined or recontextualized before they can be reclaimed or considered useful.

The benefits of caring for other beings are obvious: caring is necessary for the health, livelihood, and stability of individuals and communities, and participating in caring relationships is part of what many people feel makes life worth living. As Hume wrote, 'Whatever other passions we may be actu-ated by, pride, ambition, avarice, revenge, or lust; the soul or animating principle of them all is sympathy' (1978: 363). At face value it does seem as though caring for others as humans care is an attitude as basic as anything else we might want to label 'morally important,' and an activity at which women tend to be particularly experienced. On closer inspection, it becomes clear that 'caring' cannot be fully described without discussing its agent, its object, and the context in which it occurs. Caring, then, is most meaningfully evaluated *in situ*. Talk of caring and compassion in the abstract, devoid of attention to the object of caring and the context in which the caring occurs, is ethically uninformative.

In constructing an ethic, ecological feminists must ask if caring for other particular beings or objects is a good activity to engage in when one is trying to move from subordinate social positions. But 'caring' cannot be evaluated unless the objects and purposes of care are made clear. It is no secret that complex norms of female caring and compassion for men and children are cornerstones of patriarchal systems. Women have forgiven harm, stayed with abusers, and sacrificed their own desires because of their great ability to care for others, a supposedly feminine quality that is glorified and encouraged in nearly every corner of the globe. Claudia Card has argued that in the context of oppression the care ethic actually causes moral damage and can therefore be an unhealthy moral choice (Card 1996). Put simply, caring can be damaging to the carer if she neglects other responsibilities, including those she has to herself, by caring for another.

In addition to questions about the effects of caring on caretakers, questions must be asked about the effects of caring on the object of care, whom Nel Noddings refers to as the 'one-cared-for' (Noddings 1984). Caring for someone can be damaging to the object of care, who might be better off, or a better person, if she cares for herself. The line between empowerment and paternalism is as difficult to identify as the boundary between guidance and domination, although these relations might all be labeled 'caring,' under certain circumstances. Regarding interactions with the land and nonhuman species, caring attitudes and actions cannot be assessed without inquiries to determine if caretaking is in the best interest of those objects of care. Indeed, humans need the care of other humans in ways in which nonhumans, especially nondomesticated nonhumans, do not. Like advocates of ethics based on care, proponents of stewardship of the land as an appropriate model of ecological interaction often fail to consider nonhuman 'self'-directedness as a moral goal.

Some ecofeminist proponents of a care ethic recommend empathy and ego denial as the point of departure for reframing moral relationships. Judith Plant claims that 'feeling the life of the other' should be the starting point for ecofeminist decision-making (1989: 1). Deena Metzger, in 'Invoking the Grove,' writes of the importance of giving up the ego as a necessary prerequisite to living out a compassionate commitment to the equality of all things, a move similar to Naess' calls for the demotion of the individual self (1989: 122). But what does Metzger mean when she recommends that women give up their egos? Some of us spend much of our lives responding to exhortations to ignore and deny our 'egos' – our desires, impulses, self-interests. Female self-denial has allowed many to live out compassionate commitments to others at great expense to our relationships with ourselves, our relationships with other women, and our relationships with our environments, and various forms of feminism have been instrumental in questioning the sources and manifestations of women's self-denial. Treading on controversial psychoanalytic ground, even the work of theorists like Nancy Chodorow implies that stronger ego boundaries may enable women to reject or revise oppressive, damaging roles like motherhood, or as consumers within the beauty industry, an institution historically destructive both to women and to animals tortured in cosmetic testing (Chodorow 1978). Given the constraints of gender, race, class, and women's material conditions, the importance of feeling oneself and identifying one's own interests in ecological contexts cannot be overlooked. *These* experiences might be the most promising point of departure for ethical decision-making and theory-building. In fact, identifying one's own complicated, conflicting feelings and interests may be a necessary prerequisite to empathizing with another. If so, then 'ego denial' is contrary to the kind of empathy that allows one to appreciate the oppression or circumstance of another living being.

Proponents of an unmodified reclamation of ethics based on care and compassion may be drawing from a conception of female being rooted not in the actual material and social conditions of women living anywhere today, but from mythical ideals of femininity and historical woman. Riane Eisler claims that societies with an 'ecological consciousness' were rooted in a social structure in which 'women and "feminine" values such as caring, compassion, and non-violence were not subordinate to men and the so-called masculine values of conquest and domination' (1990: 23–24). But again, even putting aside her romanticized conception of history, we cannot neglect the fact that the meanings and ethical relevance of acts of caring and compassion are determined by their contexts and their objects. These contexts and objects vary according to the historical moment and the society and culture in which they occur. Individuals who have been socialized or constructed, to their moral detriment, to behave or to *be* certain ways, cannot easily, individually transform the social meanings and roles propagated by that being. The significance of values such as caring, mothering, and nonviolence is embedded in their current meanings, as well as in the genealogy of their meanings.

An ecological feminist ethic that holds caring for other beings as a good, and clearly sets out the appropriate objects and contexts of ethical caring relationships could certainly be informative and useful. There are very good reasons to argue that, generally speaking, men need to learn some ethical lessons from women's experiences as caretakers and apprentices to feminine practices. As Claudia Card points out, anyone's gendered 'moral luck' might result in damaged capacities (Card 1996). If the construction of gender in phallocratic societies results in unequal development of ethical skills,

130

we might argue that, given the historical, social, and cultural contexts, men ought to develop more caring attitudes, especially toward women and non-human entities. Note, however, that this contextualist approach also raises questions about what is *lacking* in the typical moral development of women and girls.

DIVERSITY AND ETHICS

Anyone who has spent time on a college campus in the last few years can tell you that ecofeminists are not alone in making ethical calls for diversity, or claiming that diversity must be valued 'above all else.' Increased public awareness and discussion of the multicultural nature of US society and the permeability of its borders, while accompanied by reactionary attempts to reduce the influx of immigrants and maintain a very limited conception of American culture, has also resulted in efforts to value cultural and ethnic diversity. But like an unqualified feminist call for caring in ethics, an unqualified call for celebrations of diversity in ecofeminism and other political movements is uninformative, if not nonsensical.

In 'Development and Western Patriarchy,' Vandana Shiva shows how what she calls the 'feminine principle,' which includes 'equality in diversity,' has been destroyed by 'Western male-oriented concepts and values,' including the Western model of economic development, which Shiva and others have labelled 'maldevelopment' (Shiva 1989). In sketching the importance of diversity, she discusses the pre-development relationship between men and women in rural India and how this relationship was characterized by equal but different (that is, diverse) social roles for the sexes. She also discusses the importance of diversity in preserving the integrity of forests and the livelihood of women who have depended upon the renewable products of the forest for survival. In this context, Shiva is recommending an ethic that promotes a diversity of social roles along with a diversity of species. But *why* promote a variety of social roles or species? It is not true that *any* variety of persons, voices, and species should be welcomed by an environmental ethic. Ecofeminism certainly could not defend that claim and also hold that patriarchy, anthropocentrism, imperialism, and racism are bad or wrong.

But rather than simply endorsing the valuing of diversity for its own sake, Shiva clearly intends to make a case for certain kinds of voices, perspectives, and species. Indeed, she seems to want to claim her own voice, to give voice to perspectives and interests generally ignored within current economic and political discourses, and to value life-affirming biological differences. Talk of diversity in the abstract, and calls simply to value diversity are uninformative and lead to misunderstandings about the value and importance of *particular* differences within diverse communities. If Shiva is correct in recommending a reorientation toward differences, then thorough discussion is needed as to which differences are life-affirming and what kinds of diversity are likely to promote environmentalist and feminist agendas.

Webster's New World Dictionary defines diversity as the 'quality, state, fact, or instance of being diverse; difference,' and 'variety.' Given this definition, 'diversity' is not something that can be intrinsically good, in an ethical sense. To claim that something is ethically valuable merely because it is unlike something else is incoherent – to be ethically valuable something must itself have a certain quality or status, even if that quality or status is contextually determined. Also, claiming that difference itself renders something morally valuable fails to give attention to the content and origins of the thing itself. As argued above, the claim that something like caring is good because it has been devalued by something bad, like patriarchy, is far too simple. Likewise, the claim that ethics should promote varieties of theories, or should promote social and ecosystemic variety as an ethical goal – two distinct arguments made by Shiva and others – puts a gloss over more substantive recommendations that certain forms of life be valued.

THEORETICAL DIVERSITY

I believe that, at heart, ecofeminist discussions of diversity are not mere calls for difference and variety; indeed, they are – or ought to be – calls for the acknowledgement and valuing of certain instances of difference, and a positive shift in general orientation toward unfamiliar or unjustifiably devalued things. Although diversity is not good in and of itself, there are at least two ways in which instances of diversity might be valuable in ecological feminism. The first is summed up as a claim about the kind of theory ecological feminism ought to be: ecological feminist theory ought to reflect the heretofore neglected diversity of women's lives and interests.

Ecofeminist positions regarding the need for diverse ethical and epistemological foundations stem in part from recent work in feminist epistemology and philosophy of science which claims that

> The activities of those at the bottom of . . . social hierarchies can provide starting points for thought – for *everyone's* research and scholarship – from which humans' relations with each other and the natural world can become visible. This is because the experience and lives of marginalized peoples, as they understand them, provide particularly significant *problems to be explained*, or research agendas.
>
> (Harding 1993b: 54)

That the social location of knowers is a significant aspect of the construction of theory, and that a 'strongly' objective position is most successfully derived through the consideration of a wide number of relevant perspectives, is widely held by feminist philosophers. Although these epistemological claims are not uncontroversial, pluralist approaches to theory-building – and to truth – are core aspects of ecological feminism's commitments to producing knowledge from women's experiences, and to addressing the multifarious ways in which women's interests and concerns intersect with ecological flourishing. These commitments ought not to be confused with a simplistic or shallow celebration of diversity. Rather, the ethical point is that given the monopoly on ideas and values typically held by those with economic and hegemonic power, opposing viewpoints are valuable because of the questions they raise, and the more beneficial alternatives they present for ethically valuable beings.

As discussed earlier, the perceived need for theory built on difference and variety stems also from critiques by women (including women of color, lesbians, poor and working-class women, Third World, disabled and Jewish women) who have criticized other feminists for assuming that all women are the same, or that *la femme* in feminism is white, middle-class, able-bodied, Western, straight, or able to identify with the interests of those with social sanction and privilege. The myth of universal Woman has resulted in feminist theory that reflects the experiences and interests of only *some* women, while claiming to be about, or for women generally.

María Lugones writes eloquently of the need for pluralist feminist theory, and the ways in which white feminist theorists misunderstand this need.

> White women used to simply and straightforwardly ignore difference. In their theorizing, they used to speak as if all women *as women* were the same. Now white women recognize the problem of difference. Whether they *recognize* difference is another matter. As white women are beginning to acknowledge the problem in their theorizing, it is interesting to see that the acknowledgement is a noninteractive one, or at least there is no clear emphasis on interactive acknowledgement . . . If the acknowledgement is noninteractive, the knowledge that I want to see in feminist theorizing is missing.
>
> (1991: 38)

In an effort to represent women more adequately, and to attend to interests and experiences that are shared by many women despite the existence of tremendous differences, ecofeminists ought actively to engage a plurality of perspectives in the formulation of feminist theory (Warren 1991). Ethical theory that prejudicially promotes or ignores the interests of some women is grossly inadequate, if not oppressive and distorting, for feminists with broad intentions concerning the deconstruction of systems of oppression other than sexism that affect women. But as Lugones further points out, inclusion – or pluralism – must be more than acknowledgements of and respect for difference. Feminist pluralism requires theory that actively engages specific forms of difference in its very structure.

When I do not see plurality stressed in the very structure of a theory, I know that I will have to do lots of acrobatics – like a contortionist or tight-rope walker – to have this theory speak to me without allowing the theory to distort me *in my complexity*.

When I do not see plurality in the very structure of a theory, I see the phantom that I am in your eyes, take grotesque forms and mime crudely and heavily your own image. Don't you?

(1991: 43)

ECOLOGICAL DIVERSITY

The second ecological feminist claim regarding diversity is a more general principle about the kinds of human and ecological communities that should be promoted by any ethic. This reason for ecological feminist valuing of diversity originates in ecological knowledge of the realities of biological interdependence, as well as commitments to justice in diverse contexts.

Interdependent relationships within the biota are incredibly numerous and complex. Though we know relatively little about the intricacies of these relationships, we do know that biota usually flourish when a great deal of species diversity exists. When this diversity is disrupted, far-reaching adjustments become necessary, and each readjustment is increasingly taxing on the biotic community as a whole. With a sensitivity to the complexity of the biotic web, and awareness of human ignorance regarding the subtleties of species, community, and interpersonal interdependencies, ecofeminists affirm the importance of diverse communities. They aim as well to create theories that reflect this humble appreciation of diversity and the subtleties of symbiosis. Given the extent to which human manipulations of environments tend to result in the eradication of whole species and ecosystems, and given that healthy ecosystems usually include a high number of different species and forms of life, ethical interactions within environments often involve the preservation or restoration of natural diversity.

Diversity is merely one marker of ecosystemic health. Environmental thinkers who promote 'diversity' are actually often arguing in favor of maximizing undisrupted, or natural states. Valuing ecological and social diversity as a healthy aspect of communities has to include an acknowledgement that healthy, thriving, integrated communities are the underlying goal, that an increase of diversity is not itself a good thing, and that most currently diverse communities have been significantly shaped by human manipulations.

TYRANNIES OF UNITY

Ethical issues become further complicated when calls for diversity are accompanied by arguments for global unity. Charlene Spretnak argues for an ecofeminist ontology based on the oneness of all being, united in a 'cosmic consciousness' in which 'only the illusions of separation divide us' (1989: 128–129). Although Spretnak at times seems to be making an ontological point (which might certainly be questioned on its own terms), many ecofeminist spiritual writers emphasize global and ecological unity as an ethical goal without realizing the implications for human communities. Who, or what qualities, are reduced or eliminated when unity of being or mind is promoted as a *political* goal, or when a unified ontology is used as the basis for ethical and political practices? Historically, the interests of members of groups considered Other by those with hegemonic power are ignored or destroyed in the interest of unification, and even those with power must sometimes sacrifice autonomy or aspects of themselves to achieve racial, ethnic and other kinds of unity.

An ethic that is adequately inclusive and anti-oppressive must leave room for certain kinds of separation, difference, and plurality to avoid the logic of unity. In fact, the kind of feminist pluralism described above is incompatible with conceiving of the divisions between us as illusory, or insignificant. Given the reductionist tendencies of oppressive systems, the health of individuals, groups, species, or ecosystem often requires conscious moves away from unification. In fact, there may be healthy reasons for some of us to seek out separation and, as discussed in the Interlude, to revel in our multiplicity, in order to enable resistance and empowerment, to strategize, and to avoid enemies. Our histories are such that solidarity, or the recognition of certain forms of connection and relation, rather than difference-obliterating unity, is an important political and ethical goal.

Behind spiritualistic talk of unity, writers like Spretnak hope to inspire greater awareness of biotic and social interdependence, interconnection, and similarity. One can hardly argue that such awareness is not a necessary aspect of feminist and environmental ethics that aim toward flourishing. In fact, talk of unity and the ways in which we're all connected in the web of life can be comforting. But calls for unity can also incite bloody riots and racial wars. Ironically, conceptions of racial, ethnic, species, and geographical unity ultimately break down on close inspection. In *Black Is/Black Ain't*, filmmaker Marlon Riggs explores the complicated, multiple meanings of being black in the United States. Although a strong sense of racial identity and similarity is communicated through the film, the blurred boundary around 'black' is as apparent as the importance of identifying with the concept. The sense of joyful solidarity and kinship expressed by the women and men interviewed in the film would in fact be compromised by a drive for unity that would downplay the vast and significant physical, political, sexual, and cultural differences among African-Americans. This is no less true of biotic communities, with their fluid boundaries and indeterminate edges. The boundaries that circumscribe systems of life, communities, and even the planet are permeable and potentially temporary even when indisputably real.

DUALISMS

Dualisms, such as masculine and feminine, yin and yan, male and female, dark and light, nature and culture, primitive and civilized, abound in the history of phallocratic thought, though the meanings and terms of the dualisms vary. Feminists, and ecofeminists in particular, have identified hierarchical dualistic thinking as endemic to systems of dominance and subordination typified by Western power discourses. These discourses define women, people of color, nature, and anything that comes to be associated with these as subordinate and less valuable. But not all ecofeminist treatment of dualistic thinking cuts as deeply as it ought. In fact, a number of ecofeminists argue not against dualistic thinking, but against the hierarchical ordering present in most dualistic systems of thought. Deena Metzger, invoking a common contemporary spiritual theme, claims that without an integration of masculinity and femininity – a healing of the gender split – humans will become deranged and destroy the planet. Ecology, she believes, 'implies the coexistence of the inside and the outside, the dark and the light, and the masculine and the feminine.' Environmentalism therefore requires 'that each of us change the essential patterns of our life which are based more upon exclusivity, distinction, elimination, separation' to 'inclusiveness, unification, and relationship' (1989: 121). Using a string of undefined abstract concepts, she calls for a dissociation of domination from dualisms, but she does not touch on the deeper problems with systematic dualistic thinking.

Dichotomies exist in the natural world. Describing them is not problematic. Nevertheless, sometimes we make (or inherit) choices about whether to conceive things dualistically, or whether linguistically to mark distinctions as noteworthy at all. Dichotomous distinctions can become ethically problematic when they form and fuel social hierarchies, but they also are damaging in so far as they become paradigms for all reality, or the basis for describing, classifying, and evaluating almost everything. Problems with dualistic thinking include the following:

(1) Dualisms are *false* dichotomies, constructed in order to maintain a power structure and a false conception of essential reality. Dualistic thinking emphasizes only extremes or caricatures of a continuum of existing entities or attributes. For example, dualistic thinking sets up a dichotomy between masculinity and femininity, despite the cultural variety in the actual content of the concepts, which corresponds to constructions of gender and sex: women naturally and appropriately embody femininity, and men embody masculinity, or so the story goes, and the punishment for acting unnaturally can be severe. Yet in actuality humans exhibit arrays of characteristics, with attributes and qualities considered 'masculine' and 'feminine' occurring in both women and men. Additionally, a conceptual template that can only expose masculinity and femininity does not allow for the recogni-

tion or creation of traits and characteristics that are neither. Dualisms characterize and limit behavior in terms of gender, but they often do not map neatly on to material reality.

(2) Dualisms constructed in systems of binary opposition often become the bases of systems of domination and subordination. Even when dualistic thinking seems nonhierarchical, any dualism can become hierarchical in a context that includes a drive toward domination. A compelling example is the way in which dichotomous 'separate but equal' gender roles of pre-colonial societies often became hierarchically ordered with the introduction of great, externally-imposed power imbalances.

(3) Positing the reconciliation of the genders as they currently exist, or the blending of feminine and masculine values into a more balanced worldview as the key to environmental and social salvation entails not only an uncritical acceptance of gender but also an assumption that given models of reality and its functions are adequate. Many dualisms are based on a scientific view of the world that favors the most simple explanations consistent with the previous findings of science over more complex explanations that call given models into question. A world full of phenomena and possibilities beyond dualisms that is none the less characterized dualistically (early and often) by myriad powerful institutions, is likely to continue to be perceived and described dualistically, and hence to animate false notions of reality. Rejecting the scientific drive to the simplest explanations, Elliot Sober argues that 'parsimony, in and of itself, cannot make one hypothesis more plausible than another,' and that 'the philosopher's mistake is to think that there is a single global principle that spans diverse scientific subject matters' (1990: 77). Additionally, feminists point out the correlation between the scientific and philosophical preoccupation with parsimony and the phallocratic arrogance of assuming that humans can comprehend the complexity of the universe. As poet Adrienne Rich writes, 'There is not "the truth," "a truth" – truth is not one thing, or even a system. It is an increasing complexity' (1986: 353).

Presupposing dualisms, or setting them up as natural, contradicts feminist commitments to deconstructing oppressive systems. In 'A New Movement, A New Hope,' Corinne Kumar D'Souza reiterates a critique made by many ecofeminists – that Western ideologies are based on hierarchical dualisms in which whatever is 'masculine, demanding, aggressive, competitive, rational, and analytic' is dominant over that which is 'feminine, responsive, cooperative, intuitive, and sympathizing.' The problem, she claims, is that favoring the 'male mode of aggression ... generates the militaristic mindset, the nuclear mentality, and war culture' that promote the degradation of anything perceived or marked as feminine. D'Souza recommends not an outright rejection of dualistic thinking, but an integration of the masculine and the feminine, with a reminder that rationality and intuition are two modes of perception, two ways of knowing that are 'not independent of each other,' not oppositional, but 'two points of a single whole' (D'Souza 1989: 35). But D'Souza's program presupposes the importance of gender despite its rejection of the domination of one gender over another, though constructions of gender themselves help set up and maintain dualistic hierarchies.

In a scathing piece against Deep Ecology in *Healing the Wounds*, Sharon Doubiago takes male Deep Ecologists to task for claiming that their ethics and ontology are based on their own musings and also on principles within 'Eastern mysticism.' Doubiago points out that many of the tenets of Deep Ecology can be found in the history of feminist thought (which is diverse enough to be intermingled with a variety of spiritual and nonspiritual traditions) and in other writing by women. However, in staking a female claim to certain ideas, Doubiago relies on an uncritical view of 'woman' and women's roles without delving into their sources and fails to identify critically the dualistic paradigm intrinsic to her own conception of women's virtues.

With regard to women's traditional roles, Doubiago writes, 'Woman traditionally listens to her inner voice. The habit is considered symptomatic; indeed, hormonal, anatomic' (1989: 40). 'Women have always thought like mountains,' she continues, referring to Aldo Leopold's model of sound ecological thinking, and like D'Souza she calls for an integration of this womanly thinking with linear male thinking (1989: 42). Doubiago admits that this 'female trait' is considered an essential part of what constitutes 'woman,' but she goes no further in an analysis of what it means for women to be thought of, and for some to think of themselves, this way. But what are inner voices and mountain-like thought, and which women use them? Why do, or should, they listen to inner voices, or think like mountains? Is it in their best interest to listen to those voices, whatever they may be? What other information are they missing while listening to inner voices and thinking like mountains?

Much recent ecofeminist work takes feminist critiques of gender to be central. In 'Is Ecofeminism Feminist?,' Victoria Davion asserts that any ecofeminist ethic must include an critical analysis of sex and gender (Davion 1994). And Dorothy Dinnerstein writes,

> Central to a humanly whole feminist vision is awareness that our traditional uses of gender form part of an endemic mental and societal disorder; part of the everyday psychopathology, the normal taken-for-granted mishugas, that is killing our world.

> (1989: 193)

In her book *Staying Alive*, Vandana Shiva illustrates the instrumentality of a 'feminine principle' ecofeminism in empowering rural Indian women and enabling them to sustain their livelihood by interrupting deforestation (Shiva 1989). One cannot ignore the successes of woman-centered environmental activism in communities that have suffered severely under Western-initiated maldevelopment. It is important that our theories do not lose sight of the practical relevance of this activism even when it relies on essentialist notions and is not based on rigorous conceptual analyses. Ecofeminist criticism should take seriously the reasons why certain simplistic theories, and rhetoric which does not thoroughly reject the status quo, are able to inspire social change and changes in the ways women interact with each other, their environments and systems of domination.

Still, taking a theory and a movement seriously requires questioning it at the deepest levels in order to create more useful theories for given contexts. Offering an alternative perspective, Lee Quinby, through a Foucaultian lens, discusses the strength of ecofeminist theory and practice that does not aim toward totalizing theory, but which engages in a decentered political struggle (1990: 123). Because ecofeminism is not a single-issue politics, she believes it calls for a 'plurality of resistance' which would target abuses of power on a multiplicity of levels and in many locations. This kind of resistance also originates from diverse perspectives, includes a variety of consistent goals, and takes many shapes. While continually challenging each other and working to create an ecologically astute and feminist ethic, ecological feminists should respect, encourage, and learn from a variety of effective methods and theories. In that way, ecofeminism could then become an alliance of varied theories and methodologies that share common goals and values, rather than a unified movement.

In *Rethinking Ecofeminist Politics*, Janet Biehl argues that those interested in the integration of feminist and other social issues with radical ecology ought to abandon ecofeminism and turn instead to Social Ecology (Biehl 1991). Represented most notably by the writings of Murray Bookchin, Social Ecology combines an anarchist critique of hierarchy and exploitation with an ethic based on biological interdependence. Some ecofeminists call themselves 'social ecofeminists,' identifying their affinity to both ecofeminism and Bookchin's social analysis. Biehl, a former social ecofeminist, has abandoned ecofeminism because of her disappointment over the seeming lack of influence of 'the best of social theory' on ecofeminism (1991: 1). She finds particularly troubling the spiritualism, biological determinism, and anti-rationalism expressed by a number of ecofeminists. But Biehl unfortunately limits her analysis of ecofeminism to a consideration of some of the least promising examples of ecofeminist theory. Most striking is her omission of the philosophical work of Karen Warren, Jim Cheney, and Val Plumwood, three examples of nonspiritualist ecological feminist theory. Biehl's critique of 'classic' ecofeminist treatises, such as Susan Griffin's *Woman and Nature*, is incredibly ungenerous, and fails to place particular quotations, and the book as a whole, in an appropriate historical and theoretical context.

Despite my disagreements with Janet Biehl, she and I both believe that ecofeminism has spawned some very bad theory. But is the existence of uninspiring, or even troubling theory sufficient reason to abandon a promising project? I think not, for several reasons. First, alongside the examples of disappointing theory, there are examples of truly insightful, moving, and carefully-argued work. As for the less promising work, it seems inevitable that some disappointing theory will emerge out of relatively new fields of inquiry. It is also preferable that conflicts arise within young fields of activism. Some writers are heartened by the wealth of disagreement, or 'diversity,' evident within ecofeminism.

I do not believe that the existence of provocative, committed, yet sloppy or even somewhat wrongheaded theory that emerges early in the congealing stages of a movement is necessarily sufficient to justify complete rejection of a political and philosophical project. Careful argumentation is important, but it is not the only salient aspect of theoretical writing. Much of the work that I criticize throughout this book evidences clear political and personal commitment to uncovering at least some of the connections between women's oppression and the devastation of the planet, and undoing the harm done in the name of progress. Such commitment is a necessary prerequisite for ecological feminist activism and for the development and implementation of strategies which will improve the status quo. Writing that communicates such commitment is important because it can be a motivator, even to women who do not agree with all of its presuppositions. The inspirational impact of the mythic and seductive imagery used in much ecofeminist writings should not be underestimated, especially when such inspiration results in useful and innovative political action.

In sum, the essentialist underpinnings of some ecofeminist discourse is less problematic than the simplicity of some of its arguments. To put the anti-essentialist point differently, concepts like 'woman,' 'femininity,' 'motherhood,' 'diversity,' and 'unity' have been used far too simplistically by a number of ecological feminist writers, especially those writing on spirituality. But this fact does not mean that there are not important ontological, ethical, and political connections among those entities, qualities, and practices categorized as 'feminine,' or associated with the devalued members of racist and patriarchal cultures.

7

ACTIVISM THAT IS NOT ONE

> Within revolutionary feminist movements, within revolution-
> ary black liberation struggles, we must continually claim the-
> ory as necessary practice within a holistic framework of
> liberatory activism. We must do more than call attention to
> ways theory is misused . . . We must actively work to call
> attention to the importance of creating a theory that can
> advance renewed feminist movements, particularly highlight-
> ing that theory which seeks to further feminist opposition to
> sexism, and sexist oppression.
>
> bell hooks

In this final chapter, I begin to explore the meanings, possibilities, potentials, and functions of ecological feminist activism. I am particularly curious about the relationships among ecological feminist theories and
practices, especially between ecological feminist ethical theory and practice,
and the means of conversation among these. I aim both to contribute to
understandings of activist and theoretical practice that are shifting and
unfixed, and to provide arguments in favor of activist ecological feminist
work. If ecological feminism is a theory, a movement and/or a critique that
aims to address the intersecting oppressions of women, nature, people of
color, the poor, and others categorized as inferior by phallocratic systems,
then what counts as ecological feminist activism? In other words, how might
nontheoretical yet intellectual and self-consciously feminist and environmentalist practice address multiplicitous and shifting causes and aspects of
oppression? How can we understand an activism that is dialectically related
to theory, and that has decentered targets and objectives? Ecological feminists need to explore these questions, and to move toward the creation of a
significant ecological feminist activist movement if ecological feminism is to
be instrumental in shaping significant social change.

A large amount of self-consciously ecological feminist work, that is, work
labeled 'ecofeminist' by the people doing it, is written work, and much of that
is the kind of work that is generally categorized as 'theoretical.' Many ecological feminist writers are concerned with ethical questions and issues,
although a growing number are exploring the possibilities of ecological feminist epistemologies and ontologies. In the following pages I will attempt to
articulate how this kind of work can intersect with other kinds of political

activity by looking closely at the relationship between ethical theory and applied ethics. Although I will be using concepts like 'theory,' 'practice,' and 'activism,' I believe that these categories are not fixed, separate, distinct, or solid. I am tempted to avoid fixing these concepts by referring to them with phrases like 'so-called theory' and 'what feminists generally refer to as "activism",' but alongside my acknowledgement of the slipperiness of the space between the concepts 'theory' and 'practice,' I want also to recognize the differences in the ways those concepts are actually used. In order to negotiate the ambiguous middle space, I will ground my uses of the concepts of theory and practice in definitions developed by John Dewey.

Webster's defines activism as 'the doctrine or policy of taking positive, direct action to achieve an end, especially a political or social end,' and direct action as 'action directed at achieving an objective; esp., the use of strikes, demonstrations, civil disobedience, etc. in disputes or struggles for rights' (Webster's New World Dictionary 1994). Activism is conscious, purposeful, political activity. Now, there is no reason to assume that holding a demonstration has any more direct impact on a situation than publishing an article does, though there are significant differences between these two forms of activity. Theoretical writing addresses its specific audience with words on paper or on a computer screen; it aims directly to engage the intellect. As a practice, it can appear incredibly disembodied, or can entail abstraction from the body. Even the author who writes forthrightly and explicitly from her bodily experience cannot be certain of the extent to which her audience will be consciously embodied, or accepting of the writer's embodiment. None the less, critical perspectives that consider the product of writing to be disembodied text created by the mind encourage a problematic, hard dualism which marks intellectual activity as separate from and superior to physical activity. Writing theory is an activity, a physical activity, though it is lived though the body in ways generally different from activities like painting or marching. Given this, it is not nonsensical to think of theory as a form of activism – as a practice.

The 'other' kind of activism – the work I've heard students refer to by saying, 'I don't want to do theory; I'm interested in activism,' is unmistakably bodily. It directly puts one face up against another, it lays its body down on the street, it yells and claps and breaks things, it sits down and stands up, it can be photographed and then seen on TV and in the newspapers. Yet this activity is not unintellectual. It can be conceptually grounded, transgressive, and influential, and its effectiveness often rests on the creativity of its language. Activism entails movement, and this movement can be theoretical and thoughtful, as well as physical.

Thus far, the relationship between ecofeminist and ecological feminist theory and activism has been somewhat backward-looking: ecofeminist theorists tend to cite various instances and forms of feminist and environmental activism and claim them as ecofeminist. Examples of activist movements claimed by ecofeminists include the Chipko movement in India, the global fight for women's reproductive freedom, the 'woman-centered' peace and antinuclear movements, and the fight for animal rights. Although these movements have not often been self-consciously constructed as ecofeminist, theorists lay claim to them in so far as the movements explicitly or implicitly acknowledge and address, at the very least, ways in which sexism and misogyny are related to human maltreatment of the environment and its members (Lahar 1991).

The lack of a significant, easily identifiable ecological feminist activist movement in the United States makes me curious about the possibility of an ecological feminist activism that is not centered around creating, disseminating, or understanding the written word. If 'ecological feminist' is not merely to serve as an umbrella term under which various forms and instances of activism are retroactively classified, what other kinds of ecological feminist activist practices are possible? I believe that ecological feminist activism is necessary and could be politically significant, and that ecological feminists should be concerned both with claiming various activisms as ecological and feminist and creating and motivating specifically, stridently, self-consciously ecological feminist activisms. An emphasis on the dialectical relationship between theory and practice can ground rich, politically strategic, thoughtful ecological feminist practice.

BETWEEN ETHICAL THEORY AND APPLIED ETHICS

Lisa Heldke argues that the philosophy of John Dewey offers a valuable analysis of the relationship between theory and practice, one which 'impel[s] a radical rethinking of the way that philosophical attention has been distributed over human endeavors,' and 'reconnect[s] the practice of philosophy to ordinary concerns – the emotional, intellectual, and practical affairs of daily life' (unpublished: 1-2). Despite the fact that much of Dewey's work is based on the premise that philosophy should start with practices, or 'common experiences,' Heldke believes he fails adequately to consider the philosophical significance of much common experience, especially of rudimentary, daily practices typically identified as the work of women, slaves, servants, and laborers. Although Heldke is critical of Dewey's own theoretical practice, she and other feminist philosophers have shown the usefulness of Dewey's critique of the hierarchical dichotomy between theory and practice, and his assertions that theory-making is actually a form of practice (Seigfried 1993). In light of Dewey's articulations of the relatedness of theory and practice, Heldke characterizes theoretical work as a form of 'thoughtful practice.' I find this concept useful for describing the kind of ecological feminism I recommend in these pages, and I also believe it opens up possibilities for understanding the thoughtfulness of practice that is not formally theoretical.

143

The dualistic understanding of theory and practice against which Dewey argues, and which is still assumed in some feminist and other political circles, rests on presuppositions similar to those behind some philosophers' characterizations of the differences between ethical theory and applied ethics. Those philosophers think of environmental ethics and feminist ethics as examples of applied ethics: in environmental ethics we apply ethical theory to environmental problems (e.g. is it ethical to cause pain to nonhuman animals?), and in feminist ethics we apply ethical theory to feminist issues (e.g. is it fair to pay women less than men for the same work?). But to conceive of the field of applied ethics in this manner is to misunderstand the relationship between ethical theory and ethical decision-making. Further, to characterize feminist, environmental and, hence, ecological feminist ethics this way is to misrepresent much of that work. In fact, as philosophical work in these fields often locates itself in spaces where abstraction and material practice intersect and inform each other, many 'practical' feminist and environmental considerations have resulted in dramatic conceptual shifts.

Philosophers tend to refer to ethical theory and applied ethics as though they are significantly separate spheres. Such separation rests partially on the assumption that ethical theory gives us abstract truths about what is right and wrong or good and bad, and those truths are applied to real ethical dilemmas in the field of applied ethics. Certainly it is no secret that ethical theory has traditionally been constructed abstractly. The work of Kant, Mill, and Rawls evinces the belief that the best way to explore notions of what is right, good, or just is to consider concepts in the abstract, guided by questions such as: to what do the words generally refer? How are they used? What might the most pure interpretation of the concepts resemble? The abstraction, universality, and presumed objectivity of such ethical theory render it closer to empirical science and hence more philosophically sophisticated than applied ethics, in which philosophers consider the details of material contingencies and the difficulties of actual ethical practices.

Abstract ethical queries are not without merit. They have at times helped to reorient intellectuals, and even larger sectors of societies, toward certain values and away from others. They have helped to clarify thinking about particular examples of ethical decision-making (especially about the ways philosophers conceptualize ethical dilemmas), about the realm of ethical thought, and about the relationships among ethics, law, religion, and other social and political systems. They have also sometimes provided helpful frameworks through which to ask whether social values and conceptions of right behavior and good character are justified, consistent, or attainable.

But ethical theory in and of itself does not actually help people live better lives. First of all, ethical theory is not necessary for ethical life. In fact, most people who could be said to live 'good' lives have had absolutely no exposure to ethical theory. Second, I would assert that those students, philosophers, and other interested parties who are exposed to formal ethical theory do not accept a theory based on its abstract elegance and then, subsequently, apply it in appropriate moments of ethical uncertainty. Rather we begin with our experiences – our practical expertise in 'applied ethics' – and we evaluate and recreate ethical theory from there. Sometimes the theory simply rings true, or certain aspects of it seep into and inform our consciousness. Often, finding theoretical explorations inadequate to address our real ethical problems, we discover places where theory could be modified. Sometimes we abandon theories altogether because they have absolutely no relevance to ethical practice. In other instances we find theories wholly irrelevant to real problem-solving, yet we continue to discuss them because of their historical significance or beautiful logic.

One might ask whether ethical theory, or the work of those who consider themselves to be experts in the field of ethics, should do anything but critically analyze ethical concepts. Isn't the work of philosophy to clarify concepts, analyze assumptions, and identify implications? But even the history of traditional, male, Western ethical theory counters such assertions. Many ethical theorists, including Socrates, Hume, Bentham, and Mill, are said to have been motivated not merely by a love of pure wisdom, but also by a desire to discover how to live good lives and a wish to motivate, inspire, and educate others. The history of ethics is the story of both descriptive and prescriptive ventures, however subtle, indirect, and faulty those prescriptions may be. Its directives have generally been attempts to answer questions about how individual and social agents might live better lives and make good decisions. With the current social and environmental crises that face nearly all inhabitants of the planet, ethical thinkers are increasingly engaged by questions about how best to solve practical, material problems and what we can learn about goodness, right and wrong, relationship and responsibility as we struggle to negotiate these problems. It is in the dialogue between ethical theory, or abstract ethical principles and values, and real-life ethical decision-making, *practice*, that we can learn how to make better ethical and political decisions. Dewey's formulation of the relationship between theory and practice is helpful to ecological feminists in so far as it helps us conceptualize a dialectic in which written theoretical work and other practical work are seen as politically and philosophically necessary.

The central claim here is not merely about the practical relevance of theory. As Dewey writes in *The Quest for Certainty*, 'Theory separated from concrete doing and making is empty and futile' (1929: 281). As Dewey's claim about the relationship between theory and practice suggests, ethical theory enables us to live better lives only when it informs and is informed by the decisions real people make in their lives – about how to interact with each other, how to act as members of groups, how to live respectfully even when conflict seems inevitable. Ecological feminist ethical theory, which is born out of the difficulty of solving real, complex, ethical problems, as well as frustration with the inadequacies of traditional ethical theories, must maintain its connection to real ethical dilemmas and those who must solve them, while grappling with the abstract concepts and questions that inevitably arise from such problem-solving.

Both environmental and feminist ethics illustrate the importance of the dialogue between ethical theory and applied ethics because both feminist and ecological perspectives have found traditional ethical theory severely lacking. Most traditional ethical theory gives us no way adequately to discuss and evaluate issues of gender and cross-species interaction because it does not even recognize the particular ethical relevance of women and nonhuman nature. Feminist philosophers were the first to discuss the extent to which traditional male ethical theorists devalue women as a group and to notice that the writings of those theorists provide very little guidance concerning the kinds of ethical problems typically faced by women. Attempts to create ethics that are more relevant to women, to include women's heretofore ignored voices in ethical theory, and to respond to other feminist critiques of traditional ethics has led to a veritable revolution in ethics. Aldo Leopold recognized that traditional Western ethical systems are inadequate when the problems at hand include nonhuman entities and that to acknowledge the inherent moral value of natural entities is to expand the range of ethical thought (Leopold 1966). Like feminist philosopher Kathryn Pyne Addelson, he too wrote of 'moral revolution' (Addelson 1991).

Feminist and environmental ethics also press us to question the very nature and relevance of ethical inquiry. Though ecological feminist theory is not a simple hybrid of feminist and environmental philosophies, I argued earlier that ecological feminist ethics incorporate the important insights, analyses, and innovations of both feminist and environmental ethics. These analyses include highlighting the faults of traditional ethical thought, but also, more importantly, identifying tremendous ethical and metaethical questions about who makes ethical decisions, where values and principles originate, and to whom or what they refer – questions appreciable most dramatically when we are ethical agents, not theorists.

AMONG THEORIES AND ACTIVISMS

Arguably the best way for ecological feminist ethics to maintain a position that transcends a dualistic understanding of theoretical and applied ethics, or theory and practice, is by strengthening its ties to various forms of ecological feminist activism and explicitly mapping out potential activist agendas and strategies. Stephanie Lahar argues that close links between theory and political activism are necessary for ecological feminism's vitality. She recommends the following examples:

146

[Ecological feminism's] criticisms must continue to be acted upon by the expression of resistance through direct action on life-threatening issues (militarism, violence against women, the nuclear industry, pollutions and toxins, environmental destruction) . . . To fulfill a reconstructive potential, a social philosophy must extend a social critique and utopian vision into imperatives for action . . . for example, community forums on social or environmental issues and those at intersections such as biotechnology; state legislation supporting the civil rights and safety of groups that historically have had little political power; the reallocation of private and public resources and funds to socially responsible uses; alternative housing and land-use arrangements, and local alternative economic systems.

(1991: 35)

Emphasizing the extent to which theory-making is thoughtful practice also entails deconstructing the privileges associated with theorizing. Possessors of those privileges have a responsibility to open up dialogues among various kinds of ecological feminist practices, making explicit both the practical potentials of theory and the theoretical value of activism without exaggerating the importance of theoretical skills or talents. As Susan Bickford writes,

The very idea of democratic participation rests on the claim that all people possess, or are capable of developing through engagement, the skills or knowledge necessary for political deliberation and decision-making. The thoughtfulness of citizens (be they lawyers, food servers, computer programmers) is what is needed for engaging in political deliberation, strategizing, and action.[1] The knowledge that a theorist has and the skills she possesses as theorist do not make her a better citizen; only practice does that. Neither does the theorist's knowledge give her a better sense of what the end of political deliberation should be. What the theorist (qua theorist) can hope to provide is a better understanding of the nature and extent of political problems, the nature of the context in which they arise, and possible long-range implications of different courses of action.

(1993: 112)

Of course, ecological feminist philosophers and theorists can participate in activist projects not only as community members, but also as skilled arguers and analysts. Philosophical training is a useful tool in a movement that

---

1 Those of us who are citizens, or who take citizenship for granted, must remember that one need not be a citizen to be a meaningful participant in the intellectual, economic and cultural life of a society.

depends on deconstructive rhetoric, persuasion, fleshing out the implications of policies, and envisioning alternative paradigms. Ecological feminist theorists should use these skills not only in the creation of articles, books, and lectures, but also in helping to make the more hand-dirtying steps toward change.

If ecological feminist theory is to meet both feminist and pragmatist epistemological agendas, as theory that begins with and addresses experience, it must be informed by practice. The reversal of Dewey's emphasis on the practical relevance of theory requires that lectures, books, and articles, articulate knowledge and data that come from participation in activist projects. Theorists interested in creating ecological feminist philosophies must allow a variety of forms of experience and insight to inform our theories. We may consider our theoretical projects as more collaborative efforts, and include our practical knowledge in our accounts and analyses. An incorporation of our own narratives can continue to enrich ecological feminist ethical theory by emphasizing the ties between ethical decision-making, abstract ethical concepts, and personal experience. Given that the problems ethical agents now face seem to transcend greatly those considered by our historical predecessors in both scope and urgency, it seems only right that the perspectives from which we come to address our problems are ambitious, broad-based, and bold.

ECOLOGICAL FEMINIST ACTIVISMS

As is the case with most political movements, the possibilities for ecological feminist activism are nearly limitless. Individuals make personal choices in light of their ecological feminist politics, and may consider their recycling, their vegetarianism, their work against sexual assault, their anti-racist work, their teaching, or their protests against toxic dumping to be part of their ecological feminist activism. In so far as ecological feminism influences personal choice it is a contributor to social, ecological change. But ecological feminists also organize together to identify and work against interlocking systems of oppression that are harmful to women, people of color, the poor, the environment, and animals. If ecological feminist analyses and agendas are to have a wide-scale effect on contemporary understandings of the mechanisms and causes of oppression, and the interrelatedness of various social and environmental issues, these agendas must be presented and pursued in ways that make these connections clear. If ecological feminism is to have a prominent place in contemporary global politics and significantly affect social and political decisions, ecological feminist activism must be identifiable, powerful, and complex. Hence I am calling for a multifaceted, decentered, loud, empowering ecological feminist activist movement. Though I do not know, nor would I want to dictate, the profile of such a movement, I believe helpful historical and contemporary models of such

148

movements exist. The activities of the now-defunct ACT-UP (AIDS Coalition To Unleash Power) and the Lesbian Avengers, two direct-action political groups based in the United States, offer interesting models of activist movements that explicitly address the existence of interlocking systems of oppression and which have been effective in educating, annoying, or recruiting target audiences (as appropriate).

Both ACT-UP and the Lesbian Avengers effectively locate themselves at the intersections among various forms of oppression. This is accomplished through self-representation as well as political posturing. For example, an ACT-UP poster proclaiming 'Kissing Doesn't Kill – Greed and Indifference Do,' pictured three biracial kissing couples: one lesbian, one gay, and one heterosexual. As these images confronted racism and homophobia while celebrating love and sexuality, the slogan locates contemporary racism and homophobia in the United States in the context of corporate, capitalist greed, and social and political attempts to keep lesbians, the poor, and gay men invisible. The text also names the fact that these interlocking forces and silences have resulted in death. It is impossible to characterize this widely-disseminated piece of political art as about just one issue; the basic message is that racism, greed, and homophobia are intrinsically related in contemporary, capitalist America.

Likewise, the work of the Lesbian Avengers, though far less slick and widely disseminated than that of ACT-UP, evidences the complexity of its analysis of the causes of lesbian invisibility (including homophobia, misogyny, class oppression, housing and health issues, and patriarchal fear of the radical potential of lesbian existence). Theater, humor, deconstructions and transgressions of gender and sexuality, and methodologies that are decidedly 'in your face' contribute to the effective destabilization of the notion of single-issue politics. Activist approaches grounded in multiplicity question not only their obvious targets, but also standard notions of activism and political movement. The Lesbian Avengers emphasizes that it is a 'direct-action, activist group . . . for women who want to be involved in activism, work in community, be creative, do shit-work, take responsibility on a regular basis, have their minds blown, change their opinions and share organizing skills' (Lesbian Avengers 1993).

It is no simple task to organize multidimensional political direct-action groups or events. In fact, complex political analyses and agendas are more likely than single-issue campaigns to spark conflict and disagreement. The activist model put forward by the Lesbian Avengers is particularly interesting in this regard, because although the group's overarching priority is directly to confront lesbian invisibility, it feels its abstract goals are best met by prioritizing action. In creating our own activist and political traditions, ecological feminists would be wise to remember the many lessons about political strategizing and organizing learned through histories of feminist movements, including points of interest ranging from methods of conflict resolution (or avoidance!) and fundraising to spray-painting and wheat-pasting techniques. As Bickford sums up:

> For feminists, it is the relation to practice (to women's lives and our attempts to change the world) that gives theory meaning . . . theorists can self-consciously counter their role as 'privileged interpreters of society' by critiquing the 'power of experts' . . . Theorists do have access to diffuse social, and specific institutional, resources . . . We have the responsibility to use those resources in the service of what we say we believe (to paraphrase Audre Lorde) and in collaboration with those with whom we both claim and are trying to create solidarity.
>
> (1993: 113)

Ultimately, it is feminist insight that motivates ecological feminism, and demands meaningful action.

ON SEXUALITY

In discussing provocative examples of multidimensional activisms, I give prominence to lesbian and gay activism for several reasons. Probably most significant is the fact that this is the sphere of activism in which I have most thoroughly invested my own personal and political energies in the last several years. Also, the complex nexus of creativity, urgency, celebration and righteousness evident in lesbian, gay, and queer activism in the US and elsewhere might be inspiring and instructive to ecological feminist activists, regardless of their sexualities. Finally, it is worth making connections between movements for sexual freedom and respect, and movements promoting the flourishing of women and nonhuman life, because both sorts of movements (despite the incredible variety within each) raise deep questions about who we are, as humans, as communities, as dependent, and as complex, *embodied* selves.

Within any human activity are embedded assumptions about nature and about what it means to be human, social, encultured, embodied, contingent, matter. As Western conceptions of humans and of cultural life are founded on beliefs that the human is somehow separate from and superior to nature, we can trace ways that the devaluation of the nonhuman realm is enacted in human social practices and institutions. We can also notice the complexity of responses to the complicated reversals and contradictions that keep the shifting nature/culture divide in place. Sexuality is particularly interesting in this regard, as it is a realm of interaction that is unavoidably bodily, and the body is so strongly associated with nature. Like nature, sex is characterized as dirty, instinctual, random, uncontrolled, and mysterious. At the same time, sexuality is unmistakably cultural. It is the space in which gender is reified, where parts or notions of human bodies interweave with their cultural and political significations, where uniquely human or human-defined characteristics and emotions, like romantic love, are enacted. Sexuality is an incredibly stylized, highly culturally-defined realm of human activity. So sexuality is considered both very natural, and very unnatural, a 'particular instance of semiosis – the more general process joining subjectivity to social signification and material reality,' and defining its placement in, and over, nature (De Lauretis 1994: xix). Hence, an analysis of sexuality is likely to provide a fruitful story about instances of and responses to constructions of nature and culture and their discursive associates. It is surprising that environmental philosophers have paid so little attention to this rich, dangerous terrain.

WORKS CITED AND OF RELATED INTEREST

Ackrill, J. L. (1975) *Aristotle on Eudaimonia*, London: Oxford University Press.

Adams, Carol J. (ed.) (1993) *Ecofeminism and the Sacred*, New York: Continuum Press.

Adams, Carol J. (1991) 'Ecofeminism and the Eating of Animals,' *Hypatia* 6(1): 125–145.

Adams, Carol J. (1990) *The Sexual Politics of Meat: A Feminist-Vegetarian Critical Theory*, New York: Continuum Press.

Adams, Carol J. and Karen J. Warren (1991) 'Feminism and the Environment: A Selected Bibliography,' *American Philosophical Association Newsletter on Feminism and Philosophy* 90(3): 148–157.

Addelson, Kathryn Pyne (1991) *Impure Thoughts: Essays on Philosophy, Feminism, and Ethics*, Philadephia: Temple University Press.

Adorno, Theodor and Max Horkheimer (1993) *The Dialectic of Enlightenment*, New York: Continuum Press.

Agarwal, Bina (1992) 'The Gender and Environment Debate: Lessons from India,' *Feminist Studies* 18(1): 119–158.

Alaimo, Stacy (1994) 'Cyborg and Ecofeminist Interventions: Challenges for an Environmental Feminism,' *Feminist Studies* 20(1): 133–152.

Alcoff, Linda (1988) 'Cultural Feminism Versus Post-Structuralism: The Identity Crisis in Feminist Theory,' *Signs* 13(31): 405–436.

Alcoff, Linda and Elizabeth Potter (1993) *Feminist Epistemologies*, New York: Routledge.

Allen, Jeffner (1986) *Lesbian Philosophy: Explorations*, Palo Alto, California: Institute for Lesbian Studies.

Allen, Paula Gunn (1991) 'Kopis'taya (A Gathering of Spirits),' in Lorraine Anderson (ed.) *Sisters of the Earth: Women's Prose and Poetry about Nature*, New York: Vintage Books.

Allen, Paula Gunn (1990) 'The Woman I Love is a Planet; The Planet I Love is a Tree,' in Irene Diamond and Gloria Feman Orenstein (eds) *Reweaving the World: The Emergence of Ecofeminism*, San Francisco: Sierra Club Books.

Allen, Paula Gunn (1986) *The Sacred Hoop: Recovering the Feminine in American Indian Tradition*, Boston: Beacon Press.

Allison, Dorothy (1994) *Skin: Talking about Sex, Class & Literature*, Ithaca, New York: Firebrand Books.

Anderson, Lorraine (ed.) (1991) *Sisters of the Earth: Women's Prose and Poetry about Nature*, New York: Vintage Books.

Annas, Julia (1993) *The Morality of Happiness*, New York: Oxford University Press.

Anscombe, G. E. M. (1958) 'Modern Moral Philosophy,' *Philosophy* 32(124): 1–19.

Antony, Louise M. and Charlotte Witt (eds) (1993) *A Mind of One's Own: Feminist Essays on Reason & Objectivity*, Boulder, Colorado: Westview Press.

Anzaldúa, Gloria (ed.) (1990) *Making Face, Making Soul/Haciendo Caras: Creative and Critical Perspectives by Women of Color*, San Francisco: Aunt Lute.

Anzaldúa, Gloria (1987) *Borderlands: the New Mestiza/La Frontera*, San Francisco: Spinsters/Aunt Lute.

Anzaldúa, Gloria (1983) 'O.K. Momma, Who the Hell Am I?: An Interview with Luisa Teish,' in Gloria Anzaldúa and Cherríe Moraga (eds) *This Bridge Called My Back: Writings by Radical Women of Color*, New York: Kitchen Table: Women of Color Press.

Anzaldúa, Gloria and Cherríe Moraga (eds) (1983) *This Bridge Called My Back: Writings by Radical Women of Color*, New York: Kitchen Table: Women of Color Press.

Arditti, Rita, Pat Brennan, and Steve Cavrak (eds) (1980) *Science and Liberation*, Boston: South End Press.

Aristotle (1980) *Nicomachean Ethics*, trans. W. D. Ross, New York: Oxford University Press.

Atwood, Margaret (1972) *Surfacing*, New York: Warner Books.

Bagby, Rachel L. (1990) 'Daughters of Growing Things,' in Irene Diamond and Gloria Feman Orenstein (eds) *Reweaving the World: The Emergence of Ecofeminism*, San Francisco: Sierra Club Books.

Baier, Annette (1994) *Moral Prejudices: Essays on Ethics*, Cambridge, Massachusetts: Harvard University Press.

Baier, Annette (1991) 'Hume, The Women's Moral Theorist?,' in Claudia Card (ed.) *Feminist Ethics*, Lawrence, Kansas: University of Kansas Press.

Baier, Annette (1985) *Postures of the Mind: Essays on Mind and Morals*, Minneapolis: University of Minnesota Press.

Bar-On, Bat Ami (1991) 'Why Terrorism is Morally Problematic,' in Claudia Card (ed.) *Feminist Ethics*, Lawrence, Kansas: University of Kansas Press.

Bass, Ellen (1982) 'Our Stunning Harvest,' in Pam McAllister (ed.) *Reweaving the Web of Life*, Philadelphia: New Society Publishers.

Beauvoir, Simone de (1989) *The Second Sex*, trans. H. M. Parshley, New York: Vintage Books.

Benhabib, Seyla (1992) *Situating the Self: Gender, Community, and Postmodernism in Contemporary Ethics*, New York: Routledge.

Benhabib, Seyla, Judith Butler, Drucilla Cornell and Nancy Fraser (eds) (1995) *Feminist Contentions: A Philosophical Exchange*, New York: Routledge.

Bentham, Jeremy (1844) *Benthamiana, or Selected Extracts from the Works of Jeremy Bentham*, John Hill Burton (ed.), Philadelphia: Lea and Blanchard.

Berland, Jody and Jennifer Daryl Slack (eds) (1994) 'Introduction,' *Cultural Studies* 8(1): 1–4.

Bickford, Susan (1993) 'Why We Listen to Lunatics: Antifoundational Theories and Feminist Politics,' *Hypatia* 8(2): 104–123.

Biehl, Janet (1991) *Rethinking Ecofeminist Politics*, Boston: South End Press.

Black, Max (1962) *Models and Metaphors*, Ithaca, New York: Cornell University Press.

Blasius, Mark (1994) *Gay and Lesbian Politics: Sexuality and the Emergence of a New Ethic*, Philadelphia: Temple University Press.

Bonanno, Alessandro, Lawrence Busch, William Friedland, Lourdes Gouveia and Enzio Mingione (eds) (1994) *From Columbus to ConAgra: The Globalization of Agriculture and Food*, Lawrence, Kansas: University of Kansas Press.

Bookchin, Murray (1991) *The Ecology of Freedom: The Emergence and Dissolution of Hierarchy*, New York: Black Rose Books.

Bookchin, Murray (1990a) *The Philosophy of Social Ecology: Essays on Dialectical Naturalism*, New York: Black Rose Books.

Bookchin, Murray (1990b) *Remaking Society*, Boston: South End Press.

Bookchin, Murray (1980) *Toward an Ecological Society*, Montreal: Black Rose Books.

Bradford, George (1989) *How Deep is Deep Ecology?*, Ojai, California: Times Change Press.

Braidotti, Rosi, Ewa Charkiewicz, Sabine Hävscher and Saskia Wieringa (1994) *Women, the Environment and Sustainable Development*, Atlantic Highlands, New Jersey: Zed Books.

Browne, Susan E., Debra Connors, and Nanci Stern (eds) (1985) *With the Power of Each Breath: A Disabled Women's Anthology*, San Francisco: Cleis Press.

Bryant, Bunyan (ed.) (1995) *Environmental Justice: Issues, Policies, and Solutions*, Washington, D.C.: Island Press.

Caldecott, Leonie and Stephanie LeLand (eds) (1983) *Reclaim the Earth*, London: The Women's Press.

Callicott, J. Baird (1994) *Earth's Insights: A Survey of Ecological Ethics from the Mediterranean Basin to the Australian Outback*, Berkeley: University of California Press.

Callicott, J. Baird (1989) *In Defense of the Land Ethic: Essays in Environmental Philosophy*, Albany: State University of New York Press.

Callicott, J. Baird (1986) 'On the Intrinsic Value of Nonhuman Species,' in B. G. Norton (ed.) *The Preservation of Species: The Value of Biological Diversity*, Princeton: Princeton University Press.

Cannon, Katie G. (1988) *Black Womanist Ethics*, Atlanta: Scholars Press.

Capra, Fritjof, Charlene Spretnak, and Rudiger Lutz (1984) *Green Politics*, New York: Dutton.

Card, Claudia (1996) *The Natural Lottery: Character and Moral Luck*, Philadelphia: Temple University Press.

Card, Claudia (1995) *Lesbian Choices*, New York: Columbia University Press.

Card, Claudia (ed.) (1994) *Adventures in Lesbian Philosophy*, Bloomington: Indiana University Press.

Card, Claudia (ed.) (1991) *Feminist Ethics*, Lawrence, Kansas: University of Kansas Press.

Card, Claudia (1990) 'Gender and Moral Luck,' in Owen Flanagan and Amelie Oksenberg Rorty (eds) *Identity, Character and Morality: Essays in Moral Psychology*, Cambridge, Massachusetts: MIT Press.

Carson, Rachel (1962) *Silent Spring*, Boston: Houghton Mifflin.

Carter, Alan (1993) 'Towards a Green Political Theory,' in Andrew Dobson and Paul Lucardie (eds) *The Politics of Nature: Explorations in Green Political Theory*, New York: Routledge.

Chase, Steve (ed.) (1991) *Defending the Earth: A Dialogue Between Murray Bookchin and Dave Foreman*, Boston: South End Press.

Cheney, Jim (1987) 'Ecofeminism and Deep Ecology,' *Environmental Ethics* 9(2): 115–145.

Childers, Mary and bell hooks (1990) 'A Conversation about Race and Class,' in Marianne Hirsch and Evelyn Fox Keller (eds) *Conflicts in Feminism*, New York: Routledge.

Chodorow, Nancy (1978) *The Reproduction of Mothering: Psychoanalysis and the Sociology of Gender*, Berkeley: University of California Press.

Code, Lorraine (1991) *What Can She Know?: Feminist Theory and the Construction of Knowledge*, Ithaca, New York: Cornell University Press.

Collard, Andree with Joyce Contrucci (1988) *Rape of the Wild: Man's Violence Against Animals and the Earth*, Bloomington, Indiana: Indiana University Press.

Collins, Patricia Hill (1991) *Black Feminist Thought: Knowledge, Consciousness, and the Politics of Empowerment*, New York: Routledge.

Commoner Barry (1971) *The Closing Circle: Nature, Man, and Technology*, New York: Knopf.

Cornell, Drucilla (1995) 'What is Ethical Feminism,' in Seyla Benhabib, Judith Butler, Drucilla Cornell, Nancy Fraser (eds) *Feminist Contentions: A Philosophical Exchange*, New York: Routledge.

Corrigan, Theresa and Stephanie Hoppe (1990) *And A Deer's Ear, Eagle's Song and Bear's Grace*, San Francisco: Cleis Press.

Corrigan, Theresa and Stephanie Hoppe (1989) *With a Fly's Eye, Whale's Wit, and Woman's Heart: Animals and Women*, San Francisco: Cleis Press.

Cronon, William (ed.) (1995) *Uncommon Ground: Rethinking the Human Place in Nature*, New York: W. W. Norton and Company.

Cronon, William (1991) *Nature's Metropolis: Chicago and the Great West*, New York: W. W. Norton and Company.

Cuomo, Chris J. (1997) 'Why War is Not Merely an Event,' *Hypatia* 11(4): 30–45.

Cuomo, Chris J. (1996) 'Toward Thoughtful Ecofeminist Activism,' in Karen J. Warren (ed.) *Ecological Feminist Philosophies*, Bloomington, Indiana: Indiana University Press.

Cuomo, Chris J. (1994) 'Ecofeminism, Deep Ecology, and Human Population,' in Karen J. Warren (ed.) *Ecological Feminism*, New York: Routledge.

Cuomo, Christine (Chris) J. (1992) 'Unravelling the Problems in Ecofeminism,' *Environmental Ethics* 15(4): 351–363.

Cuomo, Chris J. and Lori Gruen (1997) 'On Puppies and Pussies: Animals, Intimacy, and Moral Distance,' in Bat Ami Bar-On and Anne Ferguson (eds) *Daring to be Good: Feminist Ethico-Politics*, New York: Routledge.

Daly, Mary (1992) *Outercourse: The Be-Dazzling Voyage*, San Francisco: Harper Collins.

Daly, Mary (1978) *Gyn/Ecology: The Metaethics of Radical Feminism*, Boston: Beacon Press.

davenport, doris (1983) 'The Pathology of Racism: A Conversation with Third World Wimmin,' in Gloria Anzaldúa and Cherríe Moraga (eds) *This Bridge Called My Back: Writings by Radical Women of Color*, Latham, New York: Kitchen Table: Women of Color Press.

Davies, Miranda (1983) *Third World-Second Sex: Women's Struggles and National Liberation*, London: Zed Books.

Davion, Victoria (1994) 'Is Ecofeminism Feminist?,' in Karen J. Warren (ed.) *Ecological Feminism*, New York: Routledge.

Davion, Victoria (1991) 'Integrity and Radical Change,' in Claudia Card (ed.) *Feminist Ethics*, Lawrence, Kansas: University of Kansas Press.

Davis, Angela Y. (1983) *Women, Race and Class,* New York: Vintage Books.

d'Eaubonne, Françoise (1981) 'Feminism or Death,' in Elaine Marks and Isabelle de Courtivron (eds) *New French Feminisms*, New York: Schocken Books.

Delaney, C. F. (1994) *The Liberalism–Communitarianism Debate: Liberty and Community Values*, Lanham, Maryland: Rowman and Littlefield.

De Lauretis, Teresa (1994) *The Practice of Love: Lesbian Sexuality and Perverse Desire*, Bloomington: Indiana University Press.

De Lauretis, Teresa (1990) 'Upping the Anti (sic) in Feminist Theory,' in Marianne Hirsch and Evelyn Fox Keller (eds) *Conflicts in Feminism*, New York: Routledge.

De Lauretis, Teresa (1989) 'The Essence of the Triangle or, Taking the Risk of Essentialism Seriously: Feminist Theory in Italy, the U.S., and Britain,' *Differences, A Journal of Feminist Cultural Studies* 1(2): 3–37.

Devall, Bill and George Sessions (1985) *Deep Ecology: Living as if Nature Mattered*, Salt Lake City: Peregrine Smith Books.

De Waal, Frans (1989) *Peacemaking Among Primates*, Cambridge, Massachusetts: Harvard University Press.

155

Dewey, John (1929) *The Quest for Certainty*, New York: Minton, Balch and Company.

Diamond, Irene (1994) *Fertile Ground: Women, Earth, and the Limits of Control*, Boston: Beacon Press.

Diamond, Irene and Gloria Feman Orenstein (eds) (1990) *Reweaving the World: The Emergence of Ecofeminism*, San Francisco: Sierra Club Books.

Dickens, Peter (1992) *Society and Nature: Towards a Green Social Theory*, Philadelphia: Temple University Press.

Dillon, Robin (1992) 'Toward a Feminist Conception of Self-Respect,' *Hypatia* 7(1): 52–69.

Dinnerstein, Dorothy (1989) 'Survival on Earth: The Meaning of Feminism,' in Judith Plant (ed.) *Healing the Wounds: The Promise of Ecofeminism*, Philadelphia: New Society Publishers.

Dinnerstein, Dorothy (1977) *The Mermaid and the Minotaur: Sexual Arrangements and Human Malaise*, New York: Harper and Row.

Dobson, Andrew and Paul Lucardie (eds) (1993) *The Politics of Nature: Explorations in Green Political Theory*, London: Routledge.

Doubiago, Sharon (1989) 'Mama Coyote Talks to the Boys,' in Judith Plant (ed.) *Healing the Wounds: The Promise of Ecofeminism*, Philadephia: New Society Publishers.

D'Souza, Corinne Kumar (1989) 'A New Movement, A New Hope: East Wind, West Wind, and the Wind from the South,' in Judith Plant (ed.) *Healing the Wounds: The Promise of Ecofeminism*, Philadelphia: New Society Publishers.

Echols, Alice (1989) *Daring to Be Bad: Radical Feminism in America 1967–1975*, Minneapolis: University of Minnesota Press.

Eisler, Riane (1990) 'The Gaia Tradition and the Partnership Future,' in Irene Diamond and Gloria Feman Orenstein (eds) *Reweaving the World: The Emergence of Ecofeminism*, San Francisco: Sierra Club Books.

Faderman, Lillian (1991) *Odd Girls and Twilight Lovers: A History of Lesbian Life in Twentieth-Century America*, New York: Penguin.

Faderman, Lillian (1981) *Surpassing the Love of Men: Romantic Friendship and Love Between Women from the Renaissance to the Present*, New York: Morrow.

Ferry, Luc (1995) *The New Ecological Order*, trans. Carol Volk, Chicago: University of Chicago Press.

Foreman, Dave (1993) 'Putting the Earth First,' in Susan J. Armstrong and Richard G. Botzler (eds) *Environmental Ethics: Divergence and Convergence*, New York: McGraw-Hill.

Fox, Warwick (1989) 'The Deep Ecology–Ecofeminism Debate and its Parallels,' *Environmental Ethics* 11(2): 5–25.

Freeman, Martha (ed.) (1995) *Always, Rachel: The Letters of Rachel Carson and Dorothy Freeman, 1952–1964*, Boston: Beacon Press.

Friedman, Marilyn (1993) *What are Friends For?: Feminist Perspectives on Personal Relationships and Moral Theory*, Ithaca, New York: Cornell University Press.

Friedman, Marilyn (1991) 'The Social Self and the Partiality Debates,' in Claudia Card (ed.) *Feminist Ethics*, Lawrence, Kansas: University of Kansas Press.

Friedman, Marilyn (1989) 'Feminism and Modern Friendship: Dislocating the Community,' *Ethics* 99: 275–290.

Friedman, Marilyn and Penny A. Weiss (eds) (1995) *Feminism and Community*, Philadephia: Temple University Press.

Frye, Marilyn (unpublished) 'Ethnocentrism/Essentialism: The Failure of the Ontological Cure.'

Frye, Marilyn (1992) *Willful Virgin*, Trumansburg, New York: Crossing Press.

Frye, Marilyn (1991) 'A Response to *Lesbian Ethics*: Why *Ethics*?,' in Claudia Card (ed.) *Feminist Ethics*, Lawrence, Kansas: University of Kansas Press.

Frye, Marilyn (1983) *The Politics of Reality: Essays in Feminist Theory*, Trumansburg, New York: Crossing Press.

Fuss, Diana (1989) *Essentially Speaking: Feminism, Nature and Difference*, New York: Routledge.

Gaard, Greta (ed.) (1993) *Ecofeminism: Women, Animals, Nature*, Philadelphia: Temple University Press.

Gare, Arran E. (1995) *Postmodernism and the Environmental Crisis*, New York: Routledge.

Gates, Henry Louis, Jr. (1994) *Colored People: A Memoir*, New York: Alfred A. Knopf.

Gearhart, Sally Miller (1984) *Wanderground*, Boston: Alyson Publications.

Gilligan, Carol (1982) *In a Different Voice: Psychological Theory and Women's Development*, Cambridge, Massachusetts: Harvard University Press.

Gilligan, Carol, J. V. Ward, and J. McLean Taylor with B. Baridge (eds) (1988) *Mapping the Moral Domain: A Contribution of Women's Thinking to Psychological Theory and Education*, Cambridge, Massachusetts: Harvard University Press.

Goldberg, David Theo (1993) *Racist Culture: Philosophy and the Politics of Meaning*, Cambridge, Massachusetts: Blackwell Publishers.

Goodpaster, Kenneth E. (1978) 'On Being Morally Considerable,' *The Journal of Philosophy* 75(6): 308–325.

Gottlieb, Robert (1993) *Forcing the Spring: The Transformation of the American Environmental Movement*, Washington, D.C.: Island Press.

Gray, Chris Hables (ed.) (1995) *The Cyborg Handbook*, New York: Routledge.

Gray, Elizabeth Dodson (1981) *Green Paradise Lost*, Wellesley, Massachusetts: Roundtable Press.

Griffin, Susan (1989) 'Split Culture,' in Judith Plant (ed.) *Healing the Wounds: The Promise of Ecofeminism*, Philadelphia: New Society Publishers.

Griffin, Susan (1978) *Woman and Nature: The Roaring Inside Her*, New York: Harper and Row.

Grimshaw, Jean (1986) *Philosophy and Feminist Thinking*, Minneapolis: University of Minnesota Press.

Gruen, Lori (unpublished) 'Has Intrinsic Value Led Environmentalists Astray?'

Gruen, Lori (1994) 'Toward an Ecofeminist Moral Epistemology,' in Karen Warren (ed.) *Ecological Feminism*, New York: Routledge.

Gruen, Lori (1993) 'Dismantling Oppression: An Analysis of the Connection Between Women and Animals,' in Greta Gaard (ed.) *Ecofeminism: Women, Animals, Nature*, Philadelphia: Temple University Press.

Haraway, Donna J. (1991a) *Simians, Cyborgs, and Women: The Reinvention of Nature*, New York: Routledge Press.

Haraway, Donna J. (1991b) 'The Actors are Cyborg, Nature is Coyote, and the Geography is Elsewhere: Postscript to Cyborgs at Large,' in Constance Penley and Andrew Ross (eds) *Technoculture*, Minneapolis: University of Minnesota Press.

Haraway, Donna J. (1989) *Primate Visions: Gender, Race, and Nature in the World of Modern Science*, New York: Routledge.

Harding, Sandra (1993a) *The 'Racial' Economy of Science: Toward a Democratic Future*, Bloomington, Indiana: Indiana University Press.

Harding, Sandra (1993b) 'Rethinking Standpoint Epistemology: What is "Strong Objectivity?",' in Linda Alcoff and Elizabeth Potter (eds) *Feminist Epistemologies*, New York: Routledge.

Harding, Sandra (1991) *Whose Science? Whose Knowledge?: Thinking from Women's Lives*, Ithaca, New York: Cornell University Press.

Harding, Sandra (1986) *The Science Question in Feminism*, Ithaca, New York: Cornell University Press.

Harding, Sandra and Merrill Hintikka (eds) (1983) *Discovering Reality: Feminist Perspectives on Epistemology, Metaphysics, Methodology and the Philosophy of Science*, Dordrecht: Reidel Publishing Company.

Harjo, Joy (1991) 'Fire,' in Lorraine Anderson (ed.) *Sisters of the Earth: Women's Prose and Poetry about Nature*, New York: Vintage Books.

Hawkins, Ronnie Zoe (1991) 'Reproductive Choices: The Ecological Dimension,' *American Philosophical Association Newsletter on Feminism and Philosophy* 91(1): 66–73.

Held, Virginia (1993) *Feminist Morality: Transforming Culture, Society, and Politics*, Chicago: University of Chicago Press.

Heldke, Lisa (unpublished) 'Toward a Bread and Butter Pragmatism: The Significance of Practical Activity in the Philosophy of John Dewey.'

Hesse, Mary (1966) *Models and Analogies in Science*, Notre Dame, Indiana: University of Notre Dame Press.

Hoagland, Sarah Lucia (1991) 'Some Thoughts about "Caring," ' in Claudia Card (ed.) *Feminist Ethics*, Lawrence, Kansas: University of Kansas Press.

Hoagland, Sarah Lucia (1988) *Lesbian Ethics: Toward New Value*, Palo Alto, California: Institute for Lesbian Studies.

hooks, bell (1994) *Teaching to Transgress: Education as the Practice of Freedom*, New York: Routledge.

Hume, David (1978) *A Treatise of Human Nature*, L. A. Selby-Bigge and P. H. Nidditch (eds), New York: Clarendon Press.

Hume, David (1975) *Enquiries*, L. A. Selby-Bigge and P. H. Nidditch (eds), New York: Clarendon Press.

Hynes, H. Patricia (1989) *The Recurring Silent Spring*, New York: Permagon.

Irigaray, Luce (1989) *Thinking the Difference: For a Peaceful Revolution*, New York: Routledge.

Jaggar, Alison M. (1983) *Feminist Politics and Human Nature*, Totowa, New Jersey: Rowman and Allanheld.

James, Stanlie M. and Abena P. A. Busia (eds) (1993) *Theorizing Black Feminisms: The Visionary Pragmatism of Black Women*, New York: Routledge.

Jasanoff, Sheila, Gerald E. Markle, James C. Peterson and Trevor Pinch (eds) (1995) *Handbook of Science and Technology Studies*, Thousand Oaks, California: Sage Publications.

Johnson, Rebecca (1993) 'New Moon Over Roxbury, Reflections on Urban Life and the Land,' in Carol Adams (ed.) *Ecofeminism and the Sacred*, New York: Continuum Press.

Jones, Karen (1996) 'Trust as an Affective Attitude,' *Ethics* 107: 4–25.

Jordan, June (1983) 'From Sea to Shining Sea,' in Barbara Smith (ed.) *Home Girls: A Black Feminist Anthology*, New York: Kitchen Table: Women of Color Press.

Kant, Immanuel (1960) *Observations on the Feeling of the Beautiful and the Sublime*, trans. John T. Goldthwait, Berkeley: University of California Press.

Katherine, Amber (1998) 'A Too-Early Morning: A Reading of Audre Lorde's Open Letter to Mary Daly,' in Marilyn Frye and Sarah Hoagland (eds) *Feminist Interpretations of Mary Daly*, Philadelphia: Pennsylvania State University Press.

Kaufman-Osborn, Timothy V. (1993) 'Teasing Feminist Sense from Experience,' *Hypatia* 8(2): 124–144.

Keller, Evelyn Fox (1992) *Secrets of Life, Secrets of Death: Essays on Language, Gender, and Science*, New York: Routledge.

Keller, Evelyn Fox (1983) *A Feeling for the Organism: The Life and Work of Barbara McClintock*, San Francisco: W. H. Freeman.

Kelly, Petra (1994) *Thinking Green!: Essays on Environmentalism, Feminism, and Nonviolence*, Berkeley: Parallax Press.

Kheel, Marti (1989) 'From Healing Herbs to Deadly Drugs: Western Medicine's War Against the Natural World,' in Judith Plant (ed.) *Healing the Wounds: The Promise of Ecofeminism*, Philadelphia: New Society Publishers.

King, Ynestra (1990) 'Healing the Wounds: Feminism, Ecology, and the Nature/Culture Dualism,' in Irene Diamond and Gloria Feman Orenstein (eds) *Reweaving the World: The Emergence of Ecofeminism*, San Francisco: Sierra Club Books.

King, Ynestra (1989) 'The Ecology of Feminism and the Feminism of Ecology,' in Judith Plant (ed.) *Healing the Wounds: The Promise of Ecofeminism*, Philadelphia: New Society Publishers.

King, Ynestra (1981) 'Feminism and the Revolt of Nature,' in *Heresies #13: Feminism and Ecology* 4(1): 12–16.

Kittay, Eva Feder and Diana T. Meyers (eds) (1987) *Women and Moral Theory*, Savage, Maryland: Rowman and Littlefield.

Klepfisz, Irene and Melanie Kaye/Kantrowitz (1986) *The Tribe of Dina: A Jewish Women's Anthology*, Montpelier, Vermont: Sinister Wisdom Books.

Kymlicka, Will (1989) *Liberalism, Community, and Culture*, New York: Clarendon Press.

Laffoon, E. Anne (1994) 'The Rhetoric of Ecofeminism,' *The Maine Scholar* 7: 131–149.

Lahar, Stephanie (1993) 'Roots: Rejoining Natural and Social History,' in Greta Gaard (ed.) *Ecofeminism: Women, Animals, Nature*, Philadelphia: Temple University Press.

Lahar, Stephanie (1991) 'Ecofeminist Theory and Grassroots Politics,' *Hypatia* 6(1): 28–45.

Leonard, Ann (ed.) (1989) *Seeds: Supporting Women's Work in the Third World*, New York: The Feminist Press.

Leopold, Aldo (1966) *A Sand County Almanac*, New York: Ballantine Books.

Lesbian Avengers (1993) Organizing flier. For information on The Lesbian Avengers, contact: The Lesbian Avengers, c/o The Center, 208 W. 13th St., New York, N.Y. 10011.

Longino, Helen (1993) 'Subject, Power and Knowledge: Description and Prescription in Feminist Philosophies of Science,' in Linda Alcoff and Elizabeth Potter (eds) *Feminist Epistemologies*, New York: Routledge.

Lorde, Audre (1992) *Undersong: Chosen Poems, Old and New*, New York: Norton.

Lorde, Audre (1984) *Sister Outsider: Essays and Speeches*, Freedom, California: The Crossing Press.

Lugones, María (1994) 'Purity, Impurity, and Separation,' *Signs* 19(2): 458–479.

Lugones, María (1991) 'On the Logic of Pluralist Feminism,' in Claudia Card (ed.) *Feminist Ethics*, Lawrence, Kansas: University of Kansas Press.

Lugones, María (1990) 'Hablando cara a cara/Speaking Face to Face,' in Gloria Anzaldúa (ed.) *Making Face, Making Soul/Haciendo Caras: Creative and Critical Perspectives by Women of Color*, San Francisco: Aunt Lute.

Lugones, María (1987) 'Playfulness, "World"-Travelling, and Loving Perception,' *Hypatia* 2(2): 3–19.

McAllister, Pam (ed.) (1982) *Reweaving the Web of Life*, Philadelphia: New Society Publishers.

MacCormack, Carol and Marilyn Strathern (eds) (1980) *Nature, Culture, and Gender*, Cambridge: Cambridge University Press.

MacIntyre, Alasdair C. (1984) *After Virtue: A Study in Moral Theory*, Notre Dame, Indiana: University of Notre Dame Press.

Mackie, J. L. (1987) 'The Subjectivity of Values,' in George Sher (ed.) *Moral Philosophy: Selected Readings*, New York: Harcourt Brace Jovanovich.

Martin, Jane Roland (1993) 'Methodological Essentialism, False Difference and Other Dangerous Traps,' *Signs* 19(3): 630–657.

Masson, Jeffrey Moussaieff and Susan McCarthy (1995) *When Elephants Weep: The Emotional Lives of Animals*, New York: Dell Publishing.

Meadows, Donella H. and Dennis L. Meadows, Jørgen Randers, William W. Behrens III (1974) *The Limits to Growth*, New York: Signet.

Merchant, Carolyn (1990) 'Ecofeminism and Feminist Theory,' in Irene Diamond and Gloria Feman Orenstein (eds) *Reweaving the World: The Emergence of Ecofeminism*, San Francisco: Sierra Club Books.

Merchant, Carolyn (1980) *The Death of Nature: Women, Ecology, and the Scientific Revolution*, San Francisco: Harper and Row.

Metzger, Deena (1989) 'Invoking the Grove,' in Judith Plant (ed.) *Healing the Wounds: The Promise of Ecofeminism*, Philadelphia: New Society Publishers.

Meyers, Diana T. (1994) *Subjection & Subjectivity: Psychoanalytic Feminism & Moral Philosophy*, New York: Routledge.

Mies, Maria and Vandana Shiva (1993) *Ecofeminism*, Atlantic Highlands, New Jersey: Zed Books.

Mill, John Stuart (1974) *Utilitarianism and Other Writings*, New York: Meridian Books.

Moline, Jon N. (1986) 'Aldo Leopold and the Moral Community,' *Environmental Ethics* 8(3): 99–120.

Moody-Adams, Michelle (1991) 'Gender and the Complexity of Moral Voices,' in Claudia Card (ed.) *Feminist Ethics*, Lawrence, Kansas: University of Kansas Press.

Moore, Margaret (1993) *Foundations of Liberalism*, New York: Clarendon Press.

Moore, Robert B. (1985) *Racism in the English Language*, New York: Council on Interracial Books for Children.

Moutlon, Janice (1977) 'The Myth of the Neutral "Man," ' in Mary Vetterling-Braggin, Frederick A. Elliston and Jane English (eds) *Feminism and Philosophy*, Totowa, New Jersey: Littlefield, Adams.

Moya, Paula (1996) 'Postmodernism, "Realism," and the Politics of Identity: Cherríe Moraga and Chicana Feminism,' in Chandra Talpade Mohanty and M. Jacqui Alexander (eds) *Feminist Genealogies, Colonial Legacies, Democratic Futures*, New York: Routledge.

Muir, John (1954) *The Wilderness World of John Muir*, Edwin Way Teale (ed.) Boston: Houghton Mifflin.

Naess, Arne (1989) *Ecology, Community, and Lifestyle: Outline of an Eco-sophy*, trans. and ed. David Rothenberg, Cambridge: Cambridge University Press.

Naess, Arne (1986) 'The Deep Ecological Movement: Some Philosophical Aspects,' *Philosophical Inquiry* 8: 10–31.

Naess, Arne (1973) 'The Shallow and the Deep, Long-Range Ecology Movement: A Summary,' *Inquiry* 16(1): 95–100.

Naess, Arne, Pat Fleming, Joanna Macy and John Seed (1988) *Thinking Like a Mountain*, Santa Cruz: New Society Publishers.

Nash, Roderick F. (1990) *American Environmentalism: Readings in Conservation History*, New York: McGraw-Hill.

Nash, Roderick F. (1989) *The Rights of Nature: A History of Environmental Ethics*, Madison, Wisconsin: University of Wisconsin Press.

Naylor, Gloria (1989) *Mama Day*, New York: Vintage Contemporaries.

Nelson, Lin (1990) 'The Place of Women in Polluted Places,' in Irene Diamond and

Gloria Feman Orenstein (eds) *Reweaving the World: The Emergence of Eco-feminism*, San Francisco: Sierra Club Books.

Nelson, Lynn Hankinson (1993) 'A Question of Evidence,' *Hypatia* 8(2): 172–189.

Nelson, Lynn Hankinson (1990) *Who Knows: from Quine to a Feminist Empiricism*, Philadelphia: Temple University Press.

Nietzsche, Friedrich (1989) *On the Genealogy of Morals*, trans. Walter Kaufmann, New York: Vintage Books.

Noddings, Nel (1984) *Caring: A Feminine Approach to Ethics and Moral Education*, Berkeley: University of California Press.

Nussbaum, Martha C. (1990) *Love's Knowledge: Essays on Philosophy and Literature*, New York: Oxford University Press.

Nussbaum, Martha C. (1986) *The Fragility of Goodness: Luck and Ethics in Greek Tragedy and Philosophy*, New York: Cambridge University Press.

Nussbaum, Martha C. and Jonathan Glover (eds) (1995) *Women, Culture and Development: A Study of Human Capabilities*, New York: Clarendon Press.

Oliver, Mary (1992) *New and Selected Poems*, Boston: Beacon Press.

O'Loughlin, Ellen (1993) 'Questioning Sour Grapes: Ecofeminism and the United Farm Workers Grape Boycott,' in Greta Gaard (ed.) *Ecofeminism: Women, Animals, Nature*, Philadelphia: Temple University Press.

Ortner, Sherry B. (1974) 'Is Female to Male as Nature is to Culture?,' in Michelle Rosaldo and Louise Lamphere (eds) *Woman, Culture and Society*, Stanford: Stanford University Press.

Pearsall, Marilyn (ed.) (1986) *Women and Values: Readings in Recent Feminist Philosophy*, Belmont, California: Wadsworth Press.

Penley, Constance and Andrew Ross (1991) 'Cyborgs at Large: Interview with Donna Haraway,' in Constance Penley and Andrew Ross (eds) *Technoscience*, Minneapolis: University of Minnesota Press.

Phelan, Shane (1993) 'Intimate Distance: The Dislocation of Nature in Modernity,' in David Bennet and William Chaloupka (eds) *In the Nature of Things*, Minneapolis: University of Minnesota Press.

Phillips, Anne (1993) *Democracy and Difference*, University Park, Pennsylvania: The Pennsylvania State University Press.

Pierce, Christine and Donald VanDeVeer (1995) *People, Penguins, and Plastic Trees: Basic Issues in Environmental Ethics*, Belmont, California: Wadsworth Press.

Pinchot, Gifford (1990) 'The Birth of "Conservation,"' in Roderick Nash (ed.) *American Environmentalism: Readings in Conservation History*, New York: McGraw-Hill.

Plant, Judith (1990) 'Searching for Common Ground: Ecofeminism and Bio-regionalism,' in Irene Diamond and Gloria Feman Orenstein (eds) *Reweaving the World: The Emergence of Ecofeminism*, San Francisco: Sierra Club Books.

Plant, Judith (ed.) (1989) *Healing the Wounds: The Promise of Ecofeminism*, Philadelphia: New Society Publishers.

Plumwood, Val (1993) *Feminism and the Mastery of Nature*, New York: Routledge.

Quinby, Lee (1990) 'Ecofeminism and the Politics of Difference,' in Irene Diamond and Gloria Feman Orenstein (eds) *Reweaving the World: The Emergence of Ecofeminism*, San Francisco: Sierra Club Books.

Rawls, John (1971) *A Theory of Justice*, Cambridge, Massachusetts: Harvard University Press.

Raymond, Janice (1986) *A Passion for Friends: Toward a Philosophy of Female Affection*, Boston: Beacon Press.

Regan, Tom (ed.) (1984) *Earthbound: New Introductory Essays in Environmental Ethics*, Philadelphia, Temple University Press.

Regan, Tom (1983) *The Case for Animal Rights*, Berkeley: University of California Press.

Regan, Tom and Peter Singer (eds) (1976) *Animal Rights and Human Obligations*, Englewood Cliffs, New Jersey: Prentice-Hall.

Regon, Berneice Johnson (1983) 'Coalition Politics: Turning the Century,' in Barbara Smith (ed.) *Home Girls: A Black Feminist Anthology*, New York, Kitchen Table: Women of Color Press.

Rich, Adrienne (1986) 'Women and Honor: Some Notes on Lying,' in Marilyn Pearsall (ed.) *Women and Values: Readings in Recent Feminist Philosophy*, Belmont, California: Wadsworth Press.

Rich, Adrienne (1978) *The Dream of a Common Language: Poems, 1974–1977*, New York: Norton.

Rich, Adrienne (1976) *Of Woman Born: Motherhood as Experience and Institution*, New York: Norton.

Riggs, Marlon (1995) *Black Is – Black Ain't: A Personal Journey Through Black Identity* (videorecording), San Francisco: California Newsreel.

Riley, Shamara Shantu (1993) 'Ecology is A Sistah's Issue Too: The Politics of Emergent Afrocentric Womanism,' in Carol Adams (ed.) *Ecofeminism and the Sacred*, New York: Continuum Press.

Ritvo, Harriet (1987) *The Animal Estate: The English and Other Creatures in the Victorian Age*, Cambridge, Massachusetts: Harvard University Press.

Roach, Catherine (1991) 'Loving Your Mother: On the Woman–Nature Connection,' *Hypatia* 6(1): 46–59.

Rooney, Phyllis (1993) 'Feminist-Pragmatist Revisionings of Reason, Knowledge, and Philosophy,' *Hypatia* 8(2): 15–37.

Rothschild, Joan (1983) *Machina Ex Dea: Feminist Perspectives on Technology*, New York: Pergamon Press.

Ruddick, Sara (1989) *Maternal Thinking: Toward a Politics of Peace*, Boston: Beacon Press.

Ruether, Rosemary Radford (1975) *New Woman, New Earth: Sexist Ideologies and Human Liberation*, New York: Seabury Press.

Salleh, Ariel Kay (1993) 'The Ecofeminism/Deep Ecology Debate,' *Environmental Ethics* 14(3): 195–216.

Salleh, Ariel Kay (1984) 'Deeper than Deep Ecology: The Eco-Feminist Connection,' *Environmental Ethics* 6(1): 339–345.

Sandel, J. Michael (1982) *Liberalism and the Limits of Justice*, New York: Cambridge University Press.

Sartre, Jean-Paul (1987) 'Existentialism Is a Humanism,' in George Sher (ed.) *Moral Philosophy: Selected Readings*, New York: Harcourt Brace Jovanovich.

Scheman, Naomi (1993) *Engenderings: Constructions of Knowledge, Authority, and Privilege*, New York: Routledge.

Schumacher, E. F. (1973) *Small is Beautiful: Economics as if People Mattered*, New York: Harper & Row.

Scott, James C. (1990) *Domination and the Arts of Resistance: Hidden Transcripts*, New Haven: Yale University Press.

Scott, Joan (1990) 'Deconstructing Equality-Versus-Difference: Or, the Uses of Poststructuralist Theory for Feminism,' in Marianne Hirsch and Evelyn Fox Keller (eds) *Conflicts in Feminism*, New York: Routledge.

Scott, Joan W. (1989) 'Commentary: Cyborgian Socialists?' in Elizabeth Weed (ed.) *Coming to Terms: Feminism, Theory, Politics*, New York: Routledge.

Seager, Joni (1993) *Earth Follies: Coming to Feminist Terms with the Global Environmental Crisis*, New York: Routledge.

Seigfried, Charlene Haddock (guest ed.) (1993) *Hypatia: Special Issue on Feminism and Pragmatism* 8(2).

Sequoia, Anna with Animal Rights International (1990) *Sixty-Seven Ways to Save the Animals*, New York: HarperPerennial.

Shiva, Vandana (1994) *Close to Home: Women Reconnect Ecology, Health and Development Worldwide*, Philadelphia: New Society Publishers.

Shiva, Vandana (1988) *Staying Alive: Women, Ecology, and Development*, Atlantic Highlands, New Jersey: Zed Books.

Singer, Peter (1987) 'Animal Liberation or Animal Rights?,' *The Monist* 70(1).

Singer, Peter (1975) *Animal Liberation*, New York: New York Review Books.

Slack, Jennifer Daryl and Anne Whitt (1994) 'Communities, Environments and Cultural Studies,' *Cultural Studies* 8(1): 5.

Slicer, Deborah (1991) 'Your Daughter or Your Dog? A Feminist Assessment of the Animal Research Issue,' *Hypatia* 6(1): 108–124.

Smith, Barbara (ed.) (1983) *Home Girls: A Black Feminist Anthology*, New York: Kitchen Table: Women of Color Press.

Snitow, Ann (1990) 'A Gender Diary,' in Marianne Hirsch and Evelyn Fox Keller (eds) *Conflicts in Feminism*, New York: Routledge.

Sober, Elliot (1990) 'Let's Razor Ockham's Razor,' in Dudley Knowles (ed.) *Explanation and its Limits*, Cambridge: Cambridge University Press.

Spelman, Elizabeth V. (1988) *Inessential Woman: Problems of Exclusion in Feminist Thought*, Boston: Beacon Press.

Spiegel, Marjorie (1988) *The Dreaded Comparison: Human and Animal Slavery*, New York: Mirror Books.

Spretnak, Charlene (1991) *States of Grace: The Recovery of Meaning in the Postmodern Age*, New York: Harper Collins.

Spretnak, Charlene (1990) 'Ecofeminism: Our Roots and Flowering,' in Irene Diamond and Gloria Feman Orenstein (eds) *Reweaving the World: The Emergence of Ecofeminism*, San Francisco: Sierra Club Books.

Spretnak, Charlene (1989) 'Toward an Ecofeminist Spirituality,' in Judith Plant (ed.) *Healing the Wounds: The Promise of Ecofeminism*, Philadelphia: New Society Publishers.

Spretnak, Charlene (ed.) (1982) *The Politics of Women's Spirituality*, Garden City, New York: Anchor Press.

Stabile, Carol A. (1994) "A Garden Inclosed is My Sister": Ecofeminism and Eco-Valences,' *Cultural Studies* 8(1): 56–73.

Stack, Carol (1986) 'The Culture of Gender: Women and Men of Color,' *Signs* 11(2): 321–324.

Sterba, James P. (1995) *Earth Ethics: Environmental Ethics, Animal Rights, and Practical Applications*, Englewood Cliffs, New Jersey: Prentice-Hall.

Stoltenberg, John (1989) *Refusing to be a Man: Essays on Sex and Justice*, Portland, Oregon: Breitenbush Books.

Stone, Christopher (1974) *Should Trees Have Standing?*, Los Altos, California: William Kaufmann.

Taylor, Charles (1992) 'Atomism,' in Shlomo Avineri and Avner De-Shalit (eds) *Communitarianism and Individualism*, New York: Oxford University Press.

Taylor, Paul (1986) *Respect for Nature: A Theory of Environmental Ethics*, Princeton, New Jersey: Princeton University Press.

Taylor, Peter J. (1988) 'Technocratic Optimism, H. T. Odum, and the Partial Transformation of Ecological Metaphor after World War II,' *Journal of the History of Biology* 21(2): 213–244.

Teish, Luisa (1983) 'Women's Spirituality: A Household Act,' in Barbara Smith (ed.) *Home Girls: A Black Feminist Anthology*, New York: Kitchen Table: Women of Color Press.

Thomas, William (1995) *Scorched Earth: The Military's Assault on the Environment*, Philadelphia: New Society Publishers.

Tong, Rosemarie (1989) *Feminist Thought: A Comprehensive Introduction*, Boulder, Colorado: Westview Press.

Treblicot, Joyce (1994) *Dyke Ideas: Process, Politics, Daily Life*, Albany: State University of New York Press.

Treblicot, Joyce (ed.) (1987) *Mothering: Essays in Feminist Theory*, Totowa, New Jersey: Rowman and Allenheld.

Tuana, Nancy and Karen Warren (eds) (1991) *APA Newsletter on Philosophy and Feminism: Feminism and the Environment* 90(3).

Tucker, David F. B. (1994) *Essay on Liberalism: Looking Left and Right*, Boston: Kluwer.

Utley, Robert M. (1983) *The Indian Frontier of the American West 1846–1890*, Albuquerque, New Mexico: University of New Mexico Press.

VanDeVeer, Donald (1995) 'Interspecific Justice,' in Christine Pierce and Donald VanDeVeer (eds) *People, Penguins and Plastic Trees: Basic Issues in Environmental Ethics*, Belmont, California: Wadsworth Press.

Varner, Gary (1985) 'The Schopenhauerian Challenge in Environmental Ethics,' *Environmental Ethics* 7(3): 209–230.

Vecsey, Christopher (1991) *Imagine Ourselves Richly: Mythic Narratives of North American Indians*, New York: Harper Collins.

Walker, Alice (1988) *Living by the Word: Selected Writings 1973–1987*, New York: Harcourt Brace Jovanovich.

Walker, Alice (1982) 'Only Justice Can Stop a Curse,' in Pam McAllister (ed.) *Reweaving the Web of Life*, Philadelphia: New Society Publishers.

Warnock, Donna (1982) 'Patriarchy is a Killer: What People Concerned About Peace and Justice Should Know,' in Pam McAllister (ed.) *Reweaving the Web of Life*, Philadelphia: New Society Publishers.

Warren, Karen J. (ed.) (1996) *Ecological Feminist Philosophies*, Bloomington, Indiana: Indiana University Press.

Warren, Karen J. (1992) 'Taking Empirical Data Seriously: An Ecofeminist Philosophical Perspective,' in *Human Values and the Environment*: Conference Proceedings, Report no. 140, Madison, Wisconsin: Wisconsin Academy of Sciences, Arts and Letters.

Warren, Karen J. (guest ed.) (1991) *Hypatia: Special Issue on Ecological Feminism* 6(1).

Warren, Karen J. (1990) 'The Power and Promise of Ecological Feminism,' *Environmental Ethics* 12(2): 125–146.

Warren, Karen J. (1987) 'Feminism and Ecology: Making Connections,' *Environmental Ethics* 9(1): 3–20.

Webster's New World Dictionary of the English Language (1994) New York: Prentice-Hall.

Weed, Elizabeth (1989) *Coming to Terms: Feminism, Theory, Politics*, New York: Routledge.

Willet, Cynthia (1995) *Maternal Ethics and Other Slave Moralities*, New York: Routledge.

Wright, Beverly (1995) 'Environmental Equity Justice Centers: A Response to Inequity,' in Bunyan Bryant (ed.) *Environmental Justice: Issues, Policies, and Solutions*, Washington, D.C.: Island Press.

Worster, Don (1993) 'The Ecology of Order and Chaos,' in Susan Armstrong and Richard G. Botzler (eds) *Environmental Ethics: Convergence and Divergence*, New York: McGraw Hill.

Young, Iris Marion (1990) *Justice and the Politics of Difference*, Princeton, New Jersey: Princeton University Press.

Zimmerman, Michael E. (1994) *Contesting Earth's Future: Radical Ecology and Postmodernity*, Berkeley: University of California Press.

Zimmerman, Michael E. (1987) 'Feminism, Deep Ecology and Environmental Ethics,' *Environmental Ethics* 9(1): 21–44.

INDEX